THE
Caudills OF THE
Cumberlands

ANNE'S STORY OF LIFE WITH HARRY

THE Caudills OF THE Cumberlands

ANNE'S STORY OF LIFE WITH HARRY

TERRY CUMMINS
Foreword by Wendell Berry

BUTLER
BOOKS

ISBN 978-1-935497-68-4

Library of Congress Control Number: 2013951072

Printed in the United States of America

Published by:

Butler Books
P.O. Box 7311
Louisville, KY 40257
phone: (502) 897-9393
fax: (502) 897-9797
www.butlerbooks.com

This book is dedicated
to all who take care of
the land and its people.

Contents

Foreword

I first met Anne Caudill in the summer of 1965 at the scene of a speech by her husband, Harry Caudill. I was introduced to her and Harry by our mutual friend, Gurney Norman, and I have remained their friend ever since. Harry's death in 1990 seems not to have frayed the bond at all. The Caudills, as I already knew when I met them, were a remarkable couple. They were clearly devoted to each other, they worked together, and they were allies in their long opposition to the plundering and destruction of the coalfields of Eastern Kentucky. Anne contributed her work, research, and intelligence to Harry's indispensable books. She was also a splendid cook, and an entirely generous and welcome hostess. Through all the 46 years I have known her, I have depended on her steadfast goodwill toward our fragile and suffering world, and toward those who are trying to protect it. She is an example to us all, for she never speaks except with intelligence, courage, and perfect courtesy. My long friendship with her has been a constant pleasure and encouragement.

—*Wendell Berry*

Acknowledgements

Writing a book requires assistance, encouragement, and inspiration from other people. Criticism is important, too, even when the red marks on a manuscript outnumber the black ones. Thanks to those who read all or parts of the manuscript— Barbara O'Hara, Glenda Mills, Bettye Weber, and my daughter, Dani. Thanks to Norma Robbins, who typed parts of the quoted material that were pasted in the book. Thanks to Tiffany Taylor for her technical assistance. Thanks to Bob St. John for his assistance with the photographs.

After Anne Caudill read and made needed corrections, Glenda Mills, an editor with X-ray eyes, tore each chapter apart and her bright red marks nearly blinded me. She also inserted comments such as, "This is not a sentence!" After I converted fragments into complete sentences, Barbara O'Hara, a professional editor, English teacher and librarian, fine-tuned each chapter and encouraged me to continue telling Anne's stories. A special thanks to Susan Lindsey, who provided invaluable assistance in finalizing the book for publication.

Perhaps the book would not been written without the assistance of a computer expert and friend. Although I had access to mountains of printed material, I needed some sort of organized account of Anne's stories. I would not ask her to type out her life. I'm essentially a digital moron, but I had heard something about a voice recognition program. David Neel, owner of a very successful computer business, loaned me a little finger-sized digital recorder and said, "Try this out." Anne and I conducted our first interview, and David printed it out in an amazingly legible form. Thanks to David, we were on our way and conducted 48 additional interviews.

At ten o'clock nearly every Monday morning for more than a year, all I had to do was sit at Anne's table, eat her homemade jams and bread, drink coffee, flip on the recorder, and listen to her stories. What a delightful way to begin a Monday morning! There were 49 interviews, which resulted in nearly 1,000 printed pages. I also read or reread Harry's ten books, and searched and perused the extraordinary number of articles, interviews, letters, newspapers, documents, films, and books about Appalachia and the Caudills.

As the book progressed, I frequently called Anne to assign "homework." For instance, when I needed additional information on, say, the history of her rocking chairs, I didn't quite expect enough material to fill another chapter.

I'm grateful to my readers and editors, my computer man, my family, and the Almighty. And I'm grateful to Anne for permitting me to tell some of her stories, which never end. She kept calling to say, "I'm reminded of another wonderful story."

When we agreed to begin the project, I explained to Anne that if nothing else, the work would help keep us both young. She's a young 89 and her heart, mind, and soul remain as vibrant and spirited as ever. I'm 79 and a wreck, but truly blessed for the good fortune to tell part of Anne's story as best I could.

—*Terry Cummins*

THE
Caudills OF THE
Cumberlands

ANNE'S STORY OF LIFE WITH HARRY

CHAPTER 1

He Was a Thinking Man

"If you will marry me, I will take you to France."

"Okay!"

Anne Robertson Frye met Harry Monroe Caudill on the campus of the University of Kentucky in 1945. They had only known each other for about three weeks. Sometimes, marriage proposals seem to be rather hasty and happen in unusual places. One starry night, when Harry walked Anne back from the library to her dormitory, she said, "Let's stop. I want to tell you a story." They stopped and leaned against an old cannon barrel, which was long, thick, and undoubtedly quite heavy. Anne told Harry a story that enchanting evening about her father, Kenneth Frye, also a UK graduate, who had fought in France in World War I. Anne said to Harry that she had always wanted to go to France to see where her father served.

The powerful weapon they leaned against was from a ship used in the Spanish-American War, and had been presented to the mayor of Lexington, Kentucky, in the early 1900s. The cannon was eventually set on a rock and concrete pedestal in front of the UK administration building, and pointed away from the building over a grassy slope.

For more than 100 years, tens of thousands of students walked by, stopped to reflect, and among other shenanigans, painted the cannon various colors throughout the years. There was at least one marriage proposal under the stars at the site of that well-known landmark. During the student revolts and protests in the turbulent '60s, a group of student protesters tore the cannon from the pedestal and aimed it toward the administration building. In earlier times, the booming cannon was fired on special occasions. On one Fourth of July, a large crowd of officials, professors, and students, including Anne's father, gathered at the cannon for the celebration, climaxed by a loud boom. The firing went perfectly, except the large, long barrel had been tightly packed with horse manure and the blast fertilized part of the campus.

The University of Kentucky (UK) is a special place for the Caudill family. Anne, her mother, father, brother, two aunts, and Harry were all graduates of UK. Later, Anne and Harry's three children received degrees from the university. Harry received a law degree from UK in June 1948. After 27 years of law practice in Whitesburg, he and Anne returned to UK in 1977, and lived there for eight years while Harry taught Appalachian studies and history.

In a sense, the site of their engagement is symbolic of the lives of Anne and Harry Caudill—strong, resilient, and enduring. The impact of a boom from the huge cannon could not be more powerful and celebratory than the extraordinary lives and work of Anne and Harry Caudill. When they married in 1946, little did they suspect that 17 years later, their lives would dramatically change when people from all over the world went to Appalachia to see what *Night Comes to the Cumberlands* was all about.

After the proposal and acceptance, imagine Anne calling her mother to inform her that she was engaged to be married.

Imagine her mother asking, "Who is he and how long have you been dating?" Then imagine her mother's reaction when Anne told her, "His name is Harry and we haven't really dated that much, but I've known him for about three weeks." The marriage turned out to be one or all of the following: it was love at first sight, they were meant for each other, or it was a marriage made in heaven. Marriages made in heaven do not require a lot of preparatory time.

In March 1945, Anne and Harry were students at UK. Anne had an appointment to have her eyes examined, so she missed her first class that day and arrived early to her next class on the world's great religions.

"From time to time, I heard this nice, deep voice coming from somewhere behind me asking questions that were sensible and thought provoking, but I never turned around and stared to see who he was," Anne recalled.

As she waited for the class to start, she sat down on the steps outside the building. "While I was sitting there, here came this nice tall young man who sat down next to me. He was early, too, and we began talking. He had that nice, deep voice that I'd heard in the classroom. He told me later, 'I've never seen anybody as starry-eyed as you.'"

Sixty-eight years after that night, Anne's eyes have not changed, always revealing a perpetual light, signifying a continuing love of life.

That same night, Anne went to study at the campus library. She had a question, so she went to the front desk for help. An acquaintance was on duty that night and pointed to a student who was sitting at a back table. Jokingly, he said, "See that fellow over there. Ask him, but he's a woman hater." Anne walked over to the alleged woman hater, and found that it was Harry. She asked him the question, and, as she said, "The rest is history. We talked for the next 45 years."

Soon after their initial meeting, they exchanged gifts— books, of course. Anne gave Harry a copy of one of her favorite books of poems, *The Vagabond's House*, by Hawaiian writer Don Blanding.

"One night, he brought me a copy of the *Rubaiyat of Omar Khayyám* as translated by Edward Fitzgerald. I later learned that not only had he read it, he had memorized every one of those verses. Until the end of his life, he could quote every one of them, and not only that, he had memorized most of a different version of the *Rubaiyat* by Le Gallienne."

Young couples in love frequently give each other a nickname. Anne began calling Harry "Omar," and Harry named Anne "Annabel," from Edgar Allen Poe's poem, "Annabel Lee." Harry called Anne by that name all his life, and many people thought that was her real name. One line from the poem reads, "We loved with a love that was more than a love, I and my Annabel Lee."

One day during the brief time they had known each other, they met for lunch at the student union. One of the more pressing issues for discussion on the campus was the progress of the UK Wildcat basketball team, but it was of little interest to Anne or Harry. He pointed to the murals on the wall depicting beautiful scenes of Kentucky—its horse farms, tobacco fields, stately mansions, and the state capitol. He pointed out that none of the walls depicted scenes of Appalachia and Eastern Kentucky. Harry stressed that the university had totally ignored Eastern Kentucky. Then he began talking about politics, economics, conservation, preserving the forests, and the plight of the people in Appalachia.

Why did Anne fall in love with Harry?

She said, "You know, somehow I had never heard about all those things. It was all new to me. Remember, I was very young then and did not know all the things I know now, but he talked very passionately about these things. And that's one of the things that made me fall in love with him, because most men I knew talked about sports or just stuff that was sort of infantile actually. And this man talked like an informed adult thinking human."

During the war, nearly all able-bodied young men were away fighting. Some young men still in high school joined the military. Many young women joined the service, worked at defense jobs, or remained home helping their families. Consequently, enrollment at colleges and universities diminished significantly. In 1944–45, UK enrolled approximately 1,200 women and 200 men. Those men were either exempt from military service because of a physical disability, or, like Harry, returning after a war wound. Mathematically, a man at UK had his pick of the women. Anne said, "I always thought I was the luckiest thing in the world to be able to capture his attention when all those other girls were without a man. When I met Harry, it was gold from there."

It takes a thinking woman to marry a thinking man, and for more than 40 years, Anne and Harry devoted their lives to the issues Harry mentioned at the student union, and to several other worthy causes. Add Harry's 27 years of law practice, service in the Kentucky legislature for six years, and eight years of teaching at UK, there was little time for other endeavors and pursuits. However, Harry, with Anne's devoted assistance, found time to give more than 120 lectures and speeches, and write more than

60 magazine articles, 100 newspaper essays and editorials, and ten books.

After his first book, *Night Comes to the Cumberlands: A Biography of a Depressed Area,* was published in 1963, the interest and attention was so intense and widespread that thousands of people flooded the small town of Whitesburg in Letcher County, Kentucky. Whitesburg, a town of about 1,900 people, is located in the Cumberland Mountains in southeastern Kentucky and is about ten miles from the western border of Virginia. The Cumberland Mountains are one of several mountain ranges or plateaus encompassing Appalachia, which stretches across several states in the eastern United States.

Whitesburg is 220 miles from Louisville, 197 miles from Anne's hometown in Cynthiana, and 174 miles from Frankfort where Harry served in the legislature. Before the interstate highways, the drive up, down, and around the mountains to central and northern Kentucky took untold hours. Flying from New York into Tri-Cities near Bristol, Virginia, or Lexington, Kentucky, a lush, rich center of the Bluegrass horse farm country, a TV crew might ask, "How do we get from here to Whitesburg?" An answer could have been, "You can't get there from here."

However, curious visitors did find Whitesburg, as did hundreds of the media, including foreign journalists and film crews, religious and civic groups, educators, professors, writers, state, federal, and foreign officials, and many others. Visitors traveled over the narrow and treacherous mountain roads to see the land where "night" had come to the Cumberlands.

After publication of the book, the Caudills were flooded with letters and phone calls asking Harry to speak to groups, grant interviews, take part in forums, and lead tours of this center of deprivation and poverty hidden away in an isolated place in the richest nation on earth. Anne and Harry generously and cordially tried to accommodate as many of those visitors as they could, but it was physically and logistically impossible to grant all requests. On some occasions, if Harry could not go to give a speech, Anne went. Since one masterful storyteller married another one, Anne became a knowledgeable, forceful, and charming speaker. In 2010, she enthralled two sizeable audiences on the topic of mountaintop removal.

The legends, lore, and stories about Appalachia are endless. In 2009, Anne addressed an audience of writers and others interested in storytelling. She told the audience about one of Harry's stories taken from one of the two books he wrote of tales from a country law office. Here is how Harry told the story:

The situation unfolded in 1962 in the Letcher County Courthouse. My client came into my office with a tale of woe. His wife was a sturdy woman of strong temper, and she had become unusually enraged at him because of an escapade involving one of the young women of the neighborhood. In her wrath, she had armed herself with a bargain-counter .22-caliber pistol with a barrel about one and one-half inches long. She had loaded it with short cartridges because they were cheaper, and awaited his return home. When, humming softly, he entered the front door, she presented her pistol and vowed to kill him. He took flight through the kitchen and out the back door with his wife in hot pursuit. He fled along a path that led around a hillside to his Buick, while the wife of his bosom fired her shooting iron into his back. Neighbors reported that at each shot he emitted piercing shrieks and wails for mercy. This continued until the five cartridges from her Saturday-night special were used up and he had reached his car.

He drove at breakneck speed to the hospital where he presented himself at the emergency room with loud assertions that he had been shot square through five times. The doctor had him remove his blanket-lined leather jacket and his sweater and shirt, and lie face down on the examination table. Sure enough, he had been shot five times, but not square through. The sturdy leather jacket and woolen garments had acted as a flak jacket, and the feeble cartridges fired from the anemic pistol had merely propelled the bullets partway into his shoulders. They remained half in and half out, as the doctor phrased it, and he withdrew them with tweezers. He painted the wounds with mercurochrome, applied bandages, and sent him forth. My client recovered quickly. The grand jury was in session at the time and he promptly presented himself at its antechamber. Admitted to tell his tale, he described his ordeal in florid terms and showed the jurors the five bullet holes. The panel immediately returned an indictment charging his wife with attempted murder.

Before the trial was scheduled, the pair fell in love again and the turbulent marriage was patched up. At this point, he came in to pay me to defend her for shooting him. In this new state of mind, he yearned to keep her out of the penitentiary.

The commonwealth attorney was unsympathetic. He had read the transcript of the victim's testimony to the grand jury and deemed her actions a most heinous crime, a carefully planned attempt to kill her husband. On the morning of the trial, the two sat in court together, their arms entwined, her head on his shoulder. I pleaded with the prosecutor, pointing out that they had children, were reconciled, were deeply in love, that the wounds were minor, and her conviction and imprisonment would break the hearts of her son and daughter. The victim reinforced my pleas with loud and fervent affirmations. At length, the prosecutor surrendered to the realities of the case and agreed that the charge would be reduced; the defendant paying a $200 fine for breach of the peace. Of course, she had no money and her husband had to pay the fine. When the judicial proceeding had been solemnly affirmed by the judge's signature, the clerk handed my client a receipt for the fine plus court costs. He stared with a rueful and uncomprehending gaze at the bits of paper and sighed. 'I just don't understand this law business. She shot me five times and now I have to pay over $40 a shot. It ain't fair; I don't care what anybody says.'

The demands of justice had been met. The chastened wife went back to her home and her husband went back to the coal mines.

I suspect the lady with the scales managed a little smile.

The Caudill's marriage and their lives were filled with many and varied activities and causes. Their priorities were numerous, and were pursued vigorously and relentlessly. Their priority above all others was their extended family and particularly their children—James, Diana, and Harry Frye. (Anne referred to her son as Harry Frye to distinguish him from his father.) She said that Harry's favorite time during the day was early mornings when he took the children to school. It was an opportunity to tell them stories.

Anne grew up in the Bluegrass area of Central Kentucky, nearly 150 miles from the Cumberland Mountains. She grew up reading books and hearing stories. That's what people did for entertainment before television, the Internet, and all the other kinds of mass media. Her background prepared her for the delights of a good story. When she married Harry, a masterful storyteller, their lives became a kind of ongoing fairy tale—magical and enduring. It was a marriage sustained, in part, by hearing, telling, and living a continuous series of stories, endless and primarily about their faith in and abiding love of their people, whom they served.

Anne's background prepared her for a life with Harry, who grew up in the Cumberland Mountains of Kentucky. Although Anne grew up in the Bluegrass area in Central Kentucky, she knew well the culture of a rural kind of life. Rural folks were her people. She lived with them and heard many stories about them. When she married Harry and moved to Whitesburg in the mountains, it became her home and her place. For 42 years there, she lived a rich and wonderful story.

CHAPTER 2

Birth of a Storyteller

Anne's story began on March 6, 1924, in Harrison County, Kentucky, in the small town of Cynthiana. Her father, Kenneth Castleman Frye, grew up in Shelby County, 35 miles from Louisville. Her mother, Lois Ammerman, was born on a farm near Cynthiana, the seat of Harrison County, and grew up there. Harrison County is located on the fringe of the Bluegrass area, 30 miles north of Lexington and 66 miles south of Cincinnati, Ohio. About half of the county is composed of gently rolling fields with rich productive soil, and the other half is hilly but tillable.

Anne's hometown is peaceful, quaint, and small, and the South Licking River meanders through its center. The town sits in a little valley surrounded by sloping hills. Until a few years ago, Cynthiana was one of Kentucky's major tobacco markets, and several large warehouses were located on the edge of the town. In late fall and winter, farmers transported their tobacco to the warehouses, where it was auctioned to the major tobacco companies. During the winter months, the little town became an exciting, busy place. The tobacco check was essentially the yearly payday for many farmers. If it was a good year, the paycheck celebration might include buying a few Christmas presents for the kids, followed perhaps with a stopover at a saloon.

During his early career, Henry Clay, known as the Great

Compromiser and a candidate for the presidency, practiced law in Cynthiana. However, the major historic event in Cynthiana occurred on June 11–12, 1864, when General John Hunt Morgan, known as the Thunderbolt of the Confederacy, attacked the town with his raiders. After a fierce two-day battle, the Union forces drove out the Confederates, but not before the raiders burned several of the town's buildings, and damaged two bridges that crossed the South Licking River. The battle at Keller's Bridge, which was the railroad bridge, was Morgan's last victory. He decided to remain in Cynthiana, and the next day, Union reinforcements defeated him. The Union forces suffered the loss of 1,092 men, and Morgan lost an estimated 1,000.

Anne, who was born 58 years after the Civil War, heard numerous stories about the war. Her grandmother, Emma Ammerman, born in 1857, remembered hearing the cannons roar, and a raid on her grandparents' home. Both armies survived in part by ransacking homes and farms for food and fresh horses. They would pick up some needed cash by threatening to burn a business or home unless the owner paid a considerable amount of money. When Anne's great-grandfather's home was raided, a black slave woman was prepared for them. She put all the family silver in a gunnysack and hid it under a bush where the hens pecked around. When the raiders asked about the family's horses, hidden in the back woods, she told them some other army men had taken their horses days ago. For soldiers foraging for food, a smokehouse was a prime target. When the soldiers went to clean out the smokehouse of cured meat, they noticed the hams were scattered about the yard and covered with a white substance. When asked what was on the hams, the woman replied, "Them other army men threw them out and spread that stuff on them."

When the puzzled men rode away, the slave woman picked up the hams, brushed off the flour and hung them back in the smokehouse. When "them army men" rode away, the silver, hams, and horses remained on the farm.

Anne's grandfather, Claude Frye, served in the state militia under General Castleman and helped quell numerous feuds, particularly in "Black and Bloody" Breathitt County. Family, clan, or community feuds were common in the earlier days. Throughout Appalachia, bloody feuds broke out between various families and factions, most stemming from the deeply divided loyalty to either the North or South.

Anne's mother, Lois Ammerman, grew up near the small village of Poindexter. Anne had one brother, Robert, who was three years younger. He earned a degree in engineering from UK, worked in civil engineering, and died in 1997.

Anne's mother recalled Poindexter's most thriving business, a distillery noted for its fine bourbon whiskey. However, it was a detriment to the community, because the distiller sold a quart jar of whiskey for ten cents to his neighbors. Anne said, "Very little work was ever done, because the farmers stayed half drunk."

Anne described her childhood as "a glorious and charming life. [Extended family] was the most important thing and the family all took care of each other and were perfectly harmonious. I never remember any friction. If there was any, it was hidden from me as a child."

She lived her first seven years in Asheville, North Carolina, spent a summer in New Orleans, where her father had a job, and a brief time in Ashland, Kentucky. Her father, an engineer specializing in sewer and waterworks, contracted for jobs when and where they were available. His wife, who was a teacher, and their children visited or lived with him during these jobs, provided it was convenient and did not interfere with school. Anne started the first grade in Ashville, but moved to the second grade around mid-year because they thought she was ready. When she returned to Cynthiana the following year, she was placed in the fourth grade. Anne said it was a mistake: "I never learned my multiplication tables."

During Anne's childhood and youth, she experienced life in both the town and on her Grandmother Ammerman's farm, four miles away, where she spent summers and other times. In towns and cities, home is a house. On a farm, home includes animals, pastures, crops, trees, creeks, gardens, and barns. On the farm, Anne loved the natural wonders that changed every day like turning the pages of a good book. She described the pilgrimage she took every year:

> My Grandmother Ammerman lived on a sizeable farm, where I spent a great many happy summers as a child. My father was a civil engineer and every year or two his job was in a different place and my mother would go stay with him, and Robert and I lived on the farm with my grandmother and the aunts and uncles. It was a glorious life. The curious thing that did not occur to me until I was a grown woman was that the pilgrimage we made every year was unusual; I thought that was what everybody did.

Anne learned how different country life was from living in town. One major difference was that towns and cities had the convenience of electricity and all of its amenities, whereas most rural areas did not. Workdays in towns and cities were either eight or nine hours, whereas on farms, a workday—six days each week—went from daylight to dark. Sundays were church and rest days except for feeding the animals and milking the cows in the morning and again in the late evening.

Anne's summers on the farm were not all play or sitting around reading books. She had chores to do. One of her jobs each day was to take care of the kerosene lamps, washing the black soot from the chimneys and refilling them with oil. She helped prepare the large midday dinners for the farmhands. She made gallons of sweet tea for the hot, tired farm workers. Every couple of days, someone in the family drove into town to the icehouse and bought a large chunk of ice. It was transported home wrapped in an old piece of carpet and tied to the front bumper of the car. If the ice melted, it wouldn't drip in the car.

Throughout her life, Anne got the urge to do spring cleaning every spring—the cleaning she had helped do growing up. Almost all homes were heated by wood or coal. During the long winters, soot, dust, and smoke stains accumulated throughout the house, which required a thorough cleaning and scrubbing, including the walls and furniture. Carpets were taken outside, hung on a clothesline, and beaten until most of the dust, dirt, and grit flew away through the sweet spring air.

Her attachment to and reverence for the countryside established a lifelong yearning to live amidst nature's unique and sustainable peace and solitude. Living in the country provided a place for her to expand her feeling of independence and gave her a greater sense of freedom. Later in life, Anne realized her dream. For 42 years, she lived on the land in Appalachia, a land covered with beautiful and massive trees, gently winding valleys, and ambling streams. For more than four decades, Anne could sit on her front porch and gaze across a broad valley at the highest peak of Pine Mountain.

Anne's childhood centered around three things—family, books, and storytelling. As in every individual's case, Anne's development and character were molded by heredity and environment. From early childhood, she grew up in a loving and devoted extended family—mother, father, brother, grandparents, uncles, aunts, and cousins. Her earliest memories were listening to family stories and to the stories read by a family member.

"All my ancestors were early settlers in Kentucky," she said. "From my earliest childhood, I heard the family talk about the stories that had come down from those early times and I always treasured those stories. Over the years, they collected written records of those earlier generations. Back in those days, telling stories was a form of entertainment."

Some of Anne's happiest childhood memories were the "spend days," where a gathering of aunts, cousins, mothers, and daughters met at her grandmother's home for a day. Anne described the activities of a spend day: "After a wonderful country-cooked lunch, the group would sit and talk and do their handiwork at their sewing baskets, knitting, crocheting, or whatever they were working on. I always had my little basket of doll clothes and little quilts to work on. It was such a great pleasure for me to sit and listen to the old people talk about this cousin or that cousin or something else."

Anne's early childhood was an idyllic one. She was loved and nourished by an extended family, and her early years were during the good times. However, an introduction to life's harsher realities and difficulties occurred when she was six.

The infamous day known as Black Friday occurred on

October 28, 1929. Anne recalls the day the stock market crashed and the struggles during the aftermath:

I was a little girl in the first grade and there was another little girl in my neighborhood who went to the same school, and the parents would take turns getting us to school and picking us up. On this particular day, it was the turn of the other family. She was not in the same room that I was in and her family must have been pretty well off because they had a chauffeur who picked her up and took us to school. My mother performed that duty when it was her turn. On this particular day, I got out of my class and went out to the playground, and the chauffeur was waiting there for us. A teacher followed me out and the other little girl hadn't come out yet. The teacher and this chauffeur were in conversation and he told her that Wall Street had crashed and that the little girl's father was dead. My understanding later was that he had killed himself. But, you know, as a child, I didn't understand any of that and I had a very definite impression that a big tall wall had fallen on the street and killed him."

There were several things I remember about those Depression years. Of course, our family had the farm and there was plenty of good food and a family that loved me and took care of me. The family was all happy together, but there was no money to patch the roof or mend the fences or repair the farm machinery, and everybody wore clothes they had made themselves. My mother and my aunts and my grandmother all sewed and made clothes for everybody, which was a necessity.

It may have been 1934 that was so dry the corn didn't develop. It grew to be about maybe waist or shoulder high and then it just died. It just curled up, turned yellow, and died, and tobacco the same way. They didn't have anything to feed their animals the next winter and, of course, it stunted the hay crops and all other crops.

From those Depression days up until very recently, the tobacco crop was the main cash crop on all farms. My mother's younger sister, Jane, was married to Forrest Kerns. They already had two children, and had taken on the debt of a farm they had bought. When it came time to sell the tobacco crop, Uncle Forrest took the crop to the warehouse that day, and Aunt Jane and the children came to my grandmother's house to stay. When he came home late in the afternoon from the tobacco market and walked in the door, Aunt Jane looked up and said, 'Forrest, how much?' I'll never forget the way he looked. He was white as a sheet and he said, 'Five cents.' Five cents on the pound wasn't enough to pay for the seed, much less the labor and all that. I don't know how that family survived that year. I have no knowledge of that, but it was mighty tight for them and everybody else.

I remember there was a plague of grasshoppers that added to the miseries. They came and they ate everything that hadn't dried up. I remember you'd walk through the yard and the grasshoppers would just jump all over you. In those days, women had begun wearing rayon underwear. Up until that time, they wore cotton underwear, but rayon was cheaper, and they discovered grasshoppers would eat the rayon. They'd eat big holes in it, if it were hung outside to dry. You'd have to dry it inside or put it in cotton bags to dry outside. Oh, there were miseries in those days.

There was a terrible water shortage in Cynthiana. I remember the water looked muddy when we filled a bathtub. It was at that time the city of Cynthiana decided they were going to have to build a dam to catch a bigger pool of water to supply the city. My father got the contract to build it, which was the first break he had had since the Great Depression. I don't know how it was financed, but I remember they started in that summer and they built the cofferdams, which are big wooden dams they build when the water is low to hold back the water so they can construct the main dam between the two wooden dams. And then there came a terrible rain. It rained and rained upriver, and washed those cofferdams out after they had labored all summer.

That's the first time I ever saw my father cry. I remember very well one day it was still raining and half the men in town were down there trying to sandbag the cofferdam to keep it from going out. My mother and aunts made great jugs of coffee and baskets of sandwiches to take down for the workers. I was with them when they drove down there and just as we got there, my dad came over to the car and I'll never forget. He was wearing a slicker and a yellow rain hat with the rain pouring off and I looked at him; the tears were running down his face. He said 'Lois, the dam's gone.' It had just gone out in the flood, the whole thing. A whole summer's work lost, and it was hard on him. It was hard on everybody.

Anne's father, Kenneth Frye, had some wonderful stories of his own. When Kenneth was a junior at the small Waddy High School in Shelby County in 1913, he and a friend decided they wanted to go to a bigger and better school during their senior year, so they caught a train from Waddy to Shelbyville, the county seat, and enrolled in Shelbyville High.

After only one day, they didn't like it either, and decided to skip their senior year and try enrolling in the University of Kentucky. It was a simple matter of catching the train from Waddy to Shelbyville, and then catching another train to Lexington and UK. They received directions to the university administration building, found it and walked in the door. They explained they didn't have diplomas, but felt they were well prepared to attend a university. The administrator told them that if they could pass an entrance exam, they would be admitted.

They took the exam that very day. When Kenneth looked at his exam, there was a section on Latin of which he had little interest or knowledge. However, there was one Latin story he particularly liked and had memorized—"How Caesar Built the Bridge." The Latin section of the entrance exam required translating "How Caesar Built the Bridge." Kenneth and his friend passed with flying colors and became UK students.

The only problem was that Kenneth's parents knew nothing about the extended train ride and his admission to UK. However, his parents accepted the surprising news and helped him relocate to Lexington.

Anne told the story of how her grandfather saved his bank:

There's another wonderful story about those Depression years in my father's family. My grandfather, Claude Frye, was the cashier of a bank in the village of Waddy, and had been since he was a young man. His bank was the place where all the farmers in that part of the county came to deposit money or borrow money for their crops for the next year and whatever. Now, my grandfather was a great storyteller; he liked nothing better than to sit and talk to the farmers and collect what he referred to as bear stories, and he was famous for his collection of stories.

During the early 1930s, banks all over the country began to fail. People became uneasy about the cash they had banked and were afraid they couldn't get it out because no bank ever carries enough cash on hand to pay everybody. They lent it out for various things and many, many banks failed.

My grandfather somehow got the feeling that there would be a run on his bank on Monday morning. So he waited until Saturday noon when he always closed the bank and then ordinarily drove to Shelbyville to do the week's shopping and errands with my grandmother, but on this occasion, he drove to Cincinnati. He had already talked by phone to some family friends up there. These were the sons of the Rothchild family, who had a mercantile business in Shelby County. This Jewish family had dealt with my grandfather and his father and grandfather for four generations. (One time, my father took my brother in to buy him a pair of socks in that store so that they could say they had dealt with five generations in the family.) Anyway, they were friends and the sons had gone to Cincinnati and prospered greatly. He called, told them his situation, and asked if they would lend him a large amount of cash. I don't remember what the amount was, but they agreed. On Saturday afternoon, he just went down the road as though he were going to Shelbyville. When he got to Shelbyville, he went right on to Cincinnati and came back late that evening with a suitcase full of greenbacks.

He had the keys to the bank and he slipped in, put that money in the bank in the safe, went home and went to bed. On Monday morning, sure enough, people came and they began to take their money out of their savings and their checking accounts, and there was a long line of people waiting. When they came in, he just handed the money out to them. 'Well, I guess here it is; it's yours.' He told me later, by the time he got to the end of the line, some of those people came back and put their money back in, and he said most of them did. They decided the bank was sound.

After the bank closed on Monday afternoon, he got in his car and quietly slipped back to Cincinnati. It was a long drive and took him all night to go and come back. He took the cash back, and that's the way he saved the bank. It was one of the few banks that didn't close.

Back in those earlier days up to about the late 1940s, most rural families did not have electricity, radios, or telephones. Entertainment and leisure were primarily limited to reading and social gatherings with family and friends, a trip to the country store, and church where, after the service, people lingered to talk and tell stories. For those who couldn't read, remembering and telling stories was about the only type of social enjoyment and entertainment available.

All able-bodied men who had not volunteered were drafted into the military during World War II. After boot camp, those who were illiterate, a large portion from rural areas, were taught to read before moving on to use weapons. After learning how to read and understand a military manual, these soldiers required little instruction in how to fire weapons, because most had learned that when they were old enough to lift a gun.

When Anne moved to Whitesburg in Appalachia in 1948, a sizeable number of those living in the area were illiterate. However, she heard many stories from the people living in the coal camps and up in the remote hollows, and she was married to a man for 44 years who was one of Kentucky's greatest storytellers. In the midst of conversations, she would often reveal her delightful smile and radiant expression, and said, "That reminds me of another story." A bit later in the conversation, she would again say, "That reminds me of another story."

Stories and books go together. During Anne's childhood days, family members read stories to her, and when she had the measles, her parents were warned to keep her away from bright light. During the day, the window blinds were drawn. It was too dark for her to read, so her father sat by a sliver of light below the window blind and read all of the *Little Colonel* books to her.

Before the mid-1950s, many families considered an eighth-grade education sufficient. After that, it was time to go to work. It was common to hear, "I'm the first one in my family to get a high school diploma." Before World War II, a college degree was a rarity, but Anne's family was an exception.

Anne's father was a civil engineer and her mother taught English, math, history, and other subjects for many years, as did her mother's sister. In those days in the small schools, teachers taught subjects whether they were qualified or not, but they gave it their best. Her mother's aunts were teachers, too. Anne referred to her little Aunt Anne, not five feet tall, as "an absolute dynamo." She taught English and many other subjects. She became the principal of a small country high school in the village of Buena Vista in Harrison County, and ended her career as librarian of the Harrison County High School, a consolidation of the county's smaller high schools. She retired at age 70 and lived until age 94. Until the day of her death, she could quote reams of poetry. Anne recalled, "I would take her a book of poetry and begin to read her a line or two, and she would quote the rest of it."

In Anne's life, family always came first, with books not far behind. "I've read books all my life and grew up in a house full of books. Out in the country, it was a joy to sit around and read the books of Dickens, Thomas Hardy, and Jane Austen out loud to each other while we were doing chores, sewing, breaking beans, or peeling apples, or whatever."

The couple consumed books during high school, college, and after their marriage. Anne said, "Harry read voluminously—history, biography, current affairs—always piecing together the pattern of cause and effect that had created a unique Kentucky society. From a rocking chair in our kitchen, he read aloud to me or discussed what he had read, as I attended to the needs of our children and household. This was his way, I think, of clarifying and fixing in his own mind what he read and observed. It made humdrum chores pass quickly, and for over forty years, I was educated by a born and gifted teacher."

Anne learned many valuable lessons during her school years. She recalled one in particular:

In seventh grade, we had English classes. In the sixth, we had studied all the parts of speech. I knew all about nouns, pronouns, adverbs, and adjectives, and thought I was awfully smart. I learned differently later, but thought I knew about everything when I first started seventh grade. When I went to this first English class under Miss Henry, I made the mistake to be so bold as to say, "I don't see why we have to take any more English classes; we've already learned the parts of speech." She looked at me and she said, "Miss Frye, would you decline a nickel?" I'd never heard of the word decline, which is part of the study of learning the structure of sentences; I stood up and said, "I decline this nickel." I remember she laughed uproariously, but then did she ever begin to make fun of me. She knew she was going to have to take me down a few notches. Every day for about a week, she said something belittling to me and I was so unhappy. I begged my mother to let me quit going to school in town and go to school with her in the country. My mother was too sharp for that. She said, "You're staying right where you are." Miss Henry and I became great friends, but after she had taken me down a few notches and made me realize I didn't know everything there was to know already.

Another thing that amused me, there was a lumbering lad in our class, and she put "wretched" on the board and told him to go to the board and write that word in a sentence. After giving it some thought, he wrote, "The boy wretched for the book."

My favorite activity in high school was dancing. Everybody in town danced. We had dancing classes. I was a good tap dancer and we'd have exhibition dances sometimes. We danced at school and had a stack of records in the orchestra pit in the auditorium. At recess or noon, we could go there and dance, and then every week during the school season that we didn't have a ball game, we had a sock hop and everybody went. It was ballroom dancing. Jitterbug came a bit later. About four times a year, we would have a fancy dress dance at the school. All the girls wore long dresses, most of which were made by our mothers, because they were so much cheaper.

When we would get together on weekends or in the summertime in somebody's home, our favorite entertainment was dancing. We would roll up the carpet and in my home or wherever we would put on a stack of records and dance. For refreshments, we would go to the kitchen and make candy. I just remember those years with the greatest delight.

In the spring of 1941, Anne graduated from Cynthiana High School and was valedictorian of her senior class of 27 students. She recalled, "Our country had recovered from the darkest days of the Depression and, although there were threats of war, times were good and hopes high."

In September 1941, Anne danced her way from high school to the University of Kentucky.

CHAPTER 3

You Make Your Own Decisions Now

"You make your own decisions now," Anne's mother told her after moving her into the Patterson Dormitory at UK in the fall of 1941. In that exciting—or traumatic—setting, most parents might firmly declare, "Don't make any hasty or stupid decisions." Most parents cross their fingers, however, and offer prayers during their drive back home. Parents also know that college is a place for boys and girls to meet and study together. In Anne's case, she met a boy—a man—and before they had time to study together, she made a decision. They would have plenty of time to study after marriage.

Anne's parents had utmost confidence in her maturity. Her mother did not instruct her to call them at any time before making a hasty life-changing decision. Although perhaps rather hasty, the biggest decision in Anne's life turned out to be correct one.

With so many English teachers in Anne's family and her love of books, one might assume she would major in English. She also liked science classes in high school and decided to major in a science-related field. She discussed nursing and home economics with her family, and ultimately chose home economics.

"My college life was absolutely wonderful," she said. "I lived in the dormitory, the same one where my mother had lived. My mother helped me move in and after she left, the old black man who was the janitor there looked at me and asked, 'Didn't she used to go to school here?' I answered, 'Yes, she did.' The old janitor said, 'I remember her.' I thought it was remarkable with all the girls he had seen over the years go through the dormitory, he remembered my mother."

In those days, rules at colleges were strict, particularly for girls, who were required to eat dinner in the dorm dining room and were assigned permanently to a table of six. The advantage of this arrangement was that a new student made five new friends in a brief time.

Curfew was ten o'clock. "Every night just before curfew, the girls and boys sat around and hugged until the very last minute and then when the lights flickered, in we went, and woe-be-tied if you were late," she said.

College life was exciting and all went well until December 7, 1941. Anne vividly recalled the day:

On the seventh day of December, as always, I went to the dining room for dinner, and after dinner, my friends and I were walking back across what we called the bridge, which was an overpass between the two buildings. It was used as sort of a lounge, and there was a radio there and as we went through, everybody was gathered up, looking astonished and listening to the radio, and then came the word. It must have been around one o'clock on that Sunday that Pearl Harbor had been bombed and the president had declared war. I can remember that as well as if it were this morning.

It seemed to me like Niagara Falls fell on me, and it was cold. It just washed over me—a cold feeling—because you see my father had been overseas in World War I in the army engineers at the front. He had brought back many, many pictures and, of course, I had seen many other pictures. My dad didn't talk about it very much, but I understood from childhood that the experience was so traumatic that it was beyond talking about. I can remember my mother saying that, for many years after they married, any time my father would hear a loud explosion like a car backfiring, he would hit the ground. Even if it were in the middle of the street, he would go down. It was just a reflex action and it would embarrass him horribly. I understood from my earliest childhood that war was a terrible thing and when I heard that my country was at war, it just left me cold. I'll never forget that.

Anne described the days after Pearl Harbor:

The nation began to draft soldiers and they all had to go unless they were physically disabled. Some young farmers were deferred from military service, because survival depended on crops and food. Unless men were volunteering, they were drafted into the army or some other kind of military service. So the men on the campus were enlisting wholesale and, at a certain point, they had a big ceremony where all these men who were students were in uniform. It was a farewell service for them and it was held in the old gym, which was what we used for big, big gatherings, and then President Herman Donovan spoke and others spoke about the bravery, courage, the danger, and all that. There was not a dry eye in the place.

All the men in uniform were seated on the floor and all the students, parents, and spectators were seated in the bleachers. It was a tear-jerking farewell and then the president announced that after the last music had been performed, the audience was to remain seated while the soldiers all 'pass out.' Well, everybody howled, just howled. It was an emotional release from all the disturbing things we had heard.

All the soldiers marched out and got on buses, which took them to trains, which took them to wherever they were stationed, and that's the last we saw of many men on campus. I'll remember that day forever.

Although Anne was nearly two years younger than Harry was, both entered UK in 1941. Anne had skipped the second grade, and Harry was confined to his home with tuberculosis during his junior year at Whitesburg High School. However, they did not meet until four years later, in 1945.

Harry Monroe Caudill was born on May 3, 1922, to Cro Carr and Martha Blair Caudill. They lived on the side of a mountain above Wat Long Hollow, about a mile from Whitesburg. Wat Long Hollow was named after an early settler, Watson Long. Cro was named for Cro Carr, a Scotsman in charge of building Middlesboro.[1]

Harry had a baby sister and one brother who both died at a

---

1.   Middlesboro was established by an English mining company. It was the first
     town to begin mining coal in Kentucky.

young age. Truman, another brother lived for many years. Harry, the youngest, entered his first day of school at the age of six. After his mother took him to the Whitesburg Grade School, he returned home two hours later. His startled mother asked for an explanation. His response was plain and simple, "I'm frew with school." She marched him back the next day, and Harry attended 12 years of public school and six years at UK, two of them in law school.

Caudill is one of the more common names in Appalachia. Families were quite large in the early days. Women frequently died during childbirth or early in their lives. It was common for a man to marry two or three times and raise two large families. The Caudill clan numbered in the hundreds; Harry had 140 first cousins.

Harry's ancestry went back to James Caudill, who settled in the area in 1792. Anne has the records of the pensions and service of James and his brother Steven, both of whom fought in the Revolutionary War.

Growing up at Wat Long Hollow, Harry heard thousands of stories, remembered most, if not all, and developed an intense interest in the culture and history of Appalachia. His grandfather, Henry R. S. Caudill, served as a lieutenant in the Civil War, but died before Harry's birth. Henry served under Colonel Ben Caudill (relationship not known) and fought with General John Hunt Morgan at the Battle in Cynthiana, Anne's hometown.

Henry R. S. Caudill and his unit were captured by the Union on July 7, 1863, near Gladeville, Virginia. They were moved from prison to prison until they were released from Johnson Island, Ohio, on September 16, 1864. Colonel Ben Caudill's diary described the horrid conditions of the prisons, where many prisoners died from starvation. Some of the soldiers' wives sewed gold pieces in the folds of their uniforms, and he told how some prisoners bought food, including rats, to avoid starving. The story goes that Harry R. S. bought a rat from another prisoner; he was convinced it saved his life. When Harry R. S. was released, he began walking to his home in Letcher County, but became so weak he could walk no further. A widow took him in and nursed him back to health. In gratitude, the next year Harry R. S. walked back to Abington, a distance of over 60 miles, helped the widow harvest her crops, and then walked back home.

Harry's Aunt Phoebe Combs was Henry Caudill's oldest daughter. She visited Harry and Anne often and stayed a week or more at a time with them. Her visits were delightful ones because Aunt Phoebe, then in her 80s, told story after story.

Aunt Phoebe told them about how her mother's Confederate father was killed in the Civil War. Her mother was 11 when the Yankee regulators came to round up those who were deserters of their own army and kill those of the enemy. Aunt Phoebe's grandfather and his brother had been given permission to return home to put in the crops. This arrangement was permitted during the Civil War, as crops were about the only means of livelihood a family had.

The regulators were riding through the area and heard that two Rebels were nearby. They rode to the respective homes and killed both soldiers. Aunt Phoebe's grandmother ran to her fallen husband. When she raised his head, he died in her lap.

On one occasion, when Aunt Phoebe was having a discussion with another lady, they began criticizing the government. Her father said, "Phoebe, don't ever let me hear you criticize the government again."

"Why, Papa, you fought against the Union."

"Yes, I know I did, and I was a damn fool. This is the greatest country on earth."[2]

Harry's parents did not have the financial means to send him to college. However, UK offered him a scholarship in agriculture, which was enough to make a start. Harry enjoyed agriculture courses in high school and was a member of the Future Farmers of America. His agriculture teacher, Jerry Montgomery, was an exceptional teacher and required his students to have a farm project. Harry raised the first purebred hogs in Letcher County.

Each year, outstanding FFA members gathered in Louisville for a statewide conference. It was a thrill for farm boys in Kentucky, some of whom had never seen a big city. Harry and eight other students represented the FFA of Whitesburg High. At the conference, various contests relating to farm projects, public speaking, and other competitions took place. Harry was also on the Whitesburg High debate team, and experienced in speaking and debating.

Before boarding the train to Louisville, Harry bought a *Life* magazine at a drugstore. The feature story in the magazine was about the war in Europe, which our country would enter shortly thereafter. Having a keen interest in history and current affairs, Harry digested the contents of the magazine. When the contests in Louisville began, the Whitesburg team took the stage for the debate. When the topic was pulled out of a hat, it was the war in Europe. There was little doubt who won the debate. In later years, Harry became a renowned speaker and orator. At the

---

2.   Anne said, "He was the only Rebel I've ever heard about admitting he was wrong."

FFA's final banquet at the Kentucky Hotel, Harry was awarded the highest honor, the Star Future Farmer of the Year Award. His talents, accomplishments, and potential were recognized early in his life.

After attending UK for one year, Harry volunteered for the United States Army on July 11, 1942, but was not called to active duty until March 1943. After basic training in South Carolina, military officials recommended Harry for officers' training school, but it did not materialize. When his training ended, Harry went to the front gate of the base to catch a bus and wind his way to Whitesburg for a few days leave. A car whizzed by, stopped, and then backed up to the gate. The driver rolled down the window and shouted, "Hey, Harry, you want a ride to Whitesburg?" Harry ran to the car and noticed there were roosters in the back.

Dr. Dale Collier, the driver, was widely known as the county's "baby catcher." He would hurriedly go up any hollow in his Model A Ford to bring another life into the world. He was a big man with a loud and commanding voice. To get away from his demanding practice for a day or two, he would take off with some of his prize roosters and transport them to cockfights. South Carolina was a haven for cockfighting in those days, and fortunately, for Harry, if he didn't mind riding with roosters with natural sharp spurs on their legs, his ride back home was free.

When Harry's leave was up, he returned to the base, and his unit boarded a train with black shades covering the windows to prevent German spies from following troop movements. Success in any war depends to an extent on surprising the enemy. Even Harry and his unit did not know their destination when they boarded their ship.

Upon landing in North Africa, the troops heard a broadcast over a loudspeaker. The voice was the infamous Axis Sally, a German propagandist whose role was to undermine the morale of allied troops. Axis Sally heartily welcomed the Americans to a war that she said they would never win.

While fighting in North Africa, Harry and a buddy were assigned to sentry duty. The stars seemed to hang brightly overhead. After walking their line, they sat down on two large stones for a brief rest, and noticed the stones were carved and perfectly square. Harry realized they were sitting on top of two magnificent columns buried by erosion from the Atlas Mountains to the south. After leaving North Africa, his unit (under General Mark Clark) was transferred to Minturno, Italy, to fight against the Germans. There he saw how barren and rocky the hills and mountains of Italy had become after centuries of erosion. Those experiences remained with him, fostering a commitment to do whatever he could to prevent erosion (particularly from strip mining) from destroying his beloved mountains in Appalachia.

On May 17, 1944, Harry was wounded near Santa Maria Infante, north of Minturno, Italy. Margaret Bourke White, the well-known journalist and photographer for *Life* magazine, was in the area, and one of her photographs of the battle appeared on the front cover of the magazine. Harry suspected that he was the soldier in the slit trench (also known as a foxhole) that appeared on the front cover. He always dug his slit trench narrower and deeper than did most other soldiers.

As American forces were attempting to drive the German army inland, a firefight began and then subsided. Perhaps the Germans were in retreat. When Harry raised his left leg over the edge to exit his trench, a shell hit him. A tourniquet was applied and it was well into the night before he was carried to a field hospital.

The army doctors wanted to amputate his leg immediately, but Harry begged and pleaded with them not to do it. After his transfer to a hospital in Naples, the doctors insisted on amputation. He begged and pleaded again, so they patched him up as best they could and shipped him to Charleston, South Carolina.

The ship used to transport the wounded, a former ocean liner, had only one means of entertaining the troops. The ship had a few records that were played over and over through a loudspeaker. A popular song in the 1940s practically drove the troops crazy, "Mairzy Doats and Dozy Doats and Liddle Lamzy Divey" (mares eat oats and does eat oats and little lambs eat ivy). When the ship landed in Charleston Harbor, a band was waiting at the dock. To cheer up the wounded troops, what did they play? "Mairzy Doats."

Harry was in a hospital in Charleston for a brief time before he was taken to a hospital in Nashville. He remained there until October 1944. His stay in hospitals lasted nearly five months. Due to continuing problems with his leg, he was in and out of other hospitals throughout his life.

Anne described Harry's lingering condition. "His left leg was badly mangled and they joined the detached muscles to the bones. The surgeon told him that no matter how painful, he had to get out and walk to strengthen his leg. He left the hospital on crutches and later progressed to using a cane. Eventually, his leg strengthened to the point where he was able to walk without a cane, but with a decided limp."

In January 1945, Harry re-enrolled at UK. Shortly thereafter, his life dramatically changed again when he met Anne. He proposed to her in February.

Throughout the war, when men were away fighting, women worked at "men's jobs" in farming, manufacturing, and other critical industries necessary for the war effort. Anne had worked the previous summer in Chicago in a chemistry lab making shell casings. With Harry finishing undergraduate and law school, Anne needed and wanted a job after she graduated in February. She had three offers, and accepted a job with Standard Oil in Roselle Park, New Jersey, in March 1945. She had four years of chemistry at UK, and was well qualified for the job.

During their separation, the love affair continued at a rather torrid pace via the US postal service. Several times each week, they exchanged love letters from New Jersey to Kentucky and from Kentucky to New Jersey. These two gifted writers expressed their love in prose, integrated with poetic rhythms. Their letters expressed happiness and love, but Harry frequently rambled off on other topics he cherished. He wrote to Anne on May 29, 1946:

> Today I ate dinner with two history professors and listened to them as they discussed interesting events in the subject they teach. Their talk was about the Civil War, the hectic cabinet meetings, Lincoln's mad wife, the personalities of Lee and Grant, of Davis and Lincoln.
>
> When I think of history, my mind almost instinctively turns to other, less spectacular aspects of the mighty panorama that has been unfolded through many a millennium. My thoughts of the Civil War do not

necessarily deal with the stooped, solemn Illinois lawyer or
the neat, precise West Point colonel whose names came to
symbolize Union and Secession. Do you remember "Jennie
Get Around"—the little ditty I mentioned to you Sunday?
I think of a 17- or 18-year-old fifer, Sy Cornett, a Yankee
soldier from what was then the nearly unbroken wilderness
of southeastern Kentucky, who at the battle of Gettysburg,
played "Jennie get around, Jennie get around I say . . ." on a
hickory fife, while the fate of half a world and the destinies
of unborn millions was decided within hearing distance
of his shrill music. That to me is history, the little things,
unremembered, unnoticed, perhaps unimportant. Yet it
cannot be denied that it was the fifer and his unnumbered
comrades and foes who reconstructed the ravaged land,
rebuilt the cities, re-plowed the land, refloated the ships
and renewed everywhere the world's unsteady belief that
life is good.

Sometimes I hear it said that the Arts are degenerating
and becoming nothing more than the vulgar expression
of commonplace ideas from commonplace people. Yet
that may be good. When a king eats with his subjects or a
magnate marries his employee, does the king or magnate
lower himself or does he climb a little higher? Where is
the ultimate greatness except in the boundless human
sea from which all greatness rises? Yet it is odd indeed, I
suppose, to contemplate seeking distinction in a mass of
the undistinguished. Perhaps then, my darling, the great
things, the great works of art (your music and paintings)
come from men whose feet are planted in the un-resting

mass of Sy Cornetts while their hearts are inspired by the grandeur of the Lincolns and their souls comprehend all the scene. I do not know.

Darling, Sunday night I determined as I held you in my arms on the porch that someday I would build a house for you and take you to it and stay with you, with never a good-bye or good-night. And some day we shall, too. And we'll make that house, whether it's a pine shanty or a brick mansion, a good place in which to live together.

Anne not only wrote Harry during her time in New Jersey, she wrote letters to her family and friends. In a letter to her mother in September 1945, she explained her work:

> The first of last week, I was asked to learn a new kind of work. Eventually, I am almost certain I will be given the entire responsibility. It is a highly complicated, very precise and very interesting test, which is still in the experimental stages. It will take about a month to learn enough about it to do just the actual testing without learning to plot, graph, and summarize results. I am amazed they picked me to do it, because there are a number of girls who have been here longer.
>
> It is a test which indicates the purity of hydrocarbons (the complex compounds which compose petroleum) by freezing point. The principle is that a pure hydrocarbon always freezes at the same temperature. The amount of deviation in freezing point of the sample tested is an indication of its purity. Some are as high as 99.999% pure.

Anne's description of the experiments continued and she said, "It is intensely interesting, though." In a letter to her parents on September 6, she said, "Standard Oil has cut our work hours from 52 to 44, and we don't work Saturdays."

Anne lived in a nice rooming house with five other girls who also worked for Standard Oil. They had a good time in and around New York City, attending plays and concerts, and visiting museums. They entertained frequent guests, usually boys, for dinner. Anne grew up cooking at home and on the farm. She had food preparation classes in home economics at UK, and she liked to cook. In the same six-page letter, she wrote, "We had this young man to dinner and then played bridge. I baked a ham and added this new sauce. It's a sauce of stewed raisins and sweetened grape juice, slightly thickened. Over ham, it is wonderful. Everyone raved and ate several helpings."

On December 31, 1945, New Year's Eve, the other girls at Roselle Park had dates. Anne's date was ringing in the New Year at Wat Long Hollow in Letcher County. A somewhat lonely night turned into a rather wild one.

I stayed with Mrs. Van Fleet, the owner of the boarding house, of whom I was very fond, and she and I were sitting up to watch the year end and were playing cards in her kitchen. She got out a bottle of apricot brandy. I had never had any apricot brandy before. I'd had a little bit of some other things, but not much, having been brought up in a non-drinking family, and what little drinking I had done was on the side while I was in college.

Anyway, that apricot brandy was delicious and I kept sipping along and all of a sudden I looked over at Mrs. Van

Fleet's stove and it was dancing back and forth. The legs were just dancing back and forth, and I thought I'd had too much to drink. It was the only time in my life that I was truly inebriated, which, I guess everybody needs to do at least once in their lives.[3]

While Anne was working in New Jersey, Harry's leg continued giving him problems. The Veterans Administration sent him to Mt. Alta Hospital in Washington where he remained for several weeks. Each Sunday morning at three o'clock, Anne took a taxi to the train station at Newark, caught the train to Washington, spent the day with Harry and returned to her room at the boarding house late that night.

One day, Harry called Anne to inform her he had fallen out of bed and broken his collarbone. The full cast on his leg had slipped over the edge of the bed and out he went. The fall transferred him from crutches to a wheelchair. She spent the next Sunday with him. They were having a wonderful time sitting and talking in the gardens until a woman, who had folks living in Whitesburg, felt it her duty to cheer up the boys who were recuperating from their horrible wounds in the war. Once she tracked them down, she wouldn't stop talking. She talked until Anne interrupted to say goodbye and catch her train. Anne said, "Both of us wanted to choke her."

Victory in Europe, known as VE Day, occurred on May 8, 1945. Anne and her girlfriends, as excited and relieved as everyone else, caught a train to Pennsylvania Station in New

---

3. Years later, Anne told this story to the county judge, and he said, "Yes, I know all about apricot brandy. It will make you scratch your head about a foot away from your ear."

York for the celebration, which "was an absolute mob scene." There were so many people on the streets, Anne and her friends locked arms to prevent getting lost as they barged through the 12 blocks to Times Square.

"All of us being southerners, we didn't know what we were getting into," she said. "I think half of New York State must have been on Times Square that night, all of them royally excited, and at least half of them royally drunk."

It was the night that a famous photographer caught a sailor kissing a nurse. "Oh, it could have been me because I was kissed by about 40 people that night," Anne said.

Three months later, on August 6, 1945, a US plane dropped an atomic bomb on Hiroshima, Japan. On August 9, another atomic bomb hit Nagasaki.

Anne's letter to her family on August 10 conveyed her feelings of both relief and apprehension. "I have been glued to the radio all morning since the news of Japan's acceptance of the Potsdam Proclamation. Undoubtedly, the bomb has hastened the end, but the invention is terrifying to me. It seems quite probable that the race of men will eventually blow itself off the face of the earth."

Japan surrendered on August 14, 1945. After the long, bloody, four-year war on two fronts, Americans returned to a semblance of normalcy. After four years of tremendous sacrifice, both on the home front and the battlefield, the focus dramatically changed. It was a brand new day, filled with hope and promise, and a time to live again.

Of the 16,112,566 men and women who served in World War II, 291,557 did not return. Add to that the thousands who returned with severe wounds for whom the readjustment to a civilian life was difficult. For combatants, the years of fighting and never knowing if each day would be the last took their toll. In the coziness of homes, the sleep of a battle-worn veteran was frequently interrupted by nightmarish dreams. As noted earlier, Anne's father, a WWI veteran, dropped to the street whenever he heard a car backfire. How many times did Harry flash back to the day he raised his leg out of the trench?

During this readjustment process, and with Harry returning to UK and Anne working in New Jersey, events in their lives were happening fast. Although there had been a couple of brief visits, their long-distance romance of only letters and phone calls was difficult. In May 1946, Anne left her job in New Jersey and returned to Kentucky. There were wedding plans to make.

CHAPTER 4

Do You Take This Man?

On December 1, 1946, Harry wrote to Anne's parents:

> Dear Mr. and Mrs. Frye,
>
> In September, because of a number of circumstances no longer important to either of us, Anne and I had a most regrettable misunderstanding. The unfortunate circumstances have been ironed out in a manner that has served both of us in the end, I believe.
>
> We plan to be married on December 15. It is our mutual hope that both parents will never have cause to regret our marriage. In the home that we shall someday build, we want you to be frequent and welcome guests. I look forward to seeing you soon.

The circumstances were not necessarily a misunderstanding, but more the physical and mental conditions that plagued Harry at the time. Nearly three years of trauma, followed by five months of pain and uncertainty about his ability to walk again, took a toll. His life had shifted dramatically from an extended period of living a nightmare to waking up in the halls of ivy bathed in sunshine. Within one month of returning to UK, Harry met Anne, and less than one month later they were engaged. Perhaps it was a situation of too much, too soon, causing confusion and stress. Under such circumstances, depression digs a deeper hole.

Readjusting to family and civilian life was difficult for many veterans. Spending months or years with stress, tension, and anxiety, knowing that each day and night could be the end, wears on any and every soul. Watching buddies being blown to pieces leaves wounds that never heal.

Anne decided she did not want to work in a laboratory the remainder of her life. After about a year of working in New Jersey, she returned to Kentucky to her parents' home in Ashland, Kentucky, near the Ohio and West Virginia borders. Her father had accepted employment as director of Eastern Kentucky Highways. At the time, many highways and cow paths in that area were dirt, mud, gravel, and rock. Paved roads always needed repair, which made the job much tougher.

When Harry visited Anne in Ashland, he explained, "I really had come back thinking we were going to be married, but I'm not ready to get married." Later, his letter to Anne explained that she wasn't the cause; it was his bout with depression, which, in time, would heal.

Anne needed a job and decided to pursue the field in which she had training. In July 1946, she accepted a position in Boone County, Kentucky, near Cincinnati, as a trainee for certification as a home demonstration agent. Each county employed at least one county agent for farmers and one home demonstration agent for the homemakers; the US Department of Agriculture sponsored them. A county agent assisted and trained farmers to use modern farming techniques. One significant change involved conserving the soil. The new method raised crops on the ridges, leaving the hillsides in pasture and hay. Grasses on steep hills and mountainsides prevented the top soil from eventually washing to the sea. Until about the mid-1950s, most American farmers tilled the soil in a manner similar to what Harry had observed in Italy during the war.

A home demonstration agent demonstrated homemaking techniques. The responsibilities included organizing groups of women primarily in rural areas and holding regular meetings in various homes. Once a month, the women in a community met in a member's home, enjoyed a home-cooked lunch followed by demonstrations and discussions. An agent's instructional program included everything from cooking, sewing, cleaning, and preserving foods to home economics. The meetings were also a time to socialize, have fun, share, and learn.

Success in almost any job depends, in part, on knowledge, skill, creativity, enthusiasm, cooperation, personality, and trust. Anne possessed them all. She loved meeting people and making friends. Her friendliness and compassion—evidenced by her warm smile and optimistic outlook—attracted and held those she knew and met.

Anne completed her training and work in December, and accepted a position as home demonstration agent in Montgomery County, 40 miles east of Lexington. The position was to begin in January 1947.

Even though her marriage was off or at least on hold, there had been frequent communication with Harry. One day he decided to drive 70 miles north from Lexington to Florence in Boone County, where she was training. When he arrived, he announced, "I've decided I am ready and do want to get married."

Anne had a few days off in December, and the Cynthiana *Democrat* soon reported:

The marriage of Miss Anne Robertson Frye to Mr. Harry Monroe Caudill is announced by her parents, Mr. and Mrs. K. C. Frye of Cynthiana. The simple ceremony was solemnized here, Sunday afternoon December 15, 1946, at the home of the bride's grandmother and aunts, Misses Anne and Emily Ammerman. The families and a few friends were present. The bride is a graduate of Cynthiana High School and the University of Kentucky. She is a member of Alpha Xi Delta social sorority and Phi Upsilon Omicron home economics honorary fraternity. At present, she is assistant home demonstration agent in Boone County.

Mr. Caudill, son of Mr. and Mrs. C. C. Caudill, is a graduate of Whitesburg High School and is a veteran and a law student at the University of Kentucky.

The couple took a brief honeymoon to New Orleans at Anne's suggestion. Her father had worked there a few years earlier. Anne, her mother and brother went to be with him during one summer, and she wanted to visit the city again.

During the war, all vehicle manufacturers had stopped making cars, because tanks, jeeps, planes, and other military vehicles were critical for the war effort. Car parts and tires were scarce or nonexistent. After the war, manufacturers converted back to make civilian cars and trucks, but there was a long, long waiting list to purchase one. Harry's father had only one arm and could not drive, but he owned a car for friends to drive when he needed to travel to various destinations.

After the war when Harry returned to UK, he used his father's car, an old Chevrolet manufactured in the '30s. The merry couple chugged away, not only to a blissful honeymoon, but to a surprisingly adventurous journey as well. Anne recalled:

We went down through Mississippi and a couple of things I remember about that particularly. We stopped for gasoline in a little town at a station, and here came a Christmas parade. All the schoolchildren were parading, and there were floats and so on, and Harry asked the attendant, "Don't the black children parade?" This man said in a nasty old way, "Who wants to watch a bunch of n_____s parade?" Well, that was a horror to us. At another town, there was some little item we needed to buy . . . we pulled into a little dry goods store in this little town. As we pulled in, we saw an old black man standing in front of the window, standing there just studying what was inside and it was Christmas toys. We got out of the car and as we did, this old black man went into the store just in front of us. As the clerk looked up, he looked right past this old man who had come in front of us, and spoke to us and said, "Can I help you?" My husband said, "This gentleman came in before us," and the most horrible expression came over that man's face. He was furious that we had questioned such a thing, and he turned and snarled at this man and said, "What do you want?" The man wanted to buy a doll for his grand-daughter. Of course, all the dolls were white dolls, but he bought one, and you could tell the storekeeper was really irritated. That was a lesson to me. I had black people in my life's experience and I knew some who had worked in the various homes that I was acquainted with, but they all were people we respected and treated as human beings. Harry and I were appalled; it was a lesson to me.

The honeymoon schedule included seeing the sights along the way, living it up in New Orleans, and returning to Cynthiana before Christmas. The Ammerman traditional family celebration of Christmas at Anne's grandmother's home was a highlight of each year. All was going according to plan until the old Chevy broke down. It took days to find a part. December 24–31, 1946, were memorable ones for the newlyweds.

It became obvious we weren't going to get to Cynthiana on time. We started north on Christmas Eve and, quite late, finally found a place to stay in Atlanta. Then we looked for a place to eat. By that time, it was like maybe ten o'clock, and all the restaurants were closed. We just couldn't find anything, finally found a White Castle that still had the lights on and they were just closing up when we went in. All they had left to eat was beet and onion salad. Well, I can't eat raw onions, never have been able to handle that, and so I nibbled some of the beets and went to bed hungry.

We got up the next morning, Christmas morning, and here I was way away from my family as we continued north. Of course, on Christmas morning, there is no place to eat breakfast. We started north and I got more and more hungry as we went along, and more and more homesick. I think that's the only time in my life I was ever really homesick, and I suspect part of it had to do with the fact that I was hungry.

Anyway, we were going up through the country and we

finally came to a place to get gasoline. It was just kind of a shacky little place with a couple of rusty looking gas tanks out front and there was smoke coming out of the chimney. We stopped to get some gasoline, and an old man was sitting there tending the pumps, and lo and behold, inside there was a rack with packages of cookies in cellophane bags on the counter and a box of Lifesaver mints; that was all the food in that place. I bought cookies and the Lifesaver mints and we got in the car toward home. I opened the bag of cookies and took a bite. They were inedible and tasted like Octagon soap. We went on through the country and came to a place where they had some kind of an establishment, with a pen out in front and it had a little bear in the pen, and we stopped. I felt sorry for the little bear, and I said, "Hey, let's stop and give the cookies to the bear." We went over and gave the little bear the cookies, but he wouldn't eat them either. So that was my first married Christmas morning.

Driving through the country on Christmas Day, we never found a place to eat. Harry said, "Tonight we will be at Spartanburg, South Carolina. It's right near where I was in the army at Camp Croft, and there's a wonderful restaurant there that I used to go to with my friend whose aunt ran the restaurant. Every time we came in, she supplied us with everything, the best in the house at no cost."

So finally, we got to Spartanburg, found a place to stay and went to the restaurant and there was a long line of people outside waiting to get in. As we stood there, I could smell the chicken frying and all those good smells, and I was just about to expire from hunger. We finally got in and got a place to sit and the waiter came to take our order and my husband said, "I'm going to have half a broiled chicken," and I looked up at the waiter and I said, "I'm going to have a whole broiled chicken." He looked at my husband with a raised eyebrow and Harry said, "Bring it to her; she'll eat it," and I did. So I finally had my Christmas dinner.

Since they missed Christmas at Anne's home in Cynthiana, the couple drove straight to Whitesburg and spent a wonderful time with Harry's parents.

On New Year's Day, Aunt Anne had planned a tea to honor Anne at the family home in Cynthiana.

We just had a small wedding with extended family and a few close friends of mine, and she was having this big tea in my honor on New Year's Day. Well, on New Year's Eve, about the middle of the day, we started driving there. When we got as far as Hazard, there came a terrible sleet and ice storm, and the roads became totally impassable. There was no way to get back to Whitesburg or go forward to Cynthiana. We were just stuck, and then a big snow came on top of the ice. There was nothing to do but to stay overnight in Hazard, so we stayed at the Old Grand Hotel and found out there would be a train leaving about 4:30 the next morning that would take me to Paris, Kentucky, which is just about 13 miles from Cynthiana. I called home and told them that I would be on that train and Dad could pick me up. We spent the night in the Old Grand Hotel. It was a grandly noisy place. It had radiators, the old-fashioned kind that popped, cracked, and snorted all night long. It was New Year's Eve and there were a great many people out in the streets celebrating, with drunks shouting and carrying on, and shooting going on in the streets. It was not a night for sleeping and, besides, we had to get up and walk to the train station in the snow across the river bridge and over to the depot to get me there by 4:30 a.m. Of course, Harry had to stay there until the ice melted and he could travel by car. I finally got to Cynthiana and I had a fine time with all the old family friends, and Harry came and picked me up when the roads cleared.

* * *

In January 1947, Anne began her job in Montgomery County, and Harry returned to UK to complete his law degree. Anne rented an apartment in Mount Sterling, 40 miles from Lexington. They lived apart for nearly two years except on weekends.

Anne described the two years of her "many wonderful times" in Montgomery County:[4]

I learned a great deal in the process of organizing homemakers clubs in the space of a year. That county had wanted a home demonstration agent for many years, but never had one. They had never been able to get their local government to agree to put up the money. They had a county farm extension agent for many years, a man by the

---

4. When asked about an experience or day, Anne consistently said, "I had a wonderful time."

name of Floyd McDaniel who had been there, I think, 22 years when I went there, and he was of tremendous help to me. We had to sponsor 4-H clubs in the schools, and had adjoining offices, and he knew who to take me to for help in organizing the homemakers clubs. Within a year, I had 14 clubs going.

The ladies always brought things for a big potluck lunch, and they were particularly interested, in those days, in how to redecorate their homes because during the Depression and the war, it wasn't possible to do any of that. All attention had been on winning the war and the houses had gotten dilapidated. They needed new wallpaper, and fashions had changed, and they were interested in finding new ways to decorate and modernize their homes. We did a lot of study on that. We did a lot of work on food preservation and canning. The new process of home freezing of foods was just coming in and people were just beginning to have deep freezers.

We worked on budgeting, sewing, tailoring, and keeping up with the fashionable trends in clothes and many things. They were interested in learning to make hand-hooked rugs and I trained them how to do that.

The way that works is a specialist in whatever topic the clubs decided they wanted to study during the next year would come from the state extension office to teach training sessions for the women in the clubs. Two women from each club would come and take the training on how to do that. It wasn't all left to the home agent to do all the demonstrating because the whole project program had several different aims, but one was to teach leadership to the women. A lot of the responsibility was placed on them, but it was up to the home agent to set up these training sessions, to get all the equipment and supplies available and ready.

One of the 14 clubs consisted of black women. Nobody told me that I should organize one, and nobody told me I couldn't. There were very few black clubs ever organized in the state, but I organized one and it was a wonderful group of women. I understood that in the days before civil rights there was no point in trying to tackle an integrated group. That would just have caused trouble they didn't need nor did I, but the black women were delighted to have an organization of their own.

The black women's group, known as the Cloverleaf Homemakers, always met at night because most of them didn't drive and these were largely farm women, mostly sharecroppers, but some owned their own small farms. Their husbands would have to bring them, and the ladies brought the most marvelous platters of food you ever ate. They were wonderful cooks and they loved the work, and if there was any kind of assignment of anything they were supposed to do ahead of the next meeting, it was done. Their husbands would all sit out in the yard or if it was wintertime, out in the barn or somewhere, and I could hear them laughing and talking, and it was a good time for them, too.

I went back 60 years later for the annual meeting of the Montgomery County homemakers group, and I found that most of those clubs were still in existence, including the black one, but I also found that several of the clubs had integrated, which greatly pleased me.

When Anne took the home demonstration agent position at Montgomery County, she explained to the officials that her husband was finishing law school and planned to establish a law office in Whitesburg. The county officials understood she would be leaving in a couple of years. At that time, just after the war, there were few trained in home economics available to serve as extension agents, and Anne's expected short tenure was accepted. Anne said that after she left her job in Montgomery County, "I never worked again for income, only to prevent outgo."

In 1941, when Anne and Harry enrolled in UK, they intended to complete their degrees, and possibly pursue professions in home economics and agriculture. Had they done so, perhaps their lives would have taken a much different turn. They could have raised a family in one of Kentucky's beautiful, rural counties, worked in their chosen fields as teachers or home and farm agents, and later sent their children to UK. It could have been a peaceful, comfortable, and satisfying life. What could have been did not materialize. Their lives were comfortable ones and relatively peaceful considering the nature of Harry's profession and particularly the numerous civic causes with which they were involved.

Many significant events occurred in their lives from their enrollment at UK in 1941 to their marriage in 1946. After finishing law school, Harry returned home to Whitesburg, temporarily living with his parents. He had plans and work to do, setting up a law office, buying a piece of land in the country, and building a home, all while waiting for his first law client to walk in. The GI bill provided some of the funds to complete law school. Additionally, Harry received a moderate amount for his disability. When Anne quit her job and joined Harry, their income significantly diminished. The early days of the marriage were a bare-bones existence. In Whitesburg, seven other lawyers were already successfully established. If Harry's law practice floundered, making payments on their loan would have been difficult. Anne's new unpaid position entailed caring for the new home, growing food, making curtains and clothes, and finding ways to become an integral part of the community. She also had to prepare for the arrival of their new baby.

Anne and Harry grew up during the Great Depression of the 1930s. Those who lived during those trying times learned how to live frugally, a lesson one never forgets. Money and jobs were scarce or nonexistent. Pennies were counted and hoarded, while the paint peeled and roofs leaked. Those who could grew their own food, and almost everyone made, patched, and re-patched their clothes. In some homes, beans, potatoes, cornbread, and milk were served three times each day. A rare slab of baloney or side meat was a delicacy. In some places, unemployment reached nearly 35 percent. Men stood day after day in lines for jobs, and then stood in line to get a bucket of soup to take home to hungry families.

During the Depression, Anne lived a relatively comfortable life. There were brief times, however, when her father was unemployed. Building roads and most other structures had practically ceased. Although relatively young, Anne was well aware of the financial struggles of her aunts, uncles, cousins, and neighbors. Not only was it a time of uncertainty, it was a time of fear. Neither Anne nor anyone else who lived through the Depression ever forgot the austerity and struggle the people suffered.

Before the mid-1950s, the major responsibilities of the vast majority of women were cooking, sewing, and making babies. It was a long way from a laboratory in New Jersey and a USDA job to cooking, sewing, and making babies, but Anne adjusted to her new routine.

Living in her new, somewhat barren home, Anne designed and made maternity dresses in a style so that after the baby was born, she could cut them down into regular dresses. She made new curtains from tobacco canvas to cover the windows.

Tobacco canvas is a strip of soft white cloth used to cover plant beds when tobacco seeds were planted in early spring. The relatively inexpensive canvas is 100 feet long and 12 feet wide. Tobacco plants are transplanted to a well-tilled field when they are about eight inches tall. In the spring in Kentucky, nearly every farm was dotted with one or more of those long white canvases. Newcomers invariably asked, "What are those long, white strips out there on the ground?" The answer: "They are canvas coverings to protect tobacco seedlings from the frost and cold, but you can also make them into curtains, because they're much cheaper than other fabrics."

During her young life, Anne had lived for brief times in Ashville, Lexington, Chicago, New Orleans, and New Jersey. Those experiences provided her with a vast array of broad cultural and social benefits. Would moving to Whitesburg be a culture shock and a difficult adjustment? After a brief time there, would she yearn to go home again? Her roots were planted in Cynthiana in fertile and nourishing soil. Whitesburg, however, was similar to Cynthiana and other small towns in many respects. Anne discovered that the major difference between Cynthiana and Whitesburg was that when she went beyond the city limits of Whitesburg, it was into a much different place with a distinct culture considerably unlike what she had previously experienced.

Both towns were populated with doctors, lawyers, bankers, business owners, and more prosperous people than the simple folks living on the small farms along the creeks, coal camps, and rural areas. The country folks purchased basic needs at the country or company store in the coalfields, but on Saturdays, those from the hollows and hills flocked to the towns and filled the streets, as did most rural folks throughout Kentucky. It was the day to gather, talk, and buy some extra things. With a dollar or two left over after a week's work, a family could watch a cowboy picture show followed by a big, icy-cold soft drink and candy bar. Saturday night in town was the highlight of each week for almost all rural Kentuckians.

The inhabitants of Letcher County were predominately "mountaineers," a term used by other Kentuckians to distinguish those living in Appalachia. With schools and education available, Whitesburg sent several of its young to colleges and universities. A considerable number of Letcher County natives, and some from the deprived rural areas, became highly successful in various professional and business fields. However, very few of those future doctors, lawyers, teachers, and business people who went away returned to the mountains, but Harry and a few others did. Those like Harry brought with them people like Anne, who contributed to improving education, healthcare, and many other valuable services to help those vast numbers who existed meagerly in a setting with little or no opportunity, except for the sporadic times when the coal business boomed.

The populace of Appalachia was noted for its high level of illiteracy. This was due to pitiful standards of education and a culture that considered formal learning unnecessary to scratch out a living working a mountainside farm or digging coal inside a treacherous mine. Learning to read opened many doors and completing four, five, or six grades was considered all the schooling most people ever needed. It wasn't that the people were incapable. Tradition and the long historical culture taught that education was not necessarily the key to a happy and successful life. Too many bright, able people, however, had little opportunity for schooling.

When Anne arrived in Whitesburg, she unloaded her possessions at Cro and Martha Caudill's home, and lived there for 10 months until their new home was completed. Anne found her new temporary home warm and gracious. "They welcomed me with open arms and I loved them dearly and they loved me. They were wonderful to me, just wonderful people."

During the wait to move into their new home, in addition to opening his law office, Harry took Anne around the community, introducing his young bride to his friends and neighbors. Seeing "Aunt" Larce Hogg, a longtime friend, standing in her yard, he stopped, rolled down the window, and beckoned her to the car. She had been married to a much older Civil War veteran and raised eight boys on her own. With a bonnet on her head and a hoe in her hand, she looked in the window, and asked Anne, "Well, Lord, honey, can you cook?"

Not only was Anne settling in, meeting the town and country people, and adjusting to her new surroundings, she discovered a somewhat different style of language. Many of the original settlers of Appalachia migrated from the British Isles. The carryover of the Anglo Saxon dialect was the predominant manner of speaking in the mountains. Many words were pronounced differently with a distinct accent. Anne knew many of the older generation living in the hollows that retained the speech patterns and way of life from earlier times. Harry had numerous relatives living throughout the area. In the post-war years, these cultural aspects began to change.

Anne's new home was not noticeably alien to her. She grew up with rural folks and was acquainted with people from Appalachia who had wandered north to seek a better life on the farms in Central Kentucky. She also made friends with students from Appalachia at UK. In all Kentucky counties, it was common to hear folks speak with three distinct accents: those with a better education living in the towns and county seats, those from the rural areas, who often quit school early to work on farms, and the migrants from Appalachia.

In *Night Comes to the Cumberlands,* a passage described the culture in which Anne lived when she moved from the Bluegrass and the bright lights of big cities to the Cumberland Mountains:

> Thus the mountaineers who filtered into Kentucky about 1800 were, in most instances, already removed from literacy by two or three generations—assuming that their forefathers had been among the handful who had learned to read and write in the British Isles. For most of them, literacy had never existed.
>
> These forces had been at work long before the mountaineer's ancestors reached these shores, and for three or four generations before settling in Kentucky. By 1840, they had accomplished their work. The twig had been bent. The tree had grown, and the course of the mountaineer's development was determined. Consider then these forces

in synopsis: The illiterate son of illiterate ancestors, cast loose in an immense wilderness without basic mechanical or agricultural skills, without the refining, comforting, and disciplining influence of an organized religious order, in a vast land wholly unrestrained by social organization or effective laws, compelled to acquire skills quickly in order to survive, and with a Stone Age savage as his principal teacher. From these forces emerged the mountaineer as he is to an astonishing degree even to this day.

While Anne was adjusting to the new and different environment and making friends, Harry was involved in establishing his law practice and building a new home. The coal business was picking up from small truck mines. The mined coal was loaded on trucks and transported to a tipple at a railroad.[5]

Harry's father had been defeated in the county clerk race. He decided to enter the coal business with another partner and invited Harry to join the venture. If his law practice did not succeed as expected, a coal business would be another enterprise to fall back on.

To begin the business, it was necessary to purchase a truck. After the war, the government disposed of a considerable amount of equipment, including trucks, office furniture, and many other items no longer needed. It was a very good deal for veterans, so Harry drove to Tennessee to see about buying a surplus truck to transport coal and make money. It was a sure thing, and the surplus office would call him, but they didn't call him, so he called them—again and again. One day, the railroad depot

5.   A tipple is a high chute built to dump coal into a truck or railcar.

called him. They had a railcar practically full of boxes addressed to Harry.

If the US government had fought the war as they distributed the excess equipment, the country might have gone down to defeat. Rather than calling Harry and telling him to come get the truck, they packed the parts in boxes, saving him the time and effort of going to Tennessee and driving his truck back to Letcher County. After Harry, his father, and their partner hired a mechanic to assemble the truck, they were in the coal business.

Materials finally became available and carpenters were employed to build the Caudills' dream home. That is, all materials were available except nails. Except for military bases, constructing any buildings practically ceased during the war. It took time for manufacturers to convert back to production of all domestic products. The house moved along until time to drive the next nail. Harry got a call that a load of nails had been delivered over in Virginia. Anne and Harry closed the law office door, jumped in the car, hurriedly traveled to Virginia and bought a keg of nails. Upon returning to the building site, their builders had been hired by a neighbor.

Finally, in May 1949, the Caudills moved into their new home, four miles from Whitesburg near Mayking. It was a small village with a few homes, a store, and post office near a coal mine and tipple.[6]

The home the Caudills were to occupy for the next 42 years was built on 32 acres of land and sat about one-quarter of a mile off the main road and up the side of a mountain. Directly behind the home, tall trees stretched toward the sky, and Pine

---

6. Mayking is now practically a ghost town.

Mountain stands across the valley in front of the home. The 32 acres had more than sufficient space to raise a garden and provide a pasture. It took a couple of years of growing soybeans to nourish their worn-out land back to fertility and productivity, resulting in enough fruits and vegetables to feed several families.

The one-story house was well planned and sturdily built. Fortunately, it was spacious and had ample room for five family members and overnight guests. When they planned and built their home, Anne and Harry had no way of knowing, never a guess, that 16 years later their home would become an attraction to hundreds of houseguests from many states and other parts of the world.

When they moved in, Anne needed to decorate, make curtains, put the house in order, and get acquainted with the neighbors. She saw little distinction between a friend from Washington DC or New York, and a neighbor and friend down the road. A few small, modest homes stood down the hill and to the right along the highway to Whitesburg. The Hall family lived at the head of a nearby hollow.

Generally, mountain people are friendly, considerate, sociable, and generous, but quite independent. Soon after the Caudills moved into their home, the Hall family trudged up the hill to pay a call on their new neighbors—and to use their phone.

In those days, many folks living way up in the hollows, crooks, and crannies had no access to electricity or telephones, and little or no access to medicine; they made their own. Concoctions and mixtures of roots, berries, bark, and leaves cured most ailments. To relieve severe pain, an ample amount of moonshine did the trick.

Traditionally, in the course of their lives, mountain folks

relied on myths, legends, fables, and superstitions. "Signs" guided their lives, efforts, and labors. The sun, moon, and signs of the Zodiac signaled when fish would bite better and when it was time to plant corn. Beans were always planted during the dark of the moon. Many of the mountain people could not read the Bible, but attended the little churches scattered about. They heard preaching about the Ten Commandments, the shepherds and the manger, and understood that God's wrath could smite them. However, few paid that much attention to the Creator, because they were too busy surviving.

Anne invited in the Hall family, and they sat a spell and talked. It was obvious to Rose Hall that Anne was well along with child. Wanting to be helpful, she told Anne, "Put an ax under your bed before delivering." When Anne asked why, the mother of several children said, "It will take the pain away."

On July 20, 1949, James Kenneth Caudill came into the world. Knowing the quality of healthcare in the area and her mother's availability for aftercare, Anne chose to give birth in the Cynthiana Hospital. When it was time, Anne forgot to tell her doctor to put an ax under her bed. The baby was named after Harry's older brother James, who had died of appendicitis at age 14, and Kenneth, Anne's father. James was born soon after the Caudills moved into their new home on the hill at Mayking.

A few weeks later, Rose Hall dropped in again to offer assistance and give advice. She noticed that newborn James had a little cough. She said, "I'll tell you what you need to do for that cough. You need to get some groundhog grease and rub it on that baby's throat." Anne thanked her and said she would look for some. James stopped coughing a day or so later, without an application of groundhog grease.

Good neighbors make good friends, and other neighbors stopped by to render aid and advice. Another neighbor dropped in, and Anne lamented that her baby took all of her time. Her neighbor had four children and offered this bit of wisdom, "If one baby takes all your time, four can't take anymore."

The proud father had his own time to fill. Establishing a successful law office would take more than nine months, but clients soon came to seek Harry's counsel. If one took all his time, dozens and dozens could not take any more.

CHAPTER 5

A Mother and Father,
a Lawyer and Politician

When James was born, Anne fulfilled the role of a loving mother, cleaned the house, and prepared superb dinners for Harry, who was weary from the tribulations of the law office. On occasion, Anne had shopping to do and needed to become active in social and civic affairs.

Harry worked diligently building up his practice, and it began flourishing, as all manner of folks from the illiterate to the educated and those in between began to drop in with legal problems, or just to sit and talk. Considerable numbers of the area's inhabitants often created troubles with the law. Harry defended many of them and prosecuted others. In his 28 years of law practice in Kentucky mountain courthouses, he defended 76 murder cases and assisted in the prosecution of 34 others. He grew up listening to and retaining memorable accounts of lore, and his associations with these unique clients and characters added to his rich depository of stories, which could fill volumes. The following is a condensed version of the story of Harry's client Sam Tate, taken from one of Harry's books, *The Mountain, the Miner, and the Lord.*

Sam's favorite things in life were moonshine, money, and

women, not necessarily in that order. At age 19, he happened to meet a pretty-as-a-picture young girl at a country store, and it was love at first sight and perhaps marriage, if he had to do it legally. Sam seldom bothered with legality in anything he did. He could hardly wait to consummate his love, but Nellie, of high moral character, told him, "You can have me after marriage by a preacher on a license out of the courthouse. I won't have this business of layin' a broomstick down on the floor and steppin' across it together, then sayin' we're married. It ain't fer me." With overflowing passion, Sam explained to Nellie they would be married "this very day." Since he couldn't wait any longer to bed down with Nellie, he mounted his horse and headed to Whitesburg lickety-split to get a marriage license. Nellie was very excited, too, and she hurried to tell her family so they could cook a "big wedding dinner with all the fixin's."

It was winter, and Sam took a shortcut down Thornton Creek where his brother lived. He stopped by his house to warm up a bit. When he backed up to the fireplace, he noticed blank papers on the mantel. They were certificates for registering cattle, which certified that a registered cow or bull was purebred and the highest quality. He thought these certification papers might be a license of some sort. He took a blank one, tucked it in his pocket, and hurriedly headed back up Rockhouse Creek.

He happened to remember that a preacher lived at the mouth of Sexton's Branch. He stopped, rapped on the door, held out a ten-dollar bill, and asked if the preacher would ride down the creek and marry him to Nellie. In the bargain, Sam told the preacher he would be an honored guest at the big wedding dinner. The preacher saddled up his old mule and they rode together down to Nellie's parents' house for the wedding. There was a lot of commotion going on there with Nellie's sisters cooking up a storm and neighbors dropping in. The guests thought it rather amazing that the excited groom could ride to Whitesburg for the license and back again in such a short time. Sam told them he nearly wore out his horse all because of his love for Nellie.

Before the ceremony, one question arose. Why was there a picture of a bull on the license, instead of a seal showing two men shaking hands with the familiar Kentucky state inscription, "United We Stand: Divided We Fall"? Sam explained that the state of Kentucky had changed it.

The ceremony was short, followed by the preacher carefully scribbling his name on the license, which made it legal. Sam had respect in the community, because he was educated all the way through the sixth grade, proving a successful man doesn't necessarily need an eighth-grade diploma. Since neither Nellie, the preacher, nor any other family member or guests could read or write, Sam filled in the blanks on the license. After the preacher scribbled his name where Sam pointed, Nellie became his lawfully wedded wife.

The marriage went well and all was loving bliss, until Nellie's older sister from Hindman in Knott County, dropped by. She had some education, too. When Nellie proudly showed her the marriage license, the older sister was astonished. The paper certified that on the date aforesaid, "Sam Tate, out of Robert and Elizabeth Tate, had been bred to Nellie." It was proper because Nellie's parents each had placed an "X" as witnesses along with the preacher's name on the proper spaces. On the line indicating the results of the union, Sam wrote, "Don't know yet."

Sam Tate shot three men to death including his own brother. Those were his most serious infractions, but there were numerous others. He had been charged with robbery, carrying concealed weapons, shooting with intent to kill, and income tax evasion. Sam had also been charged with possessing an untaxed machine gun, assault and battery, making moonshine whiskey, selling untaxed alcoholic beverages, and operating a roadhouse without a license. Add to those infractions, contributing to the delinquency of minors, operating a house of ill repute, permitting gambling on the premises, using mail to defraud, and statutory rape. His last appearance as a defendant was for illegally selling firecrackers.

Never too worried about his multiple infractions, Sam defined justice for Harry: "The more money you have, the more justice you get. If you plan to kill somebody, be sure to get plenty of money together first."

After the repeal of prohibition, Sam opened a place of business on the outskirts of Whitesburg. A customer could get almost anything he wanted at Sam's place. He was a shrewd businessman, who, during prohibition, had 22 cars running moonshine to various places around the area. After the war, when coal boomed, he bought coal from small truck mines at a low price and shipped as many as 50 railcars daily, selling the black gold at much higher prices. Sam felt somewhat naked without a roll of 1,000-dollar bills tucked away in his pocket and big diamonds glistening on his fingers.

Harry had his hands full representing Sam. His newest wife, Maxie, lived with him, as did Lizzy. Sam said it worked out mighty fine, but it didn't work forever, because later Lizzy shot Maxie dead. Nellie pleaded self-defense, but the jury didn't believe it and gave her considerable time away at prison. About two years later, Lizzy was back in Whitesburg wearing diamond rings and the latest fashions, and legally married to Sam.

Later, when Sam faced another felony charge, he had another lawyer defend him. He stopped by Harry's office for counsel, appearing to be unconcerned. When the jury returned the verdict, the foreman informed the judge they were hopelessly deadlocked, so a new trial had to be scheduled. Sam popped into Harry's office again, his face livid. He fumed that he had a special friend on the jury and had told him to "hang the jury or die." The man had given Sam his honor that he would. The other 11 jurors voted to acquit. Sam raged, "Just because I told him to hang the jury or die, that idiot wouldn't agree to anything but a hung jury. He wouldn't even agree to turn me loose scot-free." It was not unusual to see a juror of limited material means drive down the street in a new car after serving on the jury at one of Sam's trials.

At age 63, Sam Tate was shot between the eyes. He had gone to a "little two-by-four bootlegger" in Harlan County to extort $100, as was his means of business. A man perhaps worth a million or more died over $100. Whatever the money he left was never traced or found. When Sam's dignified funeral entourage passed by Harry's office window, he was conferring with an older lady who lived on the Indian Fork of Rockhouse Creek where Sam grew up. She said, "He was just as bad as a child as he was when he grew up; he never changed. There was never any limit to his devilment."

The story doesn't end there. Wanting to become involved in the community, Anne accepted her first invitation to a breakfast meeting of the Whitesburg Women's Club. Although she wasn't late for the meeting, she was one of the last to enter; two other women directly preceded her. One was the wife of the local sheriff and the other was elegantly dressed and wearing a diamond that would knock your eyes out. The other ladies were all sitting at tables chatting and laughing. When the last three ladies entered, the chatting ceased immediately—dead silence. All eyes sternly focused on Anne. She wondered, "Has my hair turned green?" Anne felt like pulling a magic act and vanishing, but discreetly took a seat in a back corner. The silence and stares were not focused on Anne after all, but on one of the women preceding her, Mrs. Sam Tate, Sam's legitimate wife, recently released from prison.

Harry was a hometown boy and widely known as Cro Caudill's boy. Cro was highly respected in the community and served three terms as county court clerk. During one election, he asked a talented friend, skilled in carving wood, to whittle several crows, which had only one wing and all were painted white. Such is the nature of politics, a one-armed man running for office symbolized by a crow with only one wing.

When Cro ran for his fourth term, he was defeated by Cossie Quillen. Quillen was a friend who had been blinded after being shot in the head. Quillen had been a leader of a Boy Scout troop, and during a campout, a drunk came along and began firing into the troop's campsite. The drunk killed one scout and shot Quillen in the head. Thus, a one-armed man relinquished the clerk's office to a blind man. The newly elected clerk relied on his wife and assistants to do the necessary paperwork.

People trusted Cro, therefore they trusted his boy, who had been wounded in the war. Trust is an absolute, particularly in the mountains. One is either trusted or not. It's black or white proposition. The word spread: Cro's young boy, a wounded war veteran, was down there in his law office and would do right by his clients.

Early in Harry's law career, an old coal miner and immigrant from Russia died with considerable savings. His wife and child had returned to Russia decades earlier. The judge assigned Harry to settle his estate consisting only of what the immigrant had saved. Harry worked through the records, which were limited, and tried unsuccessfully through the communist Russian embassy to find and reach the heirs. The judge rewarded Harry with a fee, which was a financial boost to Harry during the lean days at the beginning of his career.

After the war, recuperation, and law school, Harry had limited, if any, financial resources. Anne had saved and accumulated some war bonds during her work in New Jersey and saved her travel allowance paid during her frequent travels as home demonstration agent in Montgomery County. Financing their beautiful new home with a loan, they furnished its empty rooms with the barest essentials. Anne used her savings to help finish the home, and they accumulated hand-me-down furniture, purchased some, and Anne began working wonders with a needle and thread. She had childhood experience in making clothes, and her training and experience in home economics prepared her to use scraps and make them into attractive clothes, curtains, slipcovers, and other accessories.

During this time, Anne was also busy mothering James. When James was three, Diana Ellen was born on July 20, 1952. Anne returned to Cynthiana to give birth to Diana. When the time was nigh, Anne grabbed a magazine to read before the rush to the delivery room, and read an article about the importance of mulching strawberries. Before delivery, Anne told her mother, "When you call Harry, tell him to get straw for our strawberry bed."

With a slight tone of exasperation, her mother said, "Anne, don't you have more important things to attend to right now?"

Anne heard the doctor say, "Look at that redhead." She recalled, "My soul floated right up to a pink cloud for I always longed to have red hair."

Anne said that, from the beginning, the redhead "has ever been a pleasure and never a problem. Scarcely ever in her life has she been difficult or other than agreeable, kindhearted, caring, and cooperative. Never did I have a concern as to her behavior or honesty."

Until Diana began kindergarten, Anne remained home with her children, read to them, sewed clothes for the family, worked in the flower and vegetable gardens, and canned and froze vegetables. Anne had an opportunity to become a home demonstration agent in the area, but realized it would require too much time and decided instead to help Harry as part-time secretary.

As her neighbor had advised, if James took all of Anne's time, Diana could take no more. Their third child, Harry Frye Caudill, was not born until nine years later on May 28, 1961.

It was a time for the couple to love and attend to their children, take hikes in the woods, and read when the children went to bed. Harry continued having disturbing thoughts about the plight of his people and he began accumulating stories about their lives. After years away at school and war, with growing maturity and intellect, Harry viewed his native land differently, nearly as if the day had turned to night—the land ravaged, streams used as garbage dumps and sewer lines, one-room schools with leaky roofs, and children weak and cold. In the army, he had seen the barren hills in Italy, sheep and goats picking the few sprigs of grass from among the rocks. He thought of home and the poorly educated and impoverished people, existing primarily by digging and loading coal during the better times, which were rare.

Harry kept thinking about what he could do to make the lives of his people better. Perhaps it was a brooding process coalescing into an outlet for his basic concern and innate compassion. It became a passion that evolved into commitment to address the dire needs of his people.

The first time Harry took Anne to the mountains, a six-hour drive from the rich, lush land of her home, he introduced her to a very different way of life. They drove through the narrow valleys, through the coal towns where slag heaps burned, and railcars parked practically in the front yards. Anne noticed that the people spoke a distinct dialect, peculiar, though quite expressive and colorful. She knew she loved Harry, and he loved her and would take care of her. Like Harry, Anne was a dreamer. Dreams have no boundaries and she thought, *We'll live our dreams here.*

In the midst of the arduous work, and increasing demands and responsibilities, the Caudill family relieved the stress with amusing stories, delightful laughter, and a joyous atmosphere. Harry employed subtle humor at appropriate times in his arguments before juries. Anne attended some of Harry's trials, if for no other reason than to hear him plead a case. When Harry took the floor, the defendant, judge, jury, and spectators soon became impressed and attentive to every word he said. His frequent use of quotations from philosophers, poets, Shakespeare, and the Bible were inevitably interwoven into his pleas, arguments, and orations. Without notes, he was a master of improvisation, sneaking in statements and fabrications to embellish a point.

During one plea, with all eyes focused and all ears open,

Harry reminded the jury that scripture is the final law; take heed. "As it is written in Philadelphians, birds of a feather flock together." With approving nods from the judge and jurors, Anne could hardly contain herself. Birds of a feather flocking together is not in Genesis, Philippians, or anywhere else in the Bible, but was perhaps something Benjamin Franklin had written in Philadelphia.

Improving schools was Harry's first major cause, one with which Anne firmly concurred. Whatever the endeavor, their minds and hearts remained joined. They asked themselves, "What can we do and where can we begin to improve education, not only here, but in all of Kentucky?"

In *Night Comes to the Cumberlands,* Harry described the attitude toward education, as it was and had been for a century or more in Appalachia:

But the feud years, bloody and hideous though they were, were not given over entirely to mayhem and murder. In this era, the first faltering steps were taken toward a public school system and a few gaunt, graceless "meeting-houses" were built for public worship.

Kentucky as a whole has lagged behind the rest of the nation in almost every field of government and public service, primarily because the fiercely independent and uncooperative mentality of the frontier hunter-farmer has remained so deeply and tenaciously embedded in the mass psyche. And the frontier modes have endured in no other part of the state to such a marked degree as in the isolated and landlocked valleys of the plateau.

An essential element of the frontier mind was a jesting

abhorrence of the intellectual. Thoroughly content with the uncouth frontier world about him, the pioneer tended offhandedly to reject all discussion and consideration of ideas in the abstract. Things and people—food, whiskey, heat, cold, shelter, enmities, sexual gratification, birth and death—were the ingredients of his life. These he could understand and appreciate. Beyond them, he seldom allowed his thoughts or aspirations to stray. It is not remarkable, then, that the state was nearly a century old when the first hesitant efforts were made in the direction of Thomas Jefferson's great dream of a broadly based, free system of public schools.

A plan developed. In one sense, Harry had great interest in politics, but detested most politicians, particularly the financial entanglements involved and the cover-ups, distortions, and outright lies to which many or even most politicians fall prey. He wondered if an honest man could win. However, he realized, the best way to fight them was to join them.

"In Kentucky" is an oft-quoted poem written in 1902 by Judge James Mulligan. In the poem's seven stanzas, Mulligan writes, "the moonlight falls the softest, sunshine's ever the brightest, and friendship is the strongest in Kentucky." In the fifth stanza, he wrote:

> The bluegrass waves the bluest;
>   In Kentucky;
> Yet bluebloods are the fewest
>   In Kentucky;
> Moonshine is the clearest,

By no means the dearest,
And yet, it acts the queerest,
In Kentucky.

Everything in Kentucky is the finest, greatest, and brightest,
except a description in the last line:

Songbirds are the sweetest
In Kentucky;
The Thoroughbreds the fleetest
In Kentucky;
Mountains tower proudest,
Thunder peals the loudest,
The landscape is the grandest—
And politics—the damndest
In Kentucky."

If politics is the damndest in Kentucky, it's the g__damndest
in Letcher and other mountain counties. "All politics is local,"
said ex-Senator Tip O'Neill from Massachusetts. In Appalachia,
politics are local, internal, and at times, a life-or-death proposition.

In *The Senator from Slaughter County*, one of Harry's two works
of fiction, he based the political story on people he knew. Doc
Tom Bonham of the fictitious Slaughter County was modeled, in
part, after Dr. Benjamin Franklin Wright, who was a local and
highly respected doctor, and the kingpin of his political party.
Doc Wright was the Caudill family doctor, as well as being a
distinctive character and wily politician.

The fictitious Doc Bonham saw to it that his wife became
the county school superintendent. A political party kingpin and

a county school superintendent were, and still are in many places, the two most powerful people in a county. They control jobs and the purse strings. In many counties, the school superintendent employs more people than any other company or institution. A superintendent has to hire teachers, principals, bus drivers, cooks, janitors, and coaches, the most valuable employees in the system. One might say, "Elmer has been a good friend and supporter for years, so I'm gonna hire his daughter, who graduated from high school and had nearly a year up at Morehead College. She'll teach those kids all they need to know." The book is Anne's favorite of all those that Harry wrote.

In 1960, Harry anonymously published an article in *Harper's* magazine, "How an Election was Bought and Sold." The byline was "a Kentucky legislator." It was his first published work since years before when he wrote several articles about his war experiences for the Whitesburg's *Mountain Eagle*, a noted newspaper in the area. Not that he ever bought or sold an election, but he knew firsthand how it was accomplished. The article created considerable attention nationwide. In it, Harry described intricate and devious ways of buying or selling an election. A common way was to load the boot of a car with jugs of moonshine or half-pints of cheap Kentucky bourbon and on Election Day, stick a bottle into a voter's pocket to ensure a vote, or persuade a voter to change his mind. This practice goes back to our founding fathers. In the preface of Harry's book *Slender is the Thread*, he wrote, "George Washington was elected to the Virginia House of Burgesses in a campaign in which he dispensed four-fifths of a gallon of spirits for each vote he received."

After drinking the half pint before casting a vote, a happy, dizzy voter was more apt to vote for the generous giver. Generally, big money from the coal companies ensured victory for candidates they supported, which, in turn, obligated the victorious official to support the coal companies so they could remove a mountaintop practically wherever and whenever they pleased. Stuffing a ballot box in devious and ingenious ways was another way to win an election and not an uncommon way to seal a victory.

Feelings ran high on election days. At those big gatherings, voters fussed, fumed, and rambled around, taking frequent swigs from a bottle. A voter might think, "If my man wins, he promised me a job fixin' the roads." Many of the notorious mountain feuds stemmed from politics: Yankees against Rebels, Republicans against Democrats, clan against clan and, in some cases, internal family squabbles and fights. It was not unusual to hear gunshots on Election Day.

In 1914, the Hazard *Herald*, in Perry County, described an election incident in Letcher County: "In a fight over at Rockhouse on Election Day, four men were killed outright and one badly wounded. Talt Hall, Dunk Quillen, Marion Hall, and Albert Hall were killed and Lance Hall was shot in the arm, and Albert Hall's wife badly wounded. The trouble came up over a school trustee election."

Fully understanding the poverty-stricken quality and facilities of education, particularly in Appalachia and almost all of Kentucky, Harry realized he had to work for the improvement of education. In 1954, with Anne's blessing, Harry decided to run for the Kentucky legislature, and, without bloodshed, won a two-year term. He won again in 1956, skipped two years, and served a third term in 1960.

Political campaigns are tortuous. Sheriff George Wooten, a

county sheriff and friend of the Caudills, explained what he did when running for county judge in Leslie County:

> Lost three months and 20 days canvassing the county. Lost 1,360 hours of sleep studying about the election. Lost six acres of corn and a lot of sweet taters. Lost two front teeth in a personal encounter with an opponent. Donated to 200 preachers, gave 4,000 fans to churches. Gave away one bull, eight shoats, seven head of sheep to barbecue; gave away two pairs of suspenders, five calico dresses, five dolls, and 15 baby rattles; kissed 150 babies; kindled 25 fires; put up 14 cook stoves; cut 15 cords of wood, and promised 12 pups, but the old female only had six.
>
> Picked 25 gallons of blackberries, hauled 100 bags of dairy feed, unloaded 20 tons of lime, shook hands 9,000 times, told 500 lies, attended 27 revivals, was baptized seven times by immersion and twice some other way, contributed to foreign missions, walked 500 miles, knocked on 2,000 doors, got bit 19 times by dogs and then got defeated.[7]

Although Wooten lost that race, he was later elected judge.

In 1954, when Harry ran for state representative, Anne swung into action, too. Driving up and down the creeks and hollows, she knocked on doors, and spread the word about the dire need for better education, assuring voters her husband would get the job done in Frankfort. The legislature meets during January and February every other year, and during occasional special sessions. In 1954, when Harry went to Frankfort, Anne

---

7.   George Wooten, *Thousandsticks*, Leslie County, Kentucky, August 1953.

and her two small children moved for the two months to her parents' home in Cynthiana, approximately 40 miles from the capital in Frankfort. The family could be together some nights and on weekends. Harry also kept a room in Frankfort to stay when the sessions ran late into the night. Anne attended sessions when Harry was scheduled to speak. She and her children moved to Cynthiana again during the 1956 session. During the 1960 session, she remained in Whitesburg, because both her children were attending school.

Kentucky may be far from one of the wealthiest states in the union, but it has one of the most striking and beautiful capitol buildings. It sits majestically upon a knoll above the Kentucky River, which flows through the center of historic Frankfort. The interior walls, hallways, staircases, and massive columns are made of marble. People entering the ground floor, deep below the rotunda, might pause and reflect upon its impressive beauty and historical significance. The statue of Abraham Lincoln on the ground floor reminds visitors of this native son, who represents emancipation, granting all people freedom. Before his courageous stand, people of color were constitutionally considered three-fifths of a human being.

It did not take long for the first-term legislator from Letcher County to make an impression. Attaining prestige, power, and fame was of no concern. Harry's oratorical skills, integrity, and undivided and unyielding commitment to help his people soon gained fame of a different sort. When Harry spoke, legislators and the media listened, and after his first year as a representative, he was named "most outstanding legislator."

Anne dressed redheaded Diana in her finest little velveteen dress and drove over to Frankfort to hear Harry give an important speech. The gallery in both houses is a circular balcony high above the chamber floors. Diana had watched Peter Pan the night before on TV at her grandparents' home in Cynthiana. (The Caudills did not buy a TV until several years later, because watching it interfered with reading books.) After Anne and her beautiful little daughter took their seats in the gallery, legislators began entering the chamber. Anne described the processional as a heart-thumping experience. When Diana saw her daddy walk in, she said, "Oh, there's daddy. I'm going to fly down like Pan." When she stood up to leap over the railing, Anne grabbed the tail of her dress. "It scared me to death," she remembered.

Son James took a trip to the capitol, too. As a toddler, he was fascinated by and played with two things—toy coal trucks and chimney pots—earthenware pipes placed on the tops of chimneys. He had watched the installation of the chimney pot on his home. When he first looked at the dome on the capitol, he pointed and said, "Chimney pot."

Politics works in strange ways. To be successful, you have to know the angles, which are not geometric. Harry was assigned to the education committee to study ways to improve the schools. One way was to raise taxes. Propose raising taxes in Kentucky, or almost anywhere, and you're instigating war. Kentucky legislators had debated adopting a sales tax for years, but never made it law. Although most legislators supported improvement of schools, passing a tax was dead on arrival. Initially, only Harry and the Democratic floor leader signed the bill to pass a two-cent sales tax for schools. It was an auspicious beginning for the first-term legislator, who went to Frankfort primarily to improve schools.

In *Night Comes to the Cumberlands,* Harry explained how

the first tax passed to support a system of public education in Kentucky:

Not until 1864 did the state levy a tax for the support of its schools. This niggardly effort was so inadequate as to be grotesque. In that year, the generous lawmakers required that the owners of dogs should pay a tax of a dollar a head, and that the money thus collected from each owner, after the second dog, should go into the school fund. The state also permitted one-half of the fines collected from violators of the antigambling laws to go for the same purpose. Somewhat later, the General Assembly imposed a tax of five cents per one hundred dollars of assessed property for the support of schools. These trifling sums were all the sovereign people were willing to devote to the education of their children, and at the next session, sober second thoughts moved the legislature to require that the paupers in each county should first be supported out of the school fund and only the residue devoted to education! And this was in a state where most people simply ignored the dog-tax law and where few gamblers were ever apprehended or fined.

During this eight-year span, Harry served under three governors: Lawrence Weatherby, the legendary A. B. "Happy" Chandler, and Bert Combs. Anne knew them all, and attended meetings with them. She particularly enjoying meetings when Happy was there.

There will never be another Happy Chandler in Kentucky politics, or perhaps in politics anywhere. He was a quintessential politician and beyond what is known as a character. He was a two-term governor, a US senator, and the major league baseball commissioner; he paved the way for Jackie Robinson to become the first black major league baseball player.

At nearly every courthouse in Kentucky, Happy enthralled large crowds with his campaign orations, especially when he sang the tearjerker, "My Old Kentucky Home."

Radio announcer Cawood Ledford had worked his way from Harlan County to a job at WHAS in the big city of Louisville. Thousands of Kentuckians used to tune in to hear him call the action of UK Wildcat basketball games after first announcing, "Please stand for 'My Old Kentucky Home' sung by Governor Happy Chandler." Happy never let Kentucky forget him.

There is more than one way to skin a polecat tax. Wily political minds learn how to scheme, manipulate, and pull the wool over voters' eyes. Who would not support a bonus for veterans? They had sacrificed their all in World War II. A bill to establish a two-cent sales tax to fund a veterans' bonus passed. Tacked on to the law was the stipulation that when the bonuses were paid, the continuing tax revenues would go to schools. Chalk up a victory for Governor Weatherby, Harry, and many other supporters. It was perhaps a feeble beginning, but as the years went by, taxes increased slightly, and schools were better funded and improved considerably.

Although Harry and Happy Chandler were ardent Democrats, they frequently clashed. Harry was never hesitant to speak his mind, certainly about what he believed was right. Damn the politics. Harry and Anne were called to Louisville to meet with Happy and other political leaders. When Happy finally burst into the conference room, it was obvious he was in a rare unhappy mood. He crossed both arms over his heart and lamented, "*The Courier-Journal* is tearing my heart out." The paper had written an anti-Happy article. Later, when he asked Harry to run as his attorney general in the next election, Harry declined. He had become weary of the politics in Frankfort.

The Louisville *Courier-Journal*, Kentucky's largest newspaper, was long published by the Bingham family—Barry Sr., followed by Barry Jr., with assistance from other family members, including Mary, the wife of Barry Sr. The paper was considered one of the better newspapers in the country.

News and opinions spread daily throughout the state and the paper's influence was substantial. For many years, Alan Trout was one of its more popular columnists. He covered legislative sessions in Frankfort, wrote other interesting and colorful stories, and called himself a "barnyard scientist." Many of his articles dealt with subjects like how to grow a bushel gourd. He encouraged the people of Kentucky to grow these gourds, and he would provide the seed if a potential grower sent him a stamped envelope. When people were tending to a gourd or something else in or near a barnyard, they were not worrying about Kentucky politics. The postal service delivered hundreds of bushel gourd seeds all over the state.

The Caudills became close friends with Trout. One day while sitting in his office, Anne and Harry were discussing the scandalous goings on and the lobbying efforts, and Anne sighed and remarked, "I wish I didn't know what I've learned in this capitol building." Alan looked at her and said, "Sorrow is the price of wisdom."

Anne planted her gourd seed in her garden down by the highway, and was so proud of the washtub-sized gourd. One day, when she returned from an errand, she discovered that a dastardly thief had stolen it. Anne seldom if ever, becomes upset or angry, but she did that time. "I didn't care how many tomatoes or how much corn they took if they needed it, but not my bushel gourd," she said.

For years, the quality of Kentucky schools ranked 49th in the nation. It was disputed whether Arkansas or Mississippi ranked 50th. In the 54 one-room and two-room schools in Letcher County, many of the teachers were ill prepared. The hiring of teachers was based on local politics, and few highly qualified teachers were imported from other areas. Anne knew a principal, who when asked if being a principal was a difficult job, answered, "No, all I do is sit on the stage and look wisdom." When the free lunch program began for indigent children, Mr. Principal wrote a note to his teachers, "Please list all your indignant children."

Harry was instrumental in calling attention to and passing legislation to provide more funding for the schools. He was also influential in passing the minimum foundation law, which better equalized school funding. While wealthier urban schools received more than their fair share, the rural mountain areas received considerably less. A few more dollars shared equally began to make a difference.

One issue down and one to go. Anne and Harry only had to travel a short distance from their home to watch the sides and tops of mountains turning to rubble. Digging a tunnel to mine coal is one thing; bulldozing off a strip or the top of a mountain is another. The dirt, rocks, and trees tumble down the mountain, eventually into the streams, and occasionally down to smash against a house. One boulder that came crashing down killed a four-year-old child. Why doesn't the government stop it? Money and politics.

It is a complex dilemma. If coal miners have no jobs, they starve. Coal companies provide jobs, and if they make more money, the miners might make more money, too. Coal operators have discovered that scraping away the earth is much easier and highly profitable. The old way was much more difficult and costly, and it killed numbers of men, for which the companies took the heat. But what could they do with the dirt and rocks? They chose to let nature take its course, but sowed some seed on the mountains as a cover-up.

Harry faced a paradox. He always fought for jobs and development. He always supported and served the miners, and they supported him. He wasn't against mining coal, but was opposed to the resultant destruction of the land. However, when the word came down from a mining company headquarters in a skyscraper in a big northern city, it caused consternation and second thoughts among the miners. Miners were told that if the legislature passed strict laws against the mine owners, then they might have to close the mines. A local sentiment was, "If that Caudill feller up in Frankfort is passin' bad laws, I won't have a job."

Harry supported legislation to place some regulations and restrictions on all forms of coal mining, including safety and land reclamation. Anne was in the gallery the night he took the floor, pleading his cause and ending his speech with, "How can a man die better than facing fearful odds for the ashes of his fathers and the temples of his gods?" Harry used this quote from a poem by Thomas Macauley in which the poet told the story about Horatius guarding the bridge to Rome. The speech brought down the house.

Historically, coal mining in Appalachia has been a series of booms, busts, conflicts, strikes, feuds, battles, and small wars. During one time of trouble, gun battles developed, and Anne and Harry sat in their home listening to the gunfire. Harry worked for the cause of saving the mountains all his life.[8]

After three terms in the Kentucky legislature, Harry had had enough. Several years later, when Harry taught at UK, Stephen L. Fisher and J. W. Williamson interviewed Anne and Harry. The *Appalachian Journal* published the interview in the summer of 1981. Fisher asked Harry why he stopped running for political office, when speculation among some of the political powers considered him a candidate for a much higher office.

Harry said, "Politics is just a demeaning thing, it's terribly demeaning. You have to debase yourself to stay in politics. You have to raise money and give it to people, and do all kinds of things that are downright repugnant. And this is what makes politicians who stay in politics for very long become so cynical . . . they've plumbed the depths of human nature and they know how crass and cynical most people are." He went on to say, "When you spend much of your life raising money to give to voters—and the television nonsense of today—you can't stay in politics without becoming cynical."

Undoubtedly, the moral and ethical issues, the "buying and selling of an election," as exposed in his first major article, bothered Harry.

"You can't express opinions and stay in politics," he said. "You have to be all things to all people. You have to stand for spending programs and lowered taxes, knowing it won't work,

---

8. To this day, Anne continues working on the issue; the current scene in Appalachia has to be seen to be believed.

but you have to promise people things they shouldn't have, and if you don't, they'll vote against you."

Anne said of Harry, "I think he has served more and continues to serve more with the writings and the teaching and the constant reiteration and promotion of ideas that need to be given circulation, than he even did in the legislature."

CHAPTER 6

I Love Coal: I Love Mountains

Coal became an integral part of Anne's life for more than 60 years. Two bumper stickers tell a story, violent at times. One says, I LOVE COAL: i.e., "We love coal so much, we'll mine it any way we can." The other one says, I LOVE MOUNTAINS: i.e., "We love mountains so much, we don't want to see them destroyed." These two powerful forces continue fighting this battle, the money power versus the tree huggers.

Tunnel mines provided jobs, but took a heavy toll on the health and lives of miners. Dynamite and giant bulldozers take the sides and tops off mountains, fouling streams, destroying forests, and wounding the earth with scars that may never heal. Mountaintop removal is one thing; reclaiming the land is another. Therein lies the conflict.

Harry was never opposed to the coal business. He knew the country needed coal and it had to be mined where it was. He understood the local coal operators provided jobs and fuel for the nation. His conflict stemmed from the abuses of safety for the miners, exploitation of the workers who made low wages, and as surface mining increased, destruction of the land and ever-dwindling employment. The absentee owners, especially, raised his ire. Their profits were enormous. Based in lush offices primarily in the Northeast, they had little knowledge or interest of the dreadful conditions in which the miners worked and lived.

In *Night Comes to the Cumberlands*, Harry described the circumstances that led to the present condition:

> Much of the region's story is the story of coal. Geologists tell us that two hundred million years ago it was a plain that had risen from the floor of a long-dry inland sea. Then the tortured crust of the earth cracked and "faulted," rearing the Pine Mountain. This long, steep, ragged ridge now stretches from the Breaks of the Big Sandy River on the Virginia line some 130 miles southwesterly into Northern Tennessee. It parallels the Cumberland (or Big Black) Mountain, the southern boundary of the plateau. Water flowing away from its base over a great fan-shaped territory carved channels of three of the state's major streams and chiseled thousands of narrow valleys, the creeks and hollows of today.
>
> After the shallow sea receded it left a vast bog where vegetation flourished, died, piled up in deep beds, turned to peat, and finally, eons later, to coal. When the streams carved out the mountains and ridges of today, they sliced through magnificent seams of coal, a mineral the steel age would esteem more highly than rubies.
>
> Coal has always cursed the land in which it lies. When men begin to wrest it from the earth, it leaves a legacy of foul streams, hideous slag heaps and polluted air. It peoples this transformed land with blind and crippled men and with widows and orphans. It is an extractive industry, which takes all away and restores nothing. It mars but never beautifies. It corrupts but never purifies.

But the tragedy of the Kentucky mountains transcends the tragedy of coal. It is compounded of Indian wars, civil war and internecine feuds, of layered hatreds and of violent death. To its sad blend, history has added the curse of coal as a crown of sorrow.

On January 28, 2010, Anne drove her car to Louisville and parked it in the church lot at the Thomas Jefferson Unitarian Church. The large numbers who walked in probably noticed the "I Love Mountains" bumper sticker on her car, which referred to her strong feelings, not about coal, but about dynamiting off the tops of mountains to extract coal.

Anne frequently commented about Harry's natural gift as speaker and orator. She heard him speak many times; evidently, she absorbed some of his talent. Anne moved the large crowd that evening with her heartfelt presentation. If audience members weren't tree huggers when they walked in, they were looking for the first tree to hug when they walked out.

As a member of this church, I salute the committee for all the work they do, for all the environmental projects they undertake, and for their constant support of green tips that each of us individually and as households can use to subdue and lessen our imprint on this little green earth. Often there comes to my mind one of the first commandments as set out in the scriptures. In Genesis 2:15, it says, "And the Lord God took the man and put him in the Garden of Eden to dress it and to keep it." I'm proud of this church for hosting this rally against mountaintop removal. It is an effort to save a part of our earth. I want to take note and tell you about a clipping from this past Tuesday's *Courier-Journal*. It says federal mine safety officials are looking into comments by one of its Kentucky-based inspectors on the social networking site Facebook that declares, "Hang a tree hugger today."

Now, I wish to tell you that I stand before you and vow that I'm a dedicated, card-carrying tree hugger. I carry not one, but several cards that prove me a tree hugger, and that is a term of division and scorn, a controversial person to be much castigated and sneered at by some on one side of the controversy to which we address ourselves tonight.

My introduction to the Appalachia dilemma came in 1945 at the University of Kentucky. I had just met Harry Caudill, a wounded veteran recently returned to the UK from combat in Italy during World War II. At lunch in the school cafeteria, he began to tell me how his homeland, the eastern third of Kentucky, the mountain counties, were ignored and shortchanged by the rest of Kentucky. "Look around," he said. "These big murals decorating this dining hall have beautiful pictures of horse farms, tobacco fields, Bluegrass mansions, but no pictures of the mountain forests and streams, or of the huge coal mining industry or the people there."

He told me of President Roosevelt's ideas for turning vast stretches of the mountain land into national forest preserves and helping the people to move into other areas where they could enter the mainstream of American life.

Well, as it turned out, I spent 43 years helping him spread the message of the plight of the Appalachians to the American nation and seeking ways to bring constructive change to the lives of the people. Those decades were a marvelous adventure and a gift in my life.

During those years, I hugged many a tree. We hiked through those magnificent forests, and as tree farmers, we paid for the planting of many thousands of trees on worn-out land. We also cared deeply about our neighbors, relatives, and friends, the people of that land.

Now, I need not persuade you that the destruction of the Appalachian Mountains by surface mining is monstrously shortsighted and destructive. You wouldn't be here tonight if you did not believe passionately that this terrible destruction of the land, the forests, and the streams which sustain the oxygen–carbon dioxide exchange of our atmosphere, and the headwater sources of our streams is lethally shortsighted. We have ample historic examples of civilizations that have dwindled and disappeared because of the loss of forests and vegetative cover.

Tonight, I want to share with you some of the decades-long struggle that has brought us to this critical situation. It is a struggle between those concerned entirely with the present drive for profits, for jobs, for the cheap electricity, which you and I use each time we flip on a light switch or consume the products of our coal-powered electrical system. On the other hand, there are those who seek to sustain the land so that future generations can also live in abundance and beauty.

During World War II, Harry Caudill served in the army in Italy as a foot soldier. As he clambered over the rocky steep slopes of the Italian mountains, he observed the ruins of ancient villages long abandoned because the land was worn down to the bedrock, the forest long ago cut away, and the slopes overgrazed by sheep and goats.

When he returned to his beloved Appalachian Mountains, he saw the same destruction happening at an immensely accelerated pace by the surface mining for coal. For more than four decades, he fought to awaken the American people to this destruction of the land.

In 1954, as a member of the Kentucky legislature, he helped sponsor and pass the first legislation for reclamation for strip-mined land. Under Governor Lawrence Weatherby, it was strictly enforced and the practice greatly diminished. However, the next governor's enforcement was feeble and there was much more concern to accommodate the coal companies.

Now, these coal producers had obtained title to the minerals in the land beginning about 1880 and up through 1900 or so. They were jovial and smooth-talking agents who traveled through the hills persuading the people to sign deeds selling the minerals under their land for ten cents up to a dollar an acre.

The mountain people had been isolated, with few roads or schools for as much as a century and all too often, they signed the deeds with an X, or if they could read at all, they were not sufficiently schooled to comprehend the fine print of the so-called broad-form deeds. The purchasers obtained ownership of all the minerals underlying the surface and the right to mine them, as well as the use of the forests that grew on the surface to be used as mine props.

They left to the surface owner the right to farm the land and pay taxes on it. The Kentucky Supreme Court ruled that broad-form deeds gave the coal corporations the right to mine the minerals without permission of the surface owners. The frequent destruction of the homes and the farms of the people who lived below the strip mines were called an act of God by coal companies as the rains washed the disturbed soil, the rocks, and the uprooted trees through houses and over the gardens and farms.

Harry filed suits for those so damaged, carrying cases all the way to the Court of Appeals. When the courts ruled against the plaintiffs, Harry wrote and spoke out about the injustice of their interpretation of the broad-form deeds. It was not until 1988 that the broad-form deed was overturned.

During the 1950s and '60s, a terrible depression fell on the coalfields. After the war, much of the nation had turned to cleaner oil and gas as fuels. The railroad and steamships had become diesel powered instead of coal powered. Homeowners and manufacturers switched to cleaner fuels. The Appalachian people were left jobless by the thousands, and they fled the mountains hoping to find work in the industrial cities. Whole communities were largely depopulated, leaving behind only the old, the infirm, and the less able elements.

Just last month at the Festival of Faith here in Louisville, a panel discussion was conducted on the matter of mountaintop removal. One of the panel members, a spokesman for a company that supplies coal equipment to the coal operators, stated that the people of East Kentucky did not know they were poor until the people came down from Washington, and told them they were poor and gave them welfare checks to make them dependent. I could not let such a statement pass. I had to challenge that because I lived among those people and I know how desperate their lives had become.

In 1960, Harry Caudill introduced in the legislature the first bill to outlaw strip mining in Kentucky. Such is the power of the coal industry over Kentucky's political system that the bill did not pass. During his six years in the legislature, however, he sponsored the sales tax, which to this day supports the schools of Kentucky, and the minimum foundation law, which equalizes somewhat the expenditures for education all across the state. He also worked for compensation for miners with black lung disease, and all these things were finally enacted.

Having attracted the disfavor and attention of the corporations by his outspoken criticisms, he concluded that he would not try to counter the money they would use to defeat him in the elections and he ceased running for the legislature. He turned instead to writing. His first article published in a national magazine, "How an Election was Bought and Sold," was bylined "a Kentucky legislator." As long as he lived, he never formally agreed to who that author was.

Over the years, he wrote about 160 magazine and newspaper articles published all over the country, both locally and nationally, about the land and the people of Appalachia, their plight, and their potentials. In 1963, *Night Comes to the Cumberlands* was published. It appeared just after the time when John F. Kennedy had electioneered in West Virginia, and he had seen for the first time the terrible conditions of that coal-producing state. Kennedy promised to do something about the hopelessness and poverty in the coalfields, and the book explained how the situation had developed historically and introduced some possible remedies.[9] The book brought a throng of people to our door, all wanting to learn about the region and many offering to help. It was a frantically busy time as we opened our home to these visitors, took them on tours to the coal camps and strip mines, wrote more and more articles, letters to the editors of the papers, more books, and made frequent trips across Kentucky, and to many other states and Canada to give talks.

Meanwhile, he had a very busy law practice and I was kept busy at the typewriter, while also managing the household and family, and taking part in various civic organizations.

Soon after publication of *Night Comes to the Cumberlands*, Harry met a former coal operator on the street, who had prospered and left the county for a more prosperous and upscale location. He said, "Harry, I read your book. What you said about us coal operators is true, but nobody said we couldn't or shouldn't mine those hills. You have divided Kentucky like it hasn't been divided since the Civil War. Half the people want to elect you governor and the other half wants to lynch you." And so it ever remained. He was praised by some and castigated by others, and that condition remains to this day.

It is the division of outlook that separates those today

---

9.   Kennedy was assassinated before he could revisit Appalachia.

whose bumper stickers read "I Love Coal" from those whose bumper stickers read "I Love Mountains." However, after 50 years, *Night Comes to the Cumberlands* still sells about 1,000 copies a year and recently, a new printing was published, so there are people still listening.

At a mass meeting [where Harry spoke in defense of Old Dan Gibson], an organization evolved—The Appalachian Group to Save the Land and People. Soon a motorcade was on its way to Frankfort, stretching a mile along the winding roads as jalopies, trucks, and jeeps carried angry and anxious citizens to meet with the governor. There, Harry escorted Mrs. Bige Ritchie into Governor Breathitt's office. She sat by his desk and told him, "When the bulldozer pushed the coffin of my baby over the hill, I thought my heart would break." These people felt themselves defenseless against the big corporations who had contracted to dig the coal at the cheapest possible rate for an agency of the US government, the Tennessee Valley Authority. This grassroots organization collected money by tiny sums contributed out of meager sources to bring suit against the coal corporation.

In Martin vs. Kentucky Oak Mining Company, Harry argued the case for LeRoy Martin, a schoolteacher whose neat home and green lawn and garden had been severely damaged by a mudslide from a strip mine on a mountain above his home. The case went all the way to the Court of Appeals. The court ruled in the favor of the coal company under the provisions of the broad-form deed signed probably well over a half a century before by landowners not literate enough to comprehend what they were giving up.

The court ruled the company had to pay Martin nothing

for his loss. Kentucky thereby gave legal sanction to a crime many Americans deplore and many others eagerly commit. Finally, in 1988, the broad-form deed was overturned by a constitutional amendment approved by 82 percent of Kentucky voters. However, the oppressions of that time, added to other factors, pushed the coal industry away from deep mining—which employed many, many men—to strip mining, which employed far fewer.

The loss of jobs and the depression brought on violence in the coalfields. Coal company equipment was destroyed in the night by dynamite and by gunfire. On many nights, we could hear gunfire from the woods near our country home aimed at mining installations just across the hill. In some places, killing occurred.

Finally, in 1972, a severance tax on extraction of coal was passed by the legislature, thus keeping some small part of the profits from the mining of coal within the state of Kentucky. First introduced in 1922 by Alben Barkley, the idea had been called anti-business and socialist.[10] Barkley's effort caused the only defeat he ever had at the polls. The idea was dropped until it was brought up again by Harry in the 1950s, and he advocated for 20 years until the state finally passed the bill. It has brought many millions to the state's coffers. Much of the severance tax has returned to the mountain counties to support services there, but not all. The entire state has profited thereby.

We continued to struggle to bring change, constructive change, to the region. Nine more books followed. In 1972,

---

10. Barkley was a longtime US senator and Truman's vice president.

My Land is Dying was published. It's a small black and white photographic exposé of the destruction on a national scale, an early precursor of today's magnificent big book, *Plundering Appalachia*, and I have a copy that's circulating around out there. For those of you who have a chance to look at it, I wish you would just turn to the page where the dedication is placed. That dedication reads just opposite a picture of a tiny girl seated on a broken-down sofa in a worn-out coal shack. The dedication reads, "That they may know some people cared; this book is dedicated to all those unborn millions who will someday inhabit America's spoil banks."

In 1976, *Darkness at Dawn* was published as part of the centennial series put out by the University of Kentucky, and it took the university and the legislature to task for ignoring the eastern third of the state.

In 1983, *Theirs be the Power*, identified the people and the families who were the owners of the great corporations who raped the Appalachians. Some of those identified were so prominent sitting on the board of trustees at the University of Kentucky and having inhabited the governor's office that the University Press, not unexpectedly, declined to publish it. That fact alone sold many a copy when the book was published by the University of Illinois Press.

Two novels, two books, and a collection of short stories called *Tales From a Country Law Office* and a satire about political, economic, and social realities of life in Eastern Kentucky, titled *Lester's Progress*, followed, along with a constant stream of published articles all directed at making America aware of the Appalachian problems and potentials.

After retiring from his law practice, Harry taught at the University of Kentucky for eight years. He taught Appalachian studies and Kentucky history. To this day, some of his students continue as environmental advocates, as lawyers, teachers, and in many other ways. He continued to speak out on public issues until his last days.

Two days before his death, Whitesburg's *Mountain Eagle* published an article in which he urged the people of that county to insist that the great corporations that had robbed his county contribute to the public library system there. That plea brought $1,000 as a personal contribution from one coal company owner and he was a Kentuckian.

Today, the struggle continues. When the group goes on February 11 [2010] to Frankfort to talk with legislators, you will be in competition with coal mine owners and the power of coal. As a recent whole page ad from a coal operator proclaimed, "Don't underestimate the power of coal." An earlier quote from the head of the coal association assured the public, "We are creating land for sustainable development for future generations." Somewhere among you, I have a picture of a devastated mountaintop, a land that has its mountaintop removed, an utter desert with that quotation just under it.

In 1969, the author David McCullough visited us to look at the whole situation. He was an environmental editor for *American Heritage* magazine at the time. Later, he wrote a long article in the magazine called "The Lonely War of a Good, Angry Man." He quoted Harry: "This land is always thought of as a bleak, poor, broken-down, God-forsaken place, but the truth is, this mountain land has tremendous natural resources, not the least of which is its people, and if we can make changes in the way the land is utilized, then we can become a premiere part of the United States. We have plenty of green country, an abundance of water, a superb climate, minerals, strategic location, and extraordinary beauty. And as the shortage of open land in this nation grows more and more serious, all this magnificent country is going to have value far surpassing anything like coal and we just can't afford to sit back and watch all that be destroyed so a few people can get rich."

One of these days, the dear old federal government is going to have to come in and spend billions of dollars just to repair the damage that has already been done. And guess who will have the machines and the workmen to do the job? The same coal operators who made the mess in the first place will be hired to fix it back and the taxpayers will bear the costs.

David McCullough asked Harry why he remained in Eastern Kentucky, and as so often when Harry was questioned, he answered it with a story. Harry smiled and told a story about one of the characters from an earlier time. Old Clabe Jones took part in numerous mountain feuds after the Civil War, and it is estimated that he had killed 20 men. Later, he repented of his sins and lived to a ripe old age. But at one time during the Holbrook-Underwood War, Clabe and five men were pinned down in a cabin by the Underwood forces and some law officers were called in to help finish Clabe off. The attack began before dawn and lasted until about mid-morning. At that time, Underwood's wife was sent to ask Clabe to surrender. Harry's eyes lit up and he smiled at me again. The message Clabe sent back was, "No, we want to fight on a while longer anyway." And I guess that's the way Anne and I feel. "We want to fight on a while longer anyway!"

And now, that fight has been inherited by all of you here. The Louisville chapter of Kentuckians for the Commonwealth has done much good and effective work. The organization is of particular importance, because Louisville has the largest block of members voting in the state legislature.

I'll tell you how another Louisville organization was a primary influence in getting the first strip mine control legislation enacted. In the '60s and '70s, Harry and I went to Louisville many, many times to speak to various organizations. Each time he was asked to speak, we met with small and large groups. Harry reminded them that Louisville taxpayers bear a large share of the government expenditures that support Eastern Kentucky counties. The League of Women Voters invited him to come and talk to them about the strip mining and the problems of poverty in the eastern counties. Beverly Rosenblum was the able and energetic president.

We realized the political influence the group could wield once they had researched the project and reached consensus on taking action. Harry told them about the problems and then he said, as he had said to so many others, "Come and see for yourselves," and they did. Soon Beverly arranged a three-day trip for 27 members. They came to our home for dinner and Harry talked to them in detail about what they would see the next day. We arranged for enough four-wheel-drive vehicles to transport everybody, and the next morning, we departed from Whitesburg early.

We guided them through the coal camps where the signs of poverty were everywhere to be seen. We visited the mined-out areas of Beef Hide, Elk Creek, Rockhouse, and Yellow Creek. We had lunch at the settlement school at Cordia and talked with Alice Sloan, its founder. She had told the operators of the huge strip mine, which towered above her school, that a group would be coming to see their operation. The operator was very unreceptive to the idea, but the group was allowed to come when it was explained to him that a reporter for the *Courier-Journal* would be with the group and that a refusal would not look good if reported in the state's largest newspaper. We drove up onto the extensive flats. Almost immediately, one of the huge coal trucks drove alongside our convoy, pushing us ever closer and closer to the edge of the dangerous slope on the spoiled land.

Though I did not believe the driver would actually push us over, it was a frightening situation and the message was clear, our viewing of their operation was very unwelcome.

The group returned to Louisville, reached a consensus, and conducted a very thorough and active campaign to persuade its representatives in the legislature to pass laws for reclamation of strip mine lands. It was a beginning and since that time, various efforts at restoration were initiated with very limited success. There are huge areas of so-called orphan banks, which have never received any restoration efforts at all and today, many restored areas are overrun with debris of the mountaintop removal process.

I salute the Kentuckians for the Commonwealth for your informed persistence and ever-growing resistance all across Kentucky. Remember what Kentucky's governor Happy Chandler so often said, placing his hand on his heart, maybe even weeping a little. "When the people speak, I hear no other voice." May the people speak with many voices loud and clear. As Harry said half a century ago, the right to be free is matched by the responsibility to preserve freedom's land. Liberty in a wasteland is meaningless.

Anne's speech, followed by a video of mountaintop removal, was an excellent account of the past and a brief review of the consequences leading to the present situation. *Night Comes to the Cumberlands* was a commentary, plus a broad and detailed historical account of Appalachia. Throughout the history of Appalachia, as in any area, specific events, developments, and laws changed the course, dramatically and monumentally, of how the people lived. The early settlers began cutting the prime virgin forests and floating thousands upon thousands of logs down the Kentucky River to sawmills. When the railroads initially wound around and through the mountainous terrain and down along the creek banks, the door was open to an explosion of coal transported north, south, east, and west.

In *Night Comes to the Cumberlands*, Harry wrote:

We have seen that the mountaineer sold his great trees for a consideration little more than nominal, but if his timber brought him a small financial reward, his minerals were virtually given away. The going price in the early years was fifty cents per acre, and though the price rose, little by little, over the next three decades, it rarely surpassed five dollars. Under ordinary mining methods prevailing throughout the region during the years after 1913, the operating coal companies were able to recover from 1,000 to 1,500 tons of coal per acre foot. This means that a seam of coal five feet thick produced a minimum of 5,000 tons per acre! Where more than one seam was mined, a single acre sometimes yielded 15,000 or 20,000 tons! Even this prodigious recovery left thousands of tons underground—plus the oil, gas, and other minerals. For this vast mineral wealth, the mountaineer in most instances received a single half-dollar.

During that time, one of the greatest robberies in the United States occurred. Gunslingers, armed only with a saddlebag full of printed sheets of paper, rode in to Appalachia. Smooth-talking, educated, and well-dressed fellows from up east somewhere canvassed the cabins and shacks in the hollows. A local notary public, who not only served as an "interpreter," but also made any paper signing legal, usually accompanied the nice fellow.

A conversation at such a visit might have gone something like this:

"Since they tell me you are an honest man, I'll be honest with you. I work for a little coal company up north. My company is looking for coal, and we thought there might be some under your mountain back there. There probably isn't, but we're willing to take the chance, gamble and shoot craps, you might say. We won't bother you one bit, and you still own the farm and can raise a garden and squirrel hunt your trees. But if we get lucky and find a small seam of coal, then we will mine it without making any mess at all for you. I don't know why, but my company is willing to pay you so we can just come and look."

"You mean, pay me for that?"

"Yes, 50 cents an acre and you've got one hundred acres, so we'll write a check for $50 dollars."

"Step outside so I can talk to the good woman."

"Come back in. She says all our kids need shoes, and she needs a cookstove. Write the check."

"Now, do you want my friend here to read everything to you before you sign?"

"No, you can just write the check."

Broad-form deeds included, in part, the title to extract "all coal, oil, and gas, and all other mineral and metallic substances of every other kind and character, in, on and underlying the land." Most deeds granted coal corporations and successors in title forever, the right to enter the land and drill wells, sink shafts, drive tunnels, make excavations, make and leave heaps of mine waste, divert and pollute water courses, withdraw adjacent supports and permit the surface to subside, cut and use for mining purposes the timber growing on the surface, and the right to do any and all things necessary and convenient for mining. Finally, the coal company was relieved of all damages and claims for damages for any action described above.

However, companies provided valuable jobs and many other fringe benefits. They also built coal camps with homes and stores for their employees, and the nicer ones may have had a school, church, and a movie theater. Some had access to company doctors and hospitals scattered about. One advantage of living in a coal camp was the homes had electricity well before most other rural areas in Kentucky. Mines needed electricity and the companies installed their own generators and strung the lines through the coal camps. Large families lived in small company homes. There was no space to put a refrigerator or a washing machine, except on the front porch.

Having a paying job, a nice home, and store with all the amenities was better than scratching out a meager living on the land. The coal companies, however, had a peculiar way of paying miners. They weren't paid in greenbacks, but in various designs of metal scrip (tokens). On payday, rent, which was usually excessive, and other services were deducted from each miner's pay. What remained was paid in scrip that only the company store accepted. The corporate owners, headquartered in big cities, not only made millions from tax-free coal, but also made good weekend spending money from the miners. If a miner slacked off work, caused any trouble, or talked to a union organizer, he was immediately fired and removed from his company-owned home.

"Sixteen Tons" was a country song sung by Tennessee Ernie Ford; it was popular in the 1950s. The lyrics referred to mining sixteen tons of coal, and Ford sang about miners owing their souls to the company store.

A friend of Harry's explained, "Everything was company." The companies ruled the roost in the coalfield counties. Company money and politics selected judges, school superintendents, and other officials. People who wanted to keep their jobs voted for the company's candidates. Harry wrote that miners lived in "company towns with company houses, company streets, and company stores. They were company employees and, when they died, they were buried in a company cemetery. If people got out of line, they were put in a company jail. People went to a company church and listened to a company preacher. The big shots even prayed to a company God, and died and went to a company heaven."

The history of coal mining was essentially boom or bust, year by year. When it went bust, large numbers of families moved north, seeking jobs in factories. From 1940 to the present, thousands upon thousands moved out of Letcher County. The number of miners decreased significantly when the pick and shovel were replaced by bulldozers and other mechanized equipment. In the 1950s, there were approximately 120,000 miners; today, there are about 17,000.

Anne remembers the traffic jams in Cynthiana soon after the war. Families who had moved north to survive left their hearts in Appalachia. Highway 27 ran from the north to the south through Cynthiana. On Friday evenings, Appalachian families traveled south to go to their true home. On Sunday evenings, traffic headed north to hillbilly havens on the outskirts of industrial cities where the people could make enough money to go home again the next Friday. Anne said, "Traffic was so dense, you couldn't cross the street."

For nearly a hundred years, the broad-form deed was in effect and coal passed through Kentucky on long railcars without one cent of a severance tax left behind.

"It takes about 20 years from the time an idea is introduced for it to be acted on," Anne said. "That's the gestation period of the idea, and it takes people and organizations to keep pushing the idea to the point where the American public finally understands and moves in favor of it."

She, like Clabe Jones, intended to fight a little longer.

CHAPTER 7

One of the Richest Parts of Life

When Anne arrived in Whitesburg in December 1946, she found a new, different, and most interesting place to call home. It didn't take her long to become involved in community organizations and civic projects. She even helped establish or revitalize organizations to benefit the community. She soon began meeting and befriending people and listening to their amazing stories. She never met a stranger, whether it was a high government official, a coal miner needing legal help, or a miner's widow needing food and clothing for her children.

"Over the years," she said, "one of the richest and most wonderful parts of my life is the fact I've been free to do volunteer work. I was not working full-time at a job as most people do. Although I've had a very busy life, I found time to volunteer."

At one time or another, Anne volunteered with the Brownies, Girl and Boy Scouts, 4-H clubs, projects of various women's clubs, garden clubs, and PTAs. She organized the first career-counseling program at Whitesburg High School before they had a counselor, and organized sales of pecans by the women's club to support an orphan girl so she could attend college. She assisted a nearly blind boy of a drunken father and poverty-stricken family to attend the Kentucky School for the Blind in Louisville. She also secured clothing and school supplies for his siblings. The young man completed school, and made a living as a piano tuner.

During her years in Whitesburg, Anne did everything from civic planting of shrubs, flowers, and trees, to measuring the feet of the many children who needed shoes. She helped organize the Pine Mountain Chapter of the Daughters of the American Revolution in Whitesburg and was a charter member. She established a genealogy and historical society, and served on the board of trustees of ten Appalachian regional hospitals. She organized a hospital advisory council and served as secretary to the Congress of Appalachian Development. Throughout all her years in Whitesburg, Anne spearheaded various projects to assist destitute families and needy children.

The number of hours she volunteered to several worthy causes—particularly libraries—in Letcher County, Kentucky, and surrounding areas, at UK, in Floyd County, Indiana, is immeasurable.

Soon after meeting people and making friends in her new locale of Whitesburg, Anne was instrumental in establishing a garden club. Because of low membership, Anne suggested the club invite their husbands to a meeting, so the ladies began having a monthly potluck supper, and seldom do men refuse an opportunity to eat home cooking. The club membership increased and to this day, the Whitesburg Garden Club is one of the few in the state with active male members. Beautification projects continue in the area.

Soon after her arrival, Anne joined the Whitesburg Women's Club, and was asked to be the library committee chair. She asked, "Where is the library?" She found it in an old ramshackle World War II Quonset hut behind the town jail. Anne recalled that, two hours, twice a week, "a dear little old lady volunteer sat there in her overcoat." Not many visitors came for the few discarded books stacked on the dirty floor.

It took only one visit to the county library for Anne to announce, as she did with other dire needs in the community, "This calls for action." She learned the state would help if the local counties assessed a library tax. Raising a penny in taxes is difficult for any cause. Harry began speaking to groups encouraging passage of a small tax, and filed suit to get it on the ballot. Anne and the Women's Club petitioned the fiscal court several times to get them to put the issue on the ballot. On one occasion, a court member said to Anne, "Now look here, I don't believe in that old library. My granddaughter, she's always bringing books home from the school, and she don't even have time to watch her TV programs."

Eventually, the court put the library tax on the ballot, and, against long odds, it passed. Harry contacted the Louisville and Nashville Railroad, and convinced them to lease part of the Whitesburg depot, which was being used as a freight depot. The library moved from a Quonset hut to the waiting room at the depot, but not before the depot was cleaned, scrubbed, and painted. The local Jaycees helped clean and paint the room, furniture was moved from a defunct restaurant, the manual training class at the high school built bookshelves, and the women's club made curtains and other decorations. The building sat below the elementary and high school on the hill. Soon students began flooding the new library in the valley, where, in years gone by, passengers waited to begin a new journey.

Anne organized a board to operate the library and served as secretary. She preferred serving as secretary in most organizations to which she belonged. She thought that serving as president often became political and a hot seat. When her term ended, the judge did not reappoint her to the library board because of Harry's outspoken stands. However, she never stopped donating time and effort to libraries wherever she lived.

Despite the struggle, the library grew. In 1959, 17,000 books were checked out, including those from the bookmobiles. Five years later, the number increased to 148,000. When Letcher County built a new courthouse in 1964, the library at the railroad depot moved to a more spacious facility on the ground floor of the courthouse. When the county needed more space for the jail, they told the library to look for another place. (Perhaps if those who became inmates had read more books, the library could have remained where it was.)

Harry had collected a considerable amount of genealogical and historical information on the Caudills and other families. The new library employed its first librarian with a degree in library science, Sybil Galer, and she was a dynamo. She and Anne realized the need for a historical and genealogical society. A representative of the Mormon Church sent notice that he would present a program on genealogy to help libraries establish such a project. The library held a program for those interested, and about 30 people attended. Anne devoted considerable time in the early development of the program, so much so that Harry often called the library to say, "Tell Anne to come home; she's spent enough time at the library for one day."

A building in the center of town had burned a few years earlier. The owner eventually constructed a new, modern, fireproof building on the lot. With public and private sources of funding, the library board purchased the 9,000-square-foot building. Whitesburg's library was attractive, spacious, well equipped, and first rate. The library had a well-equipped room devoted to genealogy, and within two years, the membership of the historical society had grown to over 400 members. Many lived elsewhere but had family roots in the area.

The new library had been a pet project of Harry's before his death. Private supporters contributed $1 million, but zero from the wealthy coal corporations except $1,000 from a coal-land owner from Kentucky. Amidst the celebration and fanfare, Anne recalled, "A little girl came in and checked out an armful of books, and both her parents signed their name with an X."

On May 22, 1994, three and one-half years after Harry's death, the library was named the Harry M. Caudill Library. In a dedication speech, broadcaster Al Smith said, "Here in the hills that he called home, among the people he loved so fiercely, we know that night comes to the Cumberlands, but here was a life that inspired us to search for the dawn. The very idea of a better Appalachia was his legacy to us."

On October 27, 2008, a multipurpose room in the Harry M. Caudill Library was dedicated and named the Anne F. Caudill Assembly Room. She was honored at the dedication with speeches, praise, and a proclamation from Judge Jim Ward citing her years of service to Letcher County and the commonwealth. In essence, Anne was the mother of the Whitesburg Library, nourishing it as one would a child and watching it grow to maturity, a rich and enduring legacy.

Through the 1950s and up until the book came out in 1963, the law office, the Kentucky legislature, books, libraries, education, hospitals, the needy, the trees, forests, and the land were all intermingled as a high and proportional priority, but the Caudill family and home were always the first priority. Delightful amusing stories, told and heard, accompanied their busy lives no matter when, where, or what the Caudills pursued, and were an energizing and sustaining force during solemn or trying times.

Which came first, books or trees? For Anne and Harry, it was like being asked to name a favorite child. A tree is something special. A tree changes, but stays the same. One can see and hear its rustling, yet a tree renders solitude of a renewable and enduring kind. A tree provides a resting place and a home for other creatures. A tree produces foods and other products while consuming only renewable soil, pure air, sunrays, and raindrops. A tree is a power and force, protecting and inspiring. Wendell Berry wrote that a grove of trees is like a "chambered choir." A high mountain blanketed in mosaics of changing color and light is a living embodiment of a spiritual journey, ascending to a higher plane.

"I can't live without trees," Anne stated emphatically. Neither could Harry.

The Caudill family had to only step out their front door, and take a short walk across the pasture into the woods. In winter, spring, summer, and fall, their cares diminished when they disappeared into the mountains that were covered with blankets of the tallest trees.

Walking on pavement was extremely painful for Harry, but walking on land and through the mountains was much less so. Although in later years Harry walked without a cane, he used a staff when hiking through the woods. With the continuous stressful demands of his profession, a walk out the door and into nature's wonders was an immediate renewal for both body and mind. From the shuffling of papers to integration with spectacular views, varied wildlife, and the fresh aroma of mountain air breezing through the trees, relief was readily available. From a somewhat stifling, demanding, and routine existence, a sense of openness, space, and freedom recharged his heart and nourished his soul. Harry's thoughts and contemplations during a solitary walk in the woods eventually led to his writing *Night Comes to the Cumberlands.*

The family reverence for and attention to the woods is evident in their works. Blight began killing the majestic chestnut trees in the late 1800s, and by 1945, it had virtually wiped them out. When Harry was in the legislature, he worked with the State Forest Service and began a program planting Chinese chestnut trees in the mountains in an attempt to reclaim past glory. The project proved to be a disappointment. Later attempts at restoration, however, have been successful.

In her later years, Anne said she was proud to be a qualified, certified tree hugger and had the credentials to prove it. A sign on the gatepost at the entrance to their property read, "Established Tree Farmer." Harry wrote articles about the importance of trees in land conservation, and was happiest walking among them. Anne, Harry, landowners, members of the garden club, Boy Scout troops, and other volunteers planted an estimated 120,000 trees in barren spots in the mountains.

The garden club annually pulled weeds and planted flowers and trees in and around Whitesburg. When the town built a bypass around Whitesburg, the roadside was left barren. Anne and other club members went to the city council and asked for funding to plant trees. The mayor granted $5,000 to plant trees near the new highway. The club ordered 57 large trees and went to work, and the mayor sent a backhoe and trustworthy prisoners to help.

On one planting day, Anne's cousin and her friends were driving through the area. They went to the Caudill home and Harry told them that Anne was out planting trees. When her cousin drove to the site, Anne was bent over, mulching a newly planted tree. The sheriff was standing directly behind her with his shotgun pointed toward her rear. The family had another good story to tell and more laughs.

During those years, it was not just Anne and Harry spearheading and working on projects and causes; their children became involved as they grew. Anne was a Brownie and Girl Scout leader and helped with Boy Scout projects. She assisted with 4-H clubs and was active in the PTA.

When Anne said, "This calls for action," she meant it. If one enjoyed membership in clubs for only the social benefits, one would not want to join an organization to which Anne belonged.

During part of the 1950s, times were dire in the coalfields. When miners were not working, their families suffered. There was little money for the essentials—food, clothing, and healthcare. It was a time before government programs to help the destitute were in place or were just beginning. The poorly clothed and poorly fed children grew in numbers and became more conspicuous.

At a high school football game one cold night, Anne noticed many children from the neighborhood who couldn't afford a ticket and were standing around outside looking through the fence. "They were blue with cold and raggedy, either barefoot or almost, and they didn't have enough clothes, and looked pitiful and undernourished," she said.

It was time for the women's club to take action again. They began a campaign to collect and distribute used clothing and shoes. Club members went to stores and anywhere clothing was available. One country store donated 13 pairs of shoes. Projects of this type were time consuming, but to give a child decent shoes was worth the time. The club members went to the needy children, traced their feet on a sheet of paper, and then tried to match the size of a foot to a pair of shoes.

Anne recalls one little girl, who was "nine or 10 years old with red hair, freckles, and big blue eyes, and she was about as big around as a pencil, skinny as she could be and ragged." They took her down to the store and bought her a winter coat, which was a kind of reddish brown wool and it had a beautiful scarf with a fringe. "We put the coat on her and she looked in the mirror. I don't think I ever in my life saw anybody look so happy. She literally glowed she was so happy with the coat. It was new and right for her and made her pretty and kept her warm."

To make matters worse during the difficult times, in 1957 a horrendous flood wreaked havoc on many homes in the hollows along the creeks and rivers in the area. Those possessing little had even less after the flood came. The Red Cross sent three boxcars loaded with clothing. Anne and the woman's club spent days unloading, sorting, and distributing the items. After *Night Comes to the Cumberlands* came out, readers from many places, who were inspired to help a needy family contacted Anne. She spent considerable time corresponding with them and arranging these acts of charity.

Despite their busy lives, the Caudill family took time to get away for their favorite activity, disappearing into the woods. In Appalachia, there are beautiful areas to hike practically everywhere. Two of the Caudills' favorite hikes were at the nearby Bad Branch Falls and the Lilley Cornett Woods. A

Caudill hike was divided into two parts—the physical hike and the rest periods, which were times for stories. Harry had many stories tucked away, and when he sat down on a log in a scenic setting, his companions sat down with him and listened. One of his stories was of Lilley Cornett, the man and his woods. The following is a condensed account taken from Harry's story in his book, *The Mountain, the Miner, and the Lord.*

Lilley was no ordinary man. He had his own way of doing things, such as talking his way into the White House because he wanted to talk to the president. Lilley was born and raised on Line Fork Creek, midway between Whitesburg and Hazard. After returning from World War I, he worked several years as a coal miner, saving nearly every cent he earned, living almost entirely on potatoes, meal, and salt bacon, but he also raised a garden, chickens, pigs, and hunted game and fished.

At the time, corporate lumber companies were buying the rights to the pristine forests for a minimal amount, and then harvesting the trees for lumber, ravaging the mountains in the process. With his savings, Lilley bought some fertile bottomland along Line Fork Creek and 400 acres of adjoining mountains covered with virgin stands of tulip popular, oak, beech, hickory, and gum. He said, "As long as I live, I aim to look out and see them big trees a-growin'."

The massive trees survived his death, and in 1969, the state bought the land as a nature preserve. After persistent efforts by Anne and Harry to preserve the forest, hundreds of scientists, students, and nature lovers go there each year to visit the unique virgin forest and intricate ground cover known as Lilley's Woods.

After his mining days, Lilley took a wife known as "Ma" and she bore him several children. However, as Lilley said,

"One woman ain't hardly enough fer a man if he is any count a-tall." Consequently, Lilley began scouring around and found a handsome "wider woman" over on Cutshin Creek in Leslie County. He conducted a clandestine courtship and promised to marry her as soon as he could get divorced from Ma.

Lilley figured the quickest way to get a divorce was to take his bride-to-be to a lawyer in Hazard, and swear that she was his wife and they wanted a divorce. After signing the proper papers, a legal decree dissolved Lilley's marriage to Ma, although Ma knew nothing about it. He rushed home, showed Ma the divorce paper, and told her to leave. Being illiterate, she assumed the paper was legal, so she left her home for her father's cabin.

Before Lilley could marry his new bride, he heard that Ma had taken up with another fellow just a few miles away. Shortly thereafter, Lilley was wedded to his fresh, new bride. Then, of all things, he heard that Ma had married the other man on the very same day, which caused Lilley to stop and do some thinking.

After his big wedding dinner and other festivities, night approached. Lilley eagerly took his new wife to the marriage bed. Apparently, things did not go so well, because as Lilley said, "I discovered I had made one hell of a bad swap." He rolled out of his bed, dressed, lit a lantern, grabbed his pistol, and in darkest night, headed toward another marriage bed to rescue Ma.

He beat on the door, practically breaking it down, and when the startled groom finally opened it, Lilley stuck his pistol under the groom's nose, burst into the bedroom and ordered Ma to leave with him. Fortunately for Lilley, as he said, "By God, I got there just in the nick of time."

Returning to his home with Ma tagging along, he had to figure out a way to eliminate one of his two wives. Upon arrival, he sent his newest bride—of 18 hours—back to Cutshin Creek. All appeared to have worked out well, but nine months later, Lilley's second wife brought the baby to him and said, "He's your'n and you can raise him." Ma also had a new baby, so she nursed them both and raised them together. In her old age, Ma said of Lilley's other boy, "He has always been good to me."

Lilley Cornett is probably the only soldier ever discharged from the military by direct order of the president of the United States. Lilley was shot twice in the battle at the Argonne Forest during World War I. He explained his predicament as "a mighty unhealthy commotion for a scrapping lad from the hills to find himself in." He was sent to Walter Reed Hospital in Washington, and they kept him there for months on end. Most of his wounded buddies had been sent home. He heard the mountains calling, but could not talk the doctors into releasing him.

Patients who were well enough could get a pass occasionally to walk around and see Washington DC. Lilley devised a plan, got a pass, and went directly to the White House, past the guards and through the gate. When guns were drawn, Lilley stopped. He began explaining why he desperately needed to see the president. A distinguished figure in striped trousers, stiff shirt, and a coat with tails hanging in the back happened to be passing by as Lilley argued with the guards.

The gentleman intervened, asked Lilley to explain his request, and then—impressed with his story—said, "Follow me." Into the White House they went, as the gentleman explained that he couldn't guarantee the president would be available, but that he always wanted to meet heroic veterans. After a short wait, Lilley was sent to the president's office, which he described as a "quair-shaped room, outlined like a big egg."

President Woodrow Wilson was gracious and understanding when hearing Lilley's story about how his "guts were almost shot out," and sympathetic to his request that the president see to it that, since he was now fit, he be sent home to the mountains. The president explained that he could not overrule the doctors in cases like this, but would make some inquiries and see how it turned out. They shook hands for the second time and Lilley said, "I'm much obliged for all your kindness."

The next day was routine, but the one after that all hell broke loose when Private Lilley Cornett was summoned to the commandant's office. When he walked in, the eyes of several doctors and officers focused on the lowly and lonely private. A general sprang to his feet, demanding, "What in the God-damned hell do you mean by going to see the president of the United States? Just who in the hell do you think you are anyway?"

A few days later, Lilley was honorably discharged and sent home where he could sit back and watch his trees grow. The Lilley Cornett Woods remain a living monument to the man whose discharge paper includes a footnote—"Discharged by Order of the President."

Several years later, Anne and Harry attended a meeting in Harlan County and Jont Cornett, Lilley's younger brother, was there. Jont sat down by Harry and told him he had a story to tell, one that he had never told any living soul before. He said everybody who was involved was gone and it wouldn't matter now. When Harry's father, Cro, a staunch Democrat, was running for circuit court clerk, he went up on Line Fork Creek to campaign. Jont told him, "Now Cro, you know this is solid Republican territory, and there's no use for you to go around here in an election year, but I think we can help you out; just leave it to us. Now you go up the road a ways to where I tell you and bring us back two gallons of that good moonshine, and we'll see what we can do."

A politician will do what he has to do, so Cro went up the road, purchased two gallons, and dropped them off to Jont. On Election Day, Jont and Lilley went to the polling place with the moonshine and waited down by a sycamore tree on a creek bank. When voters came, they were directed to the sycamore tree for a big slug. Jont let it be known they were giving treats to persuade voters to choose Republican Mandy Gibson. Since the voters were going to vote for Gibson anyway, they didn't need a treat, and it made them mad. Jont said that Harry's dad got every vote but two. Harry asked Jont who the two were, and Jont said, "Now Harry, you know the Cornetts always vote Republican."

"Love thy neighbor" is a simple command. Perhaps even moonshine is a means of showing that love.

*   *   *

Loving thy neighbor was embedded in Anne's character and, thus in her spiritual life. "I always loved to go to church," Anne said. Her spiritual journey through life was the force that guided and sustained her.

Anne's roots in the church go back to her ancestors in the late 18th century. They lived in Virginia and were against slavery, which had divided the church. When anti-slavery Virginians sought to move elsewhere, Daniel Boone suggested Cane Ridge in Kentucky, where the big oak trees grew. Cane Ridge is located in the rich Bluegrass farmland of what is now Bourbon County, about 20 miles from where Anne grew up.

Her ancestors moved there and eventually took part in the

Great Revival organized by Barton Stone in 1801. An estimated 10,000 people, bringing their wagons and supplies from the surrounding area, attended the weeklong meeting. The Great Revival was considered one of the most important religious events in early American history.[11]

At the time, Alexander Campbell, a Presbyterian, had a large following in southern Kentucky. In a break from established religious practices, particularly the acceptance of slavery, Stone and Campbell established a new denomination, naming it the Christian Church (Disciples of Christ). The central focus of the church was brotherly love, compassion, and care for others.

Anne grew up in the First Christian Church (Disciples of Christ) in Cynthiana. She went to school five days a week, to Sunday school and church each Sabbath morning, and to Bible study and youth meetings each Sabbath evening. She said, "It was a wonderful church, open and inclusive in its thinking, very liberal, and I never heard hellfire preached from that church. It was always a message of brotherly love, forgiveness, and helping others. Loved it, just loved it."

She went to church camp in the summers, and her awakening to the spiritual realm occurred at a church summer camp when she was quite young. Early each morning, the young participants were required to take their Bibles to a secluded quiet spot to read and meditate.

---

11. The original Cane Ridge log church still stands. About 60 years ago, a stone structure was constructed over the original log church among the oak trees, and services and anniversary celebrations are still observed there. Anne attended some of these yearly celebrations because her religious heritage began at Cane Ridge and her ancestors were a part of it.

I remember just as well as anything. I went out one morning and the dew was on the grass. All around the bushes and the grass were the tiny little cobwebs the spiders had left, and they were hanging full of dew. The sun came up and glittered on them. It was one of the most beautiful sights I ever saw. Somehow, it came to me that the teachings of Jesus about how we should love and care for other people as the way to live our lives was the right way. Ever since that time, I have tried to live, in my own peculiar interpretation of life, that way. I've never been overly declaratory about my religious beliefs, but I do believe that what He tried to teach about how to live with our fellow man was right. That moment just came to me, not in a shaft of light, but in a glitter of dewdrops.

As a student at UK, Anne attended the Central Christian Church in downtown Lexington. She remembers the service on the Sunday after the attack at Pearl Harbor. The minister's text was from Ecclesiastes 3:4: "To everything there is a season and a time to every purpose under heaven . . . a time to weep, a time to laugh, a time to mourn." That day was a time to mourn.

Anne attended various churches when working in New Jersey, and it didn't matter which church, but any church when Sunday rolled around.

The churches in Whitesburg included almost every mainline church except Catholic and Disciples of Christ. A Catholic church was located in Jenkins, the other sizeable town in Letcher County. Anne occasionally took her children to a midnight mass at Jenkins, but she regularly attended the Whitesburg Methodist Church for about 42 years.

"I took part in the church activities and the work of the women's group, and took my children when they were young. I loved attending that church," she said.

Francesca Monjardo and other stonemasons from Italy built the beautiful stone Methodist and Presbyterian churches in Whitesburg. Earlier, those stonemasons had come to Appalachia to build bridges across the many streams in the mountains when the railroads were constructed. They also built streets, homes, and other structures. Francesca eventually changed his name to Frank Majority and built the foundation for the Caudill family home. One of Harry's interesting stories in *The Mountain, the Miner, and the Lord,* tells Frank's story. When he built the Presbyterian church, he carved out a stone in the shape of the boot of Italy and placed it near the front door. During World War II, Italians, Germans, and Japanese were enemies of the United States. Someone took a chisel and marred the boot of Italy near the front door. One must look closely to see the boot today, but it is discernible.

The little churches out in the rural areas and in coal camps were primarily various Baptist sects, including primitive, old regular, and traditional. They were tight-knit and clannish, adhering to strict sets of orders from God. These churches did not believe in seminary-trained ministers. They believed that a man was called by God to minister to and pastor a flock. A charismatic preacher could build a substantial following. If a member sinned or violated a church rule, which always came from God through the association of churches, that member could be "churched" or ex-communicated, which caused considerable strife. Disputes arose over "sins" such as women cutting their hair. When a church split, the preacher remained, or was called to form another church, and gather other followers. Anne remembered one situation when a church split; an irate woman picked up the heavy pulpit Bible and hit the preacher over the head with it.

One time, during a dental appointment, the dentist stuffed the necessary materials into Anne's mouth, and proceeded to explain how firmly he believed that women should not cut their hair. "For once in my life, it made me mad and I was just itching to say something and couldn't say a word. By the time I got all those wires out of my mouth, I concluded I shouldn't say anything."

Anne had a friend who had been a pillar in her church and whose father had donated the land and lumber to build it. Anne's friend went to visit her children in another state and attended church with them. Upon returning to her church, she discussed her visit, and her preacher took issue. "Sister, you are not allowed to fellowship with anyone outside this church." She asked if she would be permitted to attend the funeral if one of her children were to die. The preacher said, "No." Anne's friend walked out and found another church.

Anne attended many churches of various types and denominations, but never attended a snake-handling service. Harry once did. The Bible says that to reveal supreme faith, "Take up serpents." Some congregations took this literally, and members picked up one or more copperheads or rattlesnakes, and let them wind around their necks and heads. Harry explained that when Pastor Sam went out into the congregation with a big rattlesnake around his arm, and stopped by his wife to test her faith, she said, "Sam, get that nasty thing out of my face."

Harry's father was a devout old regular Baptist and his mother was Presbyterian. Harry attended services, but never joined a church. He read the Bible through numerous times and could quote chapter and verse, as Anne said, "at the drop of a hat."

Harry recalled going to an old regular Baptist church when he was young that practiced "lining" during the music service. In churches without musical instruments or hymnals, the preacher sang two lines of a hymn, and the congregation would concentrate and repeat it. The preacher was deep into a sacred song when a hound dog meandered in. The dog wandered up to the front near the preacher, who went right on lining the song until the old dog began scratching his fleas, one leg scratching, and another leg thumping against the floor. The preacher's next line was, "Put out the dog and close the door." The congregation followed with, "Put out the dog and close the door."

On occasion, Anne attended the little churches scattered throughout the mountains. In the summers, large groups attended the baptismal services at a nearby creek. "People stood on the bank for prayer and singing, and the newly saved were taken into the water just like it is described in the scriptures," she said. "I always found that to be very moving, touching."

The people spoke in tongues during the Great Revival at Cane Ridge. Anne attended churches in the mountain where people spoke in tongues. As the preaching intensified, members became emotionally charged, reaching a state of ecstasy. They would begin jerking around and speaking in tongues, which to an outsider might seem like gibberish. Anne said, "Who am I to say that doesn't do something for them? It never happened to me, but maybe I've missed something."

One of the more moving services Anne attended involved foot washing. "Some of the practices of the country churches I attended were moving, down to earth, and taught great lessons," she said. "What more humble thing can you do for another person than to wash their feet? I've seen it done and it is true brotherhood. The people go forward and the elders wash their feet and dry them. As in the scriptures, when women washed Jesus's feet."

When Anne moved to New Albany in 1991, a friend invited her to attend the First Unitarian Church in Louisville. She joined, attended the church for 12 years, and then decided to move her membership.

"It got to the point where every time I went, there were discussions causing dissension and division, and I'd go to congregational meetings and there was bitterness," she said. "I thought, this is not why I go to church."

Anne joined the Thomas Jefferson Unitarian Church on the outskirts of Louisville.

She has attended many types of churches all her life, including Catholic, Jewish, Quaker, and Hindu. Her life journey accompanied her spiritual one. She said:

> I had a great uplift every time I went, and I just like being in church. I like to be with people who are willing and interested enough to take time away from the ordinary pursuits of life, gather and listen to words that try to help them become better people. I think whatever language and whatever kind, shape, or color a church is, that is what it's all about. I always come away with a feeling I have gained something, and a feeling that I could join with the people in their appreciation of the fact that there are forces larger than we are.

CHAPTER 8

How Night Came to the Cumberlands

The way in which Harry's first and well-known book came about is an unusual and fascinating story. Perhaps it would not been written without the encouragement and persistence of the one to whom Harry dedicated the book: "This book is dedicated with affection and respect to my wife, Anne, without whose assistance and insistence it would never have been written, and to the Kentucky coal miners whose trials and tragedies are its central theme."

During Anne's first 16 years of marriage, the subject of Harry wanting to write was not discussed to any extent. When they were apart during their engagement, she knew he had exceptional talent, as evidenced by his numerous thoughtful and expressive letters. Harry had the required English classes in college, but no instruction in creative writing or other such courses. He wrote essays in school, briefs and tests in law school, and composed numerous letters in his law practice. He did not use a tape recorder, keep a diary or journal, and took few notes. When his writing began, it stemmed from his vast knowledge and insight. The content of his writing was stored in his consciousness, awaiting release. Anne's assistance and insistence was a catalyst. Raising a family, practicing law, and serving six years in the legislature consumed all his time. Writing? Maybe someday.

"I knew he loved to read poetry, biography, history, and was a great reader," Anne said. "That's one of the things that brought us together. As a matter of fact, I did not know he had written articles about his war experiences for the local newspaper after he returned home from the military hospitals."

After Harry's death, Anne began sorting through his papers and found well-written articles in the bottom of a file drawer. She also found part of a novel based on the time when he was growing up, which she knew nothing about. When his writing began, Anne remarked it came easy because he had "a natural affinity for words."

Had Harry continued in politics, the book probably would never been written. Anne explained:

> Harry had made enemies with the coal companies and they had the money to defeat him. Everyone had a hand out. His first magazine article published in *Harpers* explained not only the money power of the coal companies, but also how people would come and say, "Now Harry, the roof on our church is in terrible shape. And I've got so many people in my family and they're all for you," obviously implying, "If you'll fix the roof on our church, we'll all vote for you." Harry did not want to say what needed to be said to get elected. There's no doubt he was much more effective as a writer and speaker, and after that, nobody was ever able to put the brakes on him again.

In the two-roomed Millstone School during a rainstorm, a seed was planted that grew into a book nearly three years after conception and arduous labor. In the introduction to *Night Comes to the Cumberlands: A Biography of a Depressed Area*, Harry wrote:

> In the spring of 1960, I was invited to serve as commencement speaker at an eighth-grade graduation in a coal camp two-room building, which had sheltered two generations of their forebears. A shower sent a little torrent of water through the ancient roof onto one of the scarred desks. The worn windows rattled in their frames and the paper decorations, which had been prepared by the seventh-graders, fluttered in the drafts admitted by the long-unpainted walls. Outside, the grassless playground lay in the shadow of an immense slate dump and was fringed by a cluster of ramshackle houses. One of the graduates had been orphaned by a mining accident, and the father of another wheezed and gasped with silicosis. The fathers of three others were jobless.
>
> The little ceremony opened with the singing of "America the Beautiful," our most stirring patriotic hymn. The irony of the words, sung so lustily in such a setting, inspired the writing of this book. Perhaps it may help a little to bring the sad reality and the splendid dream a little closer together for my friends, my kinsmen, my fellow mountaineers.

At the time, Harry had no idea or thought that his experience that night would result in a book. His eyes were opened long ago to the plight of his people. That night, the light was blinding.

The next day, Harry took a long walk in the woods behind his home, and when he returned, Anne noticed a difference in his demeanor. He was solemn and distressed: America is beautiful, but not here; it is unerringly ugly in many ways. "When they sang 'America the Beautiful,' it broke my heart. What can be done? What can we do?" he asked.

Anne didn't say, "Let's write a book," but she did say, "We should start by writing these things down." They did and his musings became a book three years later. The book did not correct all ills in Appalachia, but it called attention to leaky schoolhouse roofs and a whole host of other social and economic conditions. As a result, significant and dramatic changes began to occur a few years later.

Harry's everlasting concern was the ravaged land and the ruination of the miners and their families. Thirteen years after publication of *Night Comes to the Cumberlands*, he published *Watches of the Night*, a sequel to the first book. Some critics believed it had as strong an impact as his first book. The dedication reads, "This book is dedicated to the printing press of the US Bureau of Printing and Engraving that produces the checks, food stamps, and paper money by which the Kentucky Cumberlands have survived for so many years."

In his new book, Harry described the plight of the miners:

That they would drastically alter the environment within the tunnels—vastly elevating the levels as well as the quantities of suspended dust—was apparent before the first steel giant passed under the Appalachian hills. The men who bought the new generation of mining machines disregarded the need for effective filters across every mouth and nose, the imperative that flows of air to the workmen be hugely augmented, and that efficient dust traps be developed and installed. Coal digging was profitable and dust abatement was costly, so the former was pushed and the latter was ignored.

For two decades, the mines were monstrous dens in which black choking death was accepted as a normal and inevitable companion. From the whirling teeth that tore the fuel from the glittering face and along the racks and conveyor belts that carried it to the light of day arose choking clouds that mingled with gray emanations pouring down along the spinning shafts of the roof drills. The powdery dust out of the top was pulverized slate and sandstone, the same killer unloosed by the cutters that swept the slate and sandstone parting out of the veins. These grim substances flowed together like evil genies to form a ubiquitous pall that accumulated inches thick on the tunnel ribs and the machines, permeated every stitch of the miner's clothing and choked every pore of his body. When he was lucky enough to possess a micronite filter, it was packed solid within a half-hour, then cast aside as useless. With each gulp into oxygen-starved lungs, the microscopic bits of coal and silica poured in to coat the alveoli. Day after day, the black film accumulated, inexorably reducing the capacity of the doomed lungs to function. Men slowed and stooped. Suddenly young men looked middle-aged, and the middle-aged looked old and exhausted. By the early 1960s, the Appalachians contained nearly a quarter of a million ruined coal miners, an industrial army of incapacitated and forgotten workmen.

They were lost to view for a number of reasons, beginning with the region's geographical isolation. The fold upon fold of mountains shielded the people from the more advanced aspects of their country's life, and turned away the occasional twinges of social concerns that outcropped in university and journalistic circles. Too, coal is an unglamorous subject and the men who dig it tend to be taciturn and unresponsive, qualities that repel aid. Their ultraconservatism was reflected in their congressmen, undistinguished souls who survived by acting old-timey, voting for ever-greater social security and public assistance appropriations, serving as agents to obtain government benefits for their constituents, and running errands for the coal industry. Nearly all the congressmen, with the exception of West Virginia's Ken Hechler, fitted this dismal description, and all avoided the implications of the black death they encountered on every hand when they returned to their districts.

Most important, though, was the wanton ignorance of the physicians into whose offices the victims flocked in wheezing lines. More often than not, they dismissed their patients with the unhelpful admonition that they suffered from "miner's asthma" and should stop smoking. Many opined that coal dust was harmless or benign and that its inhalation produced no ill effects beyond occasional "spells of asthma." Nor were these grotesque notions peculiar to coalfield quacks because, incredible as it may seem, they bespoke the conventional wisdom of American medicine at the time.

Writing is, or can be, a catharsis. One feels better releasing innermost feelings, emotions, passions, opinions, and criticisms. Every spare moment, Harry dictated and Anne transcribed and typed, hour after hour, day after day. Anne was pregnant with her third child and spare moments were rare, but somehow bits of time were squeezed into the busy days and nights. When she went to bed, Harry followed—dictating. Anne lay in bed with one hand taking shorthand on the tablet propped on her bulging tummy and the other hand "kept my other eye open." Harry's dictation was precise to the extent that he inserted proper punctuation marks at the correct places. Anne took it all down—for nearly two years.

A few years earlier, Anne had started serving as one of his secretaries part-time, usually two or three days per week. It was not only a time to help and be with Harry, but the interesting work provided a welcome diversion.

Working in his office, Anne wrote numerous deeds, explained the contents to their clients, and heard and learned many interesting stories from the people living in the hollows. When a deed or other legal document required signing, she would ask, embarrassed, but tactfully, "Can you sign the paper?" She heard all kinds of excuses, but gently and diplomatically helped those who were illiterate complete the signing, making it legal. Anne wrote the name of the individual on the designated line. At the side in parentheses, the individual placed a mark, usually an X. Two witnesses signed below. As a matter of pride, some of the mountain people had learned to sign their names in a scribbled and indecipherable fashion.

With all her other tasks, Anne spent many hours at her trusty typewriter. After purchasing a Dictaphone for the office, she worked at home more often than at the law office. By phone, Harry called and recorded his requests and messages, and Anne transcribed and typed them. She transcribed and typed Harry's daily correspondence, speeches, newspaper and magazine articles, and her numerous personal letters.

Back to the origins of *Night Comes to the Cumberlands*, Anne said:

> The book just evolved and grew as he worked out in his mind all the interlocking factors that had brought the region to such a sorry pass. He read local and state newspapers, the *Wall Street Journal*, and the *Manchester Guardian* published in England. He read everything he could get his hands on about the region, collecting a library about Appalachia of more than 2,000 books. He read government documents, surveys, and statistics, as well as recollections from the old timers. He read all of Arnold Toynbee's works, and frequently quoted one of his passages: "Appalachia presents the melancholy spectacle of a people who had civilization and lost it."
>
> He listened to what his clients said, the people he electioneered with, and he was an insightful observer. He considered it all as he took frequent long rambles through the woods by himself.

Anne described her role in writing up Harry's thoughts, meditations, and reflections:

> Telling it all to me as I took dictation, I think helped him to organize his thoughts. Harry did not have me read

back his dictation, except when his train of thought was interrupted. His dictation was easy to transcribe, but occasionally I questioned a sentence for clarity, or suggested he had used the same word too often. After typing the material triple-spaced, he made corrections, and I typed it again.

All through the years, he read aloud to me or summarized what he had read or heard, thus educating me. Primarily, it helped organize his thoughts and clarify his ideas. Putting it into spoken word fixed it in his mind and forced organization of thought. It helped to make him the orator that he became, able to think on his feet, leading up to the point he wanted to make by orderly progression and citing of example.

With a foot-high stack of papers on the desk, the couple gave little thought as to what they would do next. The two-year process totally focused on putting the vast quantity of material on paper. It was a natural ever-flowing stream of consciousness, a release and partial cure of a nagging malady. The material was unorganized, without subjects, topics, or chapters. Close friends Dr. Huston Westover and his wife, originally from Massachusetts, read bits of the material and encouraged Harry to have it published.

The stack remained on the desk until Anne called Margaret Willis, director of state library services, inviting her to visit Whitesburg to advise and help with the library. Willis had visited before, and she called back and asked to bring a couple of her friends who were also involved in promoting libraries. Mary Gray had begun the bookmobile project in Jefferson County by loading her limousine with books, distributing them at schools, and later taking another load and picking up the ones she had left. Mary Gray and Mary Bingham, wife of Barry Bingham, the Louisville *Courier-Journal* publisher, accompanied Margaret Willis.

While serving in the legislature, Harry had worked with Margaret Willis and Mary Bingham in passing a state library tax. He learned the state would assist local libraries if counties also passed a library tax. Harry and Anne went to work, and, surprisingly, Letcher County voted (pennies) for a library tax.

The 54 one- and two-room schools in Letcher County furnished textbooks and a school library, which usually consisted of a shelf or two of other books. Reading materials in most homes were scarce or nonexistent. When the new, shiny bookmobiles drove up the hollows, stopping at schools, country stores, and other places on a regular basis, it was like Christmas for children who loved to read.

"I traveled with the bookmobile driver into some of those places back in the mountains," Anne said. "It was so exciting to see the children come in when the bookmobile got there, and the kids loved it."

In what was later to become a frequent and established routine, the Caudills hosted the library group from Louisville, providing dinner, beds, and breakfast. In addition to the comfortable quarters and excellent food, guests were also provided a tour of the strip mines and coal camp areas. Anne could not remember many evenings without guests, relatives, friends, and vast numbers of worldwide visitors. If visitors came for only one day, Anne insisted she provide a meal. Interspersed with meals and activity were lively, entertaining, and interesting conversation, the best part of all visits.

After the library group had dinner, they adjourned to the living room and "wonderful conversation." Questions were asked, and responses given using the Caudill method. Answers requiring factual information were embellished and enhanced with related stories by the two masterful storytellers.

"Harry, you should write these stories down," Mary Bingham said. Harry then went to the office area of their large bedroom and returned with a thick, heavy stack of papers.

It was late. "Do you mind if I take these to bed?" asked Mary.

The next morning at breakfast, Mary indicated she gotten little sleep. Harry's fascinating stories had kept her awake.

Before the good-byes, Mary asked, "May I take this stack home?"

A week or so later, she called and asked permission to contact a publisher. Anne and Harry were surprised, but pleased that Mary asked to send the manuscript to a publisher, who was her daughter Sallie's husband, Whitney Ellsworth, an editor for Atlantic Monthly Press/ Little Brown.

A few weeks later, Atlantic called and wanted to publish it, but the manuscript was too long and would require two volumes. The editor suggested condensing it.

Without having any idea what it all would lead to, Anne and Harry went back to work, organizing, cutting, revising, and typing. The rest is history.

Throughout the years before the publication of the first book, Anne had household help to free her to help Harry at the office and participate in civic organizations and worthy causes. Priscilla Adams very ably helped her for several years, but had to move away.

Anne then employed Beatrice Baltimore, who became

a loving, integral part of the family. Anne considered her a godsend. Beatrice's husband was a coal miner, and the family lived in the Tom Biggs black section at McRoberts, a coal camp about ten miles from Whitesburg. Civil rights and integration were in their early stages. However, the mines were integrated, and blacks and whites worked harmoniously side by side. When Harry's father, Cro, caught his arm in a mining machine, a black man saved him.

Bea helped the Caudills for ten years until her husband died, and she returned to her original home in Selma, Alabama, to care for her mother, who lived to be 104. Bea was an excellent cook who assisted Anne with the nightly dinners during the crazy years after the book came out. Not only did she cook southern and country food, she cooked Syrian and other foods. Bea had worked for the Dawahare family from Syria. They operated a store in the town of Neon, and later established several clothing stores throughout Kentucky.

The mines brought in educated operators, engineers, doctors, and other professionals to the area. Considerable numbers of blacks from the South migrated to the region, as did people from Italy, Syria, Russia, and many other countries, to work in the mines. The area became, perhaps, one of the earliest diverse and multi-cultural regions in the rural areas of the nation. The native people were receptive, warm, and friendly with outsiders, unless they felt they were patronized and looked down upon. They didn't respect those who put on airs. The general attitude seemed to be, "Treat us right, and we'll get along."

Bea came to work one day terribly worried and alarmed. She had received a call from a family member in Selma. Her sister, Annie Wilkerson, was arrested the day before. Blacks in Alabama had recently received the right to vote and were lined up at the voting place. The sheriff came along and told the "n_____s" to get in the gutter and let the white people pass. It made Annie so mad, she jumped on the sheriff and knocked him flat. Harry told Bea not to worry; he would pay her fine. The next day, Annie was quietly released from jail.

Bea attended church regularly and taught Sunday school. When Anne or Bea worked in the kitchen, Harry often sat in the nearby rocker and read to them. One particular time, Bea was ironing as Harry read the story of Solomon from the Bible to her. "Well, Bea, what do you think of all his wives and concubines?" he asked.

"I think with all those wives and concubines, it's a good thing old Solomon didn't have anything else to do but be the king."

Anne corresponded with Bea after she moved back to Selma. One day, Anne received a lovely note from Bea's mother, Lucy. Dated in 1966, the note, handwritten by Bea or someone else, thanked Anne for all she had done for Bea and the gift that Anne had sent. Lucy, a former slave said, "I just wish I could see you face to face and talk with you. Bea has told us so much about you and your family being so nice. And you have to be one of the best, and I just love you and never had a chance to meet you. I do hope before my 100th birthday, we shall meet. Lucy Wilkerson."

When Harry was invited to speak at Auburn University some time later, he and Anne drove to Selma during the trip. Bea had prepared a marvelous dinner, some of the Caudills' favorite foods. Lucy, 104 at the time, was spry and responsive. Harry was particularly interested in Lucy's remembrances of the Civil War. She said, "When the blue soldiers left, all of our people stood by the road and cried when the blue soldiers marched by, because we knew there would be more trouble."

* * *

Who was Harry Caudill—this man who was about to attract national and international attention? Anne wrote "About the Author" in a republication of his book, *Dark Hills to Westward: The Saga of Jenny Wiley*. She recalled their time at UK, their marriage, and then continued:

Harry laughed. He relished the ridiculous and the absurd. He observed humanity and he chuckled. And he made us all laugh, for he was a master teller of tales about people, their foibles, their inconsistencies, their peculiar strengths. And he laughed with the children. As they rode to school each morning, he sang old songs, making up silly doggerel to fit the melodies as he drove along. Sometimes for days at a time, nearly everything he said came out as amusing rhyming couplets, an expression of his joyous exuberance.

And he walked in the woods, determined to strengthen his shattered leg. He walked for hours on the soft forest loam, often alone, but glad of the company of family and friends. Across our pastures and through the little gate we entered into an almost endless woodland. Sometimes, on longer expeditions, we camped and hiked to beauty spots in the Pine Mountain woods, the Red River Gorge, or the Smoky Mountains, accompanied by friends, pausing often to loiter on a fallen log and listen to Harry telling a tale of the olden days, or expounding on the magnificence and fragility of the landscape before us. This was our cherished and preferred entertainment. After the children grew up and left home, their friends remembered and sometimes came to talk with us by the fireside or on a shady summer porch.

Harry talked. His inquiring, cogitating, philosophical, and restless mind expressed a constant flow of commentary, interspersed with humor, recollections, all in vivid language. His everyday speech was a unique combination of phrases from the King James Bible, Shakespeare, and the classics, mixed with mountain colloquialisms. He talked of growing up in the Depression years in the coalfields, and of his war experiences. Both had a deep and abiding effect on his life.

As an infantry soldier, he scrambled up the slippery rock-strewn, eroded slopes of the Italian mountains where he was eventually wounded and crippled for life. He was haunted by the remains of villages he saw there, abandoned generations before because the mountains had been completely denuded of their forest cover and then grazed to the bedrock. He saw how easily the same thing could happen in his own Kentucky mountains, a process indeed already begun. The experience fired his urgent insistence in later years that surface mining be controlled, a battle he waged for decades using every tactic he could summon.

We nourished our land from worn-out hillside cornfields into rich pastures, timberlands, lawns, and gardens. We worked together growing and harvesting large gardens of marvelous vegetables to serve the table to which so many friends and sojourners were invited. For we were both farmers at heart.

Harry was outraged. As his practice grew, his clients often were coal miners and their families, or those whose land had been damaged by mining operations. He observed how welfare became a permanent way of life for too many families because there was no industrial development beyond the coal industry. He saw more and more clearly how the region and its people were exploited, how their birthright had been sold for a mess of pottage. And he longed for the people to take charge of their own destiny, to build for themselves a vibrant and growing society in which the eastern part of Kentucky would come into full and equal partnership with the rest of the state.

The Kentucky legislature seemed the place to begin. He served three terms and his deep mountain voice was heard often and noted by the newspapers. Sometimes his statements were outrageous, but they caught public attention. He made people aware of those long-ignored eastern counties. His leadership in bringing about school consolidation, the severance tax on coal, reclamation of strip-mined lands, and other changes is a matter of record.

But to be elected and stay elected, one must compromise, and he found that telling all that needed to be told irritated many powerful interests who opposed him. Instead, he turned to writing and speaking, utilizing media attention to focus public opinion across the state and bring pressure on the legislature.

As our children grew older, I felt the need to return to some kind of public life. Though the post of agricultural extension home demonstration agent was then vacant in our county, I decided not to return to the profession, choosing to work with my husband and fit my scheduled work into the needs of home and children. Soon I was a part of his busy law office staff, and as his writing career developed, I devoted much time to helping with his manuscripts and the monumental correspondence he carried on outside his legal practice. Later, during the years when he was teaching at the University of Kentucky, I searched for Appalachian-related materials, which I copied for his research files.

Harry read. He read voluminously—history, biography, current affairs—always piecing together the pattern of cause and effect that had created a unique Kentucky society. And from a rocking chair in our kitchen he read aloud to me, or discussed what he had read, as I attended to the needs of children and household. This was his way, I think, of clarifying and fixing in his own mind what he read and observed. It made humdrum chores pass quickly, and for more than forty years, I was educated by a born and gifted teacher.

Harry wrote about what he had heard, what he had witnessed, what he had read, and his readers understood. They understood how the mountain society came to be as it is, and to see some of the potential for desirable change. They responded in countless letters. They came from across the state and nation, and from foreign countries, to talk to him and to interview him for newspapers, magazines, and television. Bureaucrats, social workers, health workers, religious workers, university professors and their students, and volunteer workers came. Some remain friends to this day. Our lives were tremendously busy, sometimes exhausting, but never dull. The conversations around our dinner table were stimulating and varied, and often we had overnight guests whom we had never met before they arrived on our doorstep. Our eldest son was of an age and turn of mind to enjoy and take part in the discussions; our daughter, three years younger, accepted our busy household as a matter of course; the second son, nine years younger, recalled no other style of living.

Harry spoke. He spoke to all who would listen. As his reputation grew, he was petitioned more and more to speak in far-off places, and always he wanted me to fly or drive with him. It would have been impossible without the always-available loving attention of his parents, who lived not far away. With the assistance of ample household help, they often stayed with our children with such sincere pleasure that I felt free to help Harry.

In all of this, he remained accessible to the many clients, present and past, of his law office. In a country law practice, it is necessary to be easily available to troubled clients who have little knowledge of the intricacies of the courts. Our telephone rang constantly; each call brought some new problem or a client needing reassurance. It was a heavy burden at times. I marvel still at his vitality. Through it all, he was constantly writing or dictating. In the end, he wore himself out.

He was disappointed, sometimes discouraged to the point of bitterness, that apathy and ignorance combined to obstruct needed change. Then again he was hopeful as he saw ignorance dissolving and efforts beginning to bear fruit here and there. His were large visions. Practical ideas worth pursuing are worth the doing. I believe deeply that his life made a real difference, that his imprint is visible in the region he loved.

It was a wonderful life we shared for 44 years. I count myself as truly blessed to have been a partner in all the undertakings of a unique, complex, and gifted statesman, a man of courage constant to the end.

After *Night Comes to the Cumberlands* came out in 1963, their young son James declared, "All hell broke loose." Anne said:

Our lives became so busy with the response to Harry's writing, speaking, and activism, there was little time for any other volunteer work, especially when so many visitors came into the mountains to "see for themselves" and find ways to fight the war on poverty. My time was preoccupied with helping Harry with his writing, and traveling with him to speaking engagements and meetings in Washington and other places. I kept up with the family and cared for Harry's parents, as well as entertaining the comers and goers, often taking them on tours of the coal camps and strip mines. I loved every minute of it, so I suppose it could be considered volunteer work.

CHAPTER 9

When the Curious Came to Take the Grand Tour

After the three-year process of writing, rewriting, condensing, and revising the book, the Caudills thought their life would return to normal. Harry's law practice thrived and Anne was involved in civic affairs and worked as a part-time legal secretary to Harry. Two of the children were in school and involved in their own activities, and the youngest, Harry Frye, would begin school in three years.

Anne said that she and Harry never thought the book would ever amount to much. However, it wasn't long until they were swept into what Anne called a maelstrom.

The '60s were a turbulent time, as evidenced by the controversial Vietnam War, the civil rights movement, the war on poverty, protests, sit-ins, violence on the home front, and the assassinations of John and Bobby Kennedy and Martin Luther King. Who cared about the conditions in a remote place called Appalachia? America had enough troubles without those of a few mountaineers and coal miners.

Conservation was a priority in the '60s, and Harry's book addressed the subject. Stewart Udall, secretary of the interior under President Kennedy, wrote the foreword to *Night Comes to the Cumberlands,* which reads in part:

> Harry Caudill, a young Kentucky legislator with roots generations deep in the Cumberland coves, tells here the pathetic and disturbing story of these backcountry people—a tragic tale of the abuse and mismanagement of a resource heritage, and the human erosion that is always concomitant of shortsighted exploitation.
>
> Caudill's book is a story of land failure and the failure of men. It is reminiscent of such earlier works as Sinclair's *The Jungle,* Steinbeck's *The Grapes of Wrath,* and Agee's *Let Us Now Praise Famous Men.* Although one may differ in the interpretation, in probing areas of American life such books as these and *Night Comes to the Cumberlands* speak eloquently to the American conscience.
>
> This book is the story of what happens when men betray their responsibilities as land stewards. The price we pay for wanton spoliation is sure and certain. In the highest sense, conservation of the land is the conservation of human life. The two have always been, and will always be, inseparable.

Although it attracted immediate attention, the book became controversial soon after it came out. Academia criticized the author for not following historical and scholarly standards. Anne then criticized the scholars: "What does being a scholar entail? Harry read constantly, everything he could get his hands on about the region, collecting more than 2,000 books, booklets, government documents, all manner of surveys, statistics, as well as social and cultural stories, histories, and recollections of the old timers. He dealt with several dealers of old books to find records of Appalachia's history. He read local and state newspapers, and we subscribed to the *Wall Street Journal* and Britain's *Manchester Guardian* for coverage of US and European events."

The content was also controversial, particularly its blistering criticism of the coal barons. The local people and miners weren't critical of the content, but Harry frequently heard comments from proud friends who told him that if they had known that he was going to write a book, they would have told him stories to include.

The *New York Times* and the *Wall Street Journal* reviewed the book and both gave favorable reviews. Harry said it was one of the few times both newspapers agreed. A review from the *Communist Daily Worker* was also favorable. The reviews stirred interest, and a few days later, Harry received a call from Homer Bigart, a reporter from the *New York Times*, who had been a war correspondent in World War II and the Korean and Vietnamese wars. Bigart called from Pike County, Kentucky, where he had been touring the area for two or three days. His assignment was to report whether the content of the book was the truth. He asked to come and talk with Harry, and said, "Mr. Caudill, you haven't told half the truth about what's going on here."

Thirteen years later, Harry published *Watches of the Night.* Early in the book, he gave this account of Bigart's role:

In the fall of 1963, Harrison Salisbury, an editor of the *New York Times* handed a copy of *Night Comes to the Cumberlands* to a *Times* reporter, Homer Bigart, and suggested that he make a trip to Eastern Kentucky and report on whether the book exaggerated the region's plight.

On a clear, cool autumn day, Bigart arrived tired and hungry at my door. He had spent days wandering along rutted creek roads and the streets of dying coal towns. Twice the winner of a Pulitzer Prize and a supremely evocative writer, he had accumulated notes for a series of articles on the social and economic malaise festering in the Kentucky hills. My wife and I refreshed him with a meal and spent a marvelous evening with this superb storyteller, and in the days that followed, awaited the first of what was to become an avalanche of reporting about Appalachia in general and Eastern Kentucky in particular.

Bigart's articles appeared with front-page headlines in late October. He described a part of America that had slipped into dependency, dejection, and peonage, and, even worse, was sliding inexorably toward backwardness and ignorance. He told of gasping, dust-choked coal miners huddled in cluttered, decaying shacks, of drafty, dilapidated schools, and the pinched, drawn faces of children. He quoted a county health doctor who described children so hungry they ate the dried mud from between the rocks of chimneys. He related the plight of miners whose day at the working face in low coal produced only six or eight dollars—a time of fuel abundance when miners starved, coal operators went broke, and the TVA provided a household customer a month of electricity for about eight dollars. Bigart raised the specter of death by starvation and cold in the bleak months ahead and marveled at so vast an island of poverty in what John Kenneth Galbraith had so lately called the "affluent society."

When Bigart arrived at the Caudill home for the night, he was grateful for a drink, since most of the mountain counties were dry. Although bootlegged whiskey and moonshine were plentiful, a New Yorker might be hesitant to drive up a hollow and over a creek bed to buy a bottle of whiskey or a fruit jar full of moonshine. When reporting to the *Times*, he wrote a lead article, a blistering expose of the terrible conditions in the coalfields. The opening line was, "You can sit on a front porch in Hellier, Kentucky, and look across the threshold of Hell."

Homer Bigart's article appeared on the front page of the October 20, 1963, Sunday edition of the *New York Times*. Three days later, Bigart wrote Harry informing him that the *Times* had been flooded with letters to the editor, and that former treasury secretary, Henry Morgenthau Jr. wrote to Kennedy pleading, "in the name of humanity, I appeal to you to come to the rescue of these people promptly."

The article sent readers to bookstores. An executive of the Proctor and Gamble Corporation was so taken with the book he purchased 100 copies, and sent a copy to President John F. Kennedy, Vice President Lyndon Johnson, cabinet members and congressmen representing Appalachia. It is unknown if Kennedy ever read the book, but he read Bigart's article the day it came out. That afternoon, Kennedy summoned select staff members to the White House and ordered them to get to work on the problem.

An "Emergency Winter Relief Program," funded with $46 million, was announced a couple of days later. It provided 1,000 jobs for unemployed miners, surplus food, medical aid for children with parasitic diseases (worms), and other needs. Later, Franklin D. Roosevelt, Jr. and 40 government officials were dispatched to Kentucky to plan a permanent long-term program for the region.

President Kennedy sent personal representatives to Eastern Kentucky to arrange a visit to Harlan, Pike, and Letcher Counties to begin on December 6. Two weeks before that date, Kennedy made his fateful trip to Dallas.

After Kennedy's tragic death, President Johnson took up the cause and became the only president to visit Eastern Kentucky. During his visit to Inez in Martin County, he toured the area and was interviewed sitting on the dilapidated porch of a coal miner's decrepit cabin. If a picture is worth a thousand words, the photo of a tired, weary, and forlorn wife and mother sitting on the porch explicitly and dramatically told a story of hopelessness and despair. To this day, the photo reappears in various forms of the media.

Harry's book, Kennedy's visit to West Virginia earlier, and the Johnson visit to Inez initiated the beginning of national awareness of the dire conditions in the coal country. When the media and government officials followed, the war on poverty began. Later, Bobby Kennedy made a visit to the area to conduct hearings and meet with Harry.

The media and Washington officials began descending on the Cumberlands, and it wasn't long until Anne and Harry began traveling to Washington. Gordon Ebersole worked under Stewart Udall in the Department of the Interior. He became close friends with Anne and Harry, and visited them many times throughout the following years. Although Udall wrote the foreword to *Night*, he had never met the Caudills. Consequently, Ebersole arranged for Anne and Harry to visit Washington to meet with him. It was the Caudills' first visit to Washington after the book came out, but not the last as they made repeated visits there.

Ebersole was a long, lanky westerner, usually dressed in cowboy boots and a wide western hat. He was a trained engineer and had worked in water conservation and land reclamation projects throughout the West. He met the Caudills at the airport in an old pickup truck, as he would do several other times during their frequent trips to Washington, and took them to his home for the night. The next day, they drove to the Department of the Interior, and parked at the front in a no-parking zone. Ebersole carried a few plumbing tools in the back of his truck and said, "Don't worry; police never arrest a plumber."

When they met Stewart Udall, he was rocking back and forth in a Kennedy rocking chair.[12]

Requests for meetings began picking up, and a few months after publication, Anne received a request to do an interview for an article with Helen Leopold of the Louisville *Courier-Journal.* Anne responded on January 3, 1964.

Your request that you be allowed to do a story about me is gratifying, of course, but most surprising. My activities are not unusual at all, though I do lead a very busy life. Aside from running a household with three children and serving as Harry's legal secretary, most of my efforts have been directed toward furthering and assisting Harry in his various interests. There have been the ordinary number of involvements with civic projects and offices in various

12. President Kennedy was frequently photographed sitting in his rocking chair, which he used because of his bad back. Kennedy rockers became popular and were sold throughout the United States.

groups, and I have devoted quite a bit of time to building up our library and bookmobile service in past years, though I am not now directly involved. Presently, I am serving on the Board of Trustees of the newly organized Appalachian Regional Hospitals and much concerned with its particular problems. I have a Girl Scout Troop, too, and we have a great many guests in our informal home four miles from Whitesburg.

If this brief history appears to hold any promise of a story, I shall be happy to talk to you. At this time, I do not expect to be in Central Kentucky before January 29, when Harry will speak to the Book Review Group of the Lexington Women's Club. We will be in Lexington only a few hours on that day, since our term of court will be in progress and we will need to return immediately. If you care to come to Whitesburg, we will be delighted to have you.

A short time later when Anne looked through one of her guest books, she saw the following entry, "I live in the crazy green house at the end of the lane." It was 14-year-old Diana's assessment of her home as she experienced it after the publication of the book. Anne used the term "maelstrom" in describing the onslaught. A maelstrom is "a powerful and often violent whirlpool sucking in objects within a given radius." Perhaps the metaphor is an apt one. Objects, primarily of the human variety, were drawn in, not by a swirling whirlpool, but by the Caudills' gracious hospitality.

Their home had always been an active and hospitable place as neighbors, friends, and family members frequently visited for meals and overnight or weekends. When the book came out in 1963, guests from throughout the United States and several other parts of the world dined there. Many stayed at the crazy green house in the whirling maelstrom at the end of the lane.

Letters and requests for interviews grew into stacks. Hotels and restaurants in Whitesburg, a town then of about 2,000, were limited. The Caudills invited these guests, some of whom they'd never met, to lunch, dinner, overnight, or a weekend. People from throughout the world ate, slept, and told stories in the house on the slope with a magnificent view of Pine Mountain.

Anne said, "We always had a wonderful time and the best part was after dinner when we sat around hearing and telling stories." In return, the Caudills received numerous invitations and visited many of those whom they had hosted. A number of the guests remained lifelong friends for nearly a half century, and Anne stayed in contact with several of them.

Consequently, the lane to the house became a busy highway. A year or two later, Anne and Harry could not remember a day or night when they had not hosted a guest or guests for lunch and/or dinner and often a home stay.

Before the book came out, the phones at the office and home rang off their hooks. After the book, the phone lines to the Caudills were jammed. Anne said:

Often I marvel when I think back to those days when Harry had a tremendously busy law practice. Often he would get home late from the office or the courtroom, sometimes at eight o'clock or later. I would keep his dinner waiting for him, and he could scarcely sit down before the phone would begin to ring, with clients calling to talk about their cases, or miners asking his advice, or who knows what. Our people had little comprehension of the court system, and needed constant reassurance and explanations. Then after the book, the outside world also intruded with never-ending requests for his comments or explanations. Still, he managed to write a few pages at a time, after dinner or on weekends. We finally adopted a rule. Never, ever answer the phone during mealtime.

Harry met and talked with some of the visitors in his office, but his home was more conducive to conversations, particularly after a delicious home-cooked meal. The numerous guests, flowing in a constant stream for a number of years, were well educated, had interesting backgrounds, and usually distinct and charming personalities. Combine Anne and Harry's wealth of experiences and firsthand knowledge of the region with those of historians, authors, professors, students, government officials, journalists, media crews, noted personalities, and unique characters, and imagine what the stories and conversations were like. Each visitor had personal human-interest stories to tell. The conversations were rewarding, enlightening, and always entertaining. Some of the guests returned for additional visits, which often resulted in valuable and long-lasting friendships. These visitors came to Appalachia to discover the darker aspects of the plight of its people; however, they found rays of hope and a vibrant light shining from the home at the end of the lane. As the years went by, Anne and Harry were invited to and made several visits to the homes of those who had visited them.

In recalling their visitors, Anne said, "On one page of my four guest books, I noticed there were four visitors from the

United Nations, a writer from *National Geographic*, somebody from the *Wall Street Journal*, the president of the United Mine Workers, and the Binghams from the *Courier-Journal*." It was another typical week at the Caudills.

Anne would never name a favorite guest, but if forced to pick one of the top ten, it would probably be Charles Kuralt. He was a very popular CBS journalist, initially known for his segment, "On the Road," on Walter Cronkite's *The CBS Evening News*. Later he was the first anchor for the acclaimed *CBS News Sunday Morning*, which was on the air for 15 years.

Anne remembered him fondly. "Charles Kuralt was one of the most delightful people I've ever known. When he walked into our house, it was as if we'd known him all our life. He had an absolute talent for connecting with people."

Kuralt made several visits to Whitesburg and the Caudill home, and produced several news segments for his program. Kuralt became a wonderful friend and took a special liking to 15-year-old James, who was a great reader and read many of the same books as his dad.

During his days at Whitesburg High, James was not interested in sports, preferring to explore with his friends the surrounding mountains, streams, and the unknown passages of the cave system in Pine Mountain, known to pioneers as Hollow Mountain. Oftentimes, the reports of their adventures in such places, "turned my hair prematurely white," Anne said. When James was a high school senior, he wanted to learn to play the piano, so his mother taught him as she had Diana, and he played the classics nearly every day for several years. James studied history at home and at Whitesburg High. He learned other things, too, when escorting the guests to see the sights.

James and his dad were great friends Anne recalled, and she vividly remembered them off in another room discussing an interesting book. This was a few years before the Caudills bought a television; the educational value of a history book was more advantageous than watching *Howdy Doody*. They bought a TV in 1968 to watch the moon landing.

A few years before the moon landing, in December 1964, Kuralt and a CBS crew gathered in Letcher County to do a special program on *Christmas in Appalachia*. They filmed a dilapidated unpainted one-room school sitting precariously on the side of a hill. A pot-bellied stove sat in the center of the school and Christmas decorations made of crepe paper hung from the flimsy walls. They filmed a grandmother reading the Christmas story to her granddaughter in a drab coal camp home. They filmed weary coal miners covered with black coal dust exiting the mines after a long backbreaking workday. In the darkness of winter, some miners never saw daylight until their day off on Sundays.

Harry was interviewed beside the railroad tracks as a long train loaded with coal chugged out of the mountains, leaving not one cent in the destitute region, except the limited pay the coal miners received. Eventually, with Harry's effort, a severance tax passed, and after 60 years, a trickle in revenue returned to the mountains.

Kuralt filmed one segment of the program at a small country store beside the tracks at Hot Spot. When the crew went in, the proprietor was slicing bologna. Kuralt asked the storekeeper if people ever became indebted to him. The storekeeper continued slicing bologna and said, "Yes, they do, but you can't let people starve. I just go broke with the rest of them."

Anne called *Christmas in Appalachia* a real tearjerker. It wasn't long until a train arrived at Hot Spot. The Salvation Army had sent boxcars loaded with clothing packed in boxes. When word went out announcing the date of distribution, poor people flocked to the tracks. Like Christmas morning, the people opened their boxed presents and spread the contents out on the track. It was quite a scene as the recipients began to trade used clothing to help meet the needs of each family.

The major networks made films and several made documentaries. All these journalists and filmmakers needed Harry's counsel, direction, and assistance. When Harry was not available, the responsibility fell to Anne. The demands on their time were extraordinary, but they didn't mind. An essential component of each visit was the grand tour of the surrounding area so a first-time visitor could get a feel for the place. They traveled up and down the hollows to Fleming-Neon, Vicco, Millstone, Rockhouse, and Beef Hide. When James became old enough to drive, he relieved Mom and Dad by conducting some of the tours.

A film company arrived from Italy. Guiseppi Scotese, a movie mogul from Rome, completed his film in three days. When he departed, Scotese insisted that Anne and Harry visit him in Rome. Several years later, they did.

Two British television companies made films, British Rediffusion and the British Broadcasting Corporation. Alan Mills of British Rediffusion visited the Caudills three times. Brian Lewis of BBC first came to explore the possibility of making a film, and a few months later, returned with a crew. When Anne invited them for dinner, they were late. It was wintertime and snow covered the mountains. Anne heard people stamping snow off their boots on the front porch before the crew came in for the night. Tony Isaaks, a big red-haired fellow from Australia, apologized for their delay, explaining, "We were frightfully mired down in the snow behind the caravans and had a terrible time getting out." Caravans? They had made a wrong turn and were stuck in a trailer park.

Anne prepared many wonderful meals in her home for guests from throughout the United States and several other countries. The first time BBC's Brian Lewis visited, Anne served corn pudding, a traditional southern dish, and Brian cleaned the bowl. When the entire crew returned, Anne served corn pudding again. When the crew went back to England, Brian wrote a letter of appreciation, attaching a postscript at the bottom: "Would you send me the recipe for that delicious corn pie?"

The Caudills could not host the larger contingents, but Herman Combs Jr., son of "Big" Herman Combs, a former sheriff, gladly hosted these citified people in his motel, which was not yet on par with a Ramada. He was an accomplished con man, fabricator, and taleteller who kept his customers entertained. When film crews came to town, Herman raised his rates and was skilled in fleecing them in other ways. When one film crew arrived, he convinced them they needed a four-wheel drive jeep to get around the mountainous terrain. He worked out a deal to provide one, which he would resell upon completion of the project. He made good money on the rooms, dry cleaning, jeeps, and items of historical value. Before one crew departed, he sold them a "famous" old rifle at a high price. He claimed it was the gun "used to kill the last Indian in Letcher County." When another crew arrived, Herman said, "For you, I've saved some fresh, new poverty never filmed before."

Most of the correspondents and journalists had traveled and worked in many places throughout the world, and they had many stories to tell. Well-known writer Peter Schrag stayed with the Caudills for a long evening of good talk. The next morning at breakfast, he told them his story. He was Jewish and grew up in Germany in the late '30s when Hitler began his purge against the Jews. His father had gone to America on business and sent word that Peter and his mother must leave Germany immediately. They were not to let anybody know. They departed and struggled through the mountains at night, hiding out during the day. Eventually, they made it to France and lived.

Soon after *Night* came out, Gordon Ebersole was assigned the duty to survey conditions in Appalachia. He was to recommend a course of action to relieve poverty and develop a program for the area. Harry was an admirer of the success of the Tennessee Valley Authority and proposed a similar authority for the southern mountain area. From those meetings, the Congress for Appalachian Development was organized. CAD was designed to explore ways to develop the area. Anne served as its secretary for a number of years.

Ebersole recruited his friends, Secretary of Health, Education and Welfare Wilbur Cohen and his wife, Eloise, to visit the Caudills. Eloise took great interest and made several visits to the CAD meetings. Before one visit, Eloise solicited a large number of books from the Washington Democratic Women's Club, of which she was a member. She filled her large car with the books, drove to Whitesburg, and she and Anne delivered them to a new library named for President Kennedy in a nearby county.

After seeing the conditions of the people, many of the visitors wanted to help a destitute family or contribute in some other way.

Anne received numerous letters asking for guidance in donating. In addition to cooking, hosting, guiding, helping Harry, caring for the children, and dozens of other responsibilities, Anne gladly corresponded back and forth, and arranged for distribution of the gifts because, as she said, seeing children dressed in rags "broke my heart."

As word of *Night* spread, requests for Harry to speak were numerous. He was frequently called to Washington to appear before Congressional committees or confer with other officials. Travel became an imperative, and traveling anywhere was tedious and time-consuming. It was a two and one-half hour drive to the nearest airport, which was at Tri-Cities, centrally located between Bristol, Virginia, and Johnson City and Kingsport, Tennessee. When they had to be away from home, Anne and Harry departed with peace of mind, assured their children remained in safe, caring, and loving hands. Harry's parents, Cro and Martha, were always eager and delighted to keep watch over their grandchildren.

Harry tried to accommodate as many speaking requests as time and his schedule afforded. He understood that personal explanations and appeals were a viable means of calling attention to the plight of his people. Since their cause was a team effort, Anne accompanied him on most trips. Not only did he want and need her company, but she did most of the driving over the long, twisting roads, which helped to relieve the pain of his impaired leg. Time after time, mile after mile they talked, listened to books on tape, or one drove while the other read aloud. It was not lost time, because being together was supportive and reassuring, and provided vital strength necessary for their cause.

Anne and Harry flew to Washington again, and were met

by Gordon and his rusty, trusty pickup.[13] He delivered them to Wilbur and Eloise Cohen's home. Eloise had arranged a meeting with Felix Schneider, the Swiss ambassador, who had read Harry's book and wanted to meet him.

Harry was particularly interested in the meeting, because he knew that Eastern Kentucky was almost exactly the same size as Switzerland. Both areas were mountainous, but that was where the similarities ended. Eastern Kentucky was full of mineral wealth, coal, oil, and gas, whereas Switzerland had few mineral resources and a rather cold, snowy climate. The Kentucky mountains had the benefit of a mild climate, forested hills, and abundant resources. Why were the Swiss so well off, when Kentucky mountaineers were extremely poor? The paradox intrigued him.

The next morning, the Cohens drove Anne and Harry to the embassy, where they were expected. The butler greeted and escorted the visitors to an exquisite sitting room, announcing, "His Excellency will be with you shortly."

"His Excellency bounced in, greeting us with great effusiveness, and said, 'Come, come, come and zee my garden,'" Anne said. "He was one of the most bubbling personalities I ever met, as was his wife, Gigi." At the conclusion of their visit, Harry invited the ambassador to visit Eastern Kentucky and see firsthand what he had read about the Cumberlands.

The ambassador informed Harry that he couldn't go

---

13. So many times, Anne and Harry, dressed in their finery, squeezed into the front seat, and with their wrangler-type chauffeur under a big cowboy hat, sped through the streets of Washington. Both Anne and Harry had a keen sense of humor and unrelenting joy for life, and they considered the truck just another fun and enjoyable diversion.

anywhere in the United States without a formal invitation to speak somewhere. Harry arranged for him to speak at Pikeville College, and Felix and Gigi Schneider flew to Tri-Cities. His chauffer met them there with the limousine. When they arrived in Whitesburg, the chauffer was sitting in the back seat, and the bubbly ambassador was driving. He told them that he loved driving in the mountains.

The Schneiders spent two wonderful days and nights with the Caudills. On the second long day, they drove to Pikeville for the speech and a luncheon. During the afternoon, they toured the mountains. Since Anne did not have time to prepare dinner, her plan was to take them to the only fine restaurant in the area, 35 miles away in Wise, Virginia. She told Felix she would take them to dinner, or she could whip up some leftovers. Felix went for the leftovers. Anne remembered she had the rest of a delicious roast beef in the refrigerator, and plenty of corn, tomatoes, potatoes, and other vegetables from the garden.

It didn't take her long to fill the table and dinner was announced. The guests were seated, but before the meal began, His Excellency, overcome with an intense desire for steaming hot food, momentarily ignored proper etiquette. He took his fork, stabbed a new, buttered, little red potato, about the size of a golf ball, and popped it in his mouth, saying, "I love these little potatoes." Anne said that from that point on, she never hesitated to serve new red potatoes to any guest.

Later, Harry was invited to speak in Washington at a conference on natural beauty sponsored by Lady Bird Johnson. The final event at a swank hotel was a formal affair, sponsored by Lawrence Rockefeller. After Harry spoke, concluding the conference, Gordon and his rusty truck arrived to pick them up.

Dressed in western attire, Gordon entered the plush crowded lobby carrying a large package wrapped in newspaper.

"Here, Anne. It's your birthday, open it," Gordon said. He had painted a moonshine still on a canvas mounted on barn siding. "Anne, I took a five-dollar painting class, and they advised still life, so that's what I painted for you, a still."

Gordon worked diligently in promoting the Appalachian area, with major emphasis on the promotion of industry and tourism. Despite considerable incentives, for whatever reason, only a very few industries were established in the area. Coal remained king; bulldozers replaced miners and job opportunities dwindled. Perhaps it was due to the remote locale, poor schools, limited health facilities, and a general lack of other services. Persuading industrial managers and their families to relocate in Appalachia was difficult. Its poorly educated workforce discouraged companies from taking the risk.

To promote tourism and new industry, Gordon envisioned construction of small lakes and adjoining little towns with motels, restaurants, shops, and recreational facilities. The people were poor, but rich in their distinct cultural heritage, exemplified by colorful and fascinating lore, legends, and history. Stories about the origins of their way of life, the frequency of family and clan feuds, and the bitterness of the equally divided populace during the Civil War provided a wealth of original historical information.

The native people were highly skilled artisans, creating imaginative and original works of art, crafts, and furniture unique to the area. America's popular folk and country music had its roots in the original mountain music in Appalachia. Down in the hollows, life was drab and bleak in the coal camp towns.

Many of the songs were sad ones, but to lift the spirits, the talented and gifted pickers took dulcimers, fiddles, and banjos in hand. The music stirred the blood and spirit to foot-stompin' beats, parting the coal-black haze, letting rays of sunshine in.[14]

Another opportunity arose for Anne and Harry to go to Washington, but this time it was a visit to the White House. Before the visit, Harry had advocated a southern mountain authority similar to the TVA. There had been considerable effort on the part of governors and other government officials to bring aid to the region. Eventually, the Appalachian Regional Commission was established, resulting in some improvements in roads, schools, and the infrastructure in the area. A group of Letcher Countians wanted to express their gratitude and decided to present President Johnson with a replica of "Old Betsy," Daniel Boone's rifle.

A former longtime county judge, Arthur Dixon, who was a very talented woodworker and gunsmith, made the rifle. It was a fine work of art. The committee asked the former judge to go to Washington and present the gift, but he had never flown or been to Washington. He agreed to go if Anne and Harry would accompany him, and they did.

Anne said of LBJ, "He was a big powerful man, but genial and in control, and he just emanated a sense of power." After the trip, Judge Dixon made another Old Betsy; it remains in the Caudill family.

---

14. The elements are there, but tourism never reached the potential of what it could become. A few museums, shops, and points of interest have developed, including coal-mining museums in Jenkins and Benham. A few coal camp towns and company stores were partially restored, and a company school was converted into a charming bed and breakfast at Benham. The potential for tourism remains.

A few years later, Anne met Lady Bird Johnson again at the University of Kentucky when the first lady went there to speak. As Anne and Harry passed through the receiving line, Mrs. Johnson took Harry's hand and said, "Oh, Mr. Caudill, you are the man who planned the presentation of the rifle. It is Lyndon's favorite gift. He hung it over the door of the office in his museum in Texas. Very often he takes it down to show his visitors and explain its origin."

Lady Bird promoted beautification of America, encouraging communities to remove garbage and litter, and plant flowers, shrubs, and trees along parks and roadways, which political opponents deemed ridiculous and wasteful. Beautifying the country caught on and her project made a difference in America's landscape. Later, Anne and her Whitesburg Garden Club followed suit, planting flowers and trees to beautify their town.

When the book came out, Gordon Ebersole was one of the first on the scene and visited the Caudills several times. The long, lanky Westerner not only provided a taxi service during the several Caudill visits to Washington, but he added a kind of cowboy, cattle-herding flavor to each visit. Gordon was not only fun loving, a prankster, and ever the character, he was highly intelligent, experienced, and talented, and most importantly, a true and dear friend. Years later, when he learned of Harry's death, Gordon immediately went to Whitesburg to be with Anne. "I'll never forget him. He gave me such great help and support," she said.

CHAPTER 10

They Kept Coming to the Cumberlands

They kept coming and coming, and Anne began to lose track of who and when. Occasionally, she checked the guestbook. One notation from her daughter drew her attention, "I have lived here 16½ years, and it gets more and more weird." Diana lived her formative years in a home that, as she observed, progressed from "crazy" to "weird." During the weird years at the Caudill home, Diana was very helpful to her mother. However, she had one particular concern; every time her friends came to visit, she was washing dishes. Her mother explained that the whole family washed dishes, and if her friends were true friends, they would pitch in and help.

Anne noticed a couple of other entries: "Harry Frye Caudill—I am seven years old." Under his name was, "Mary Bingham—I am 72 years old." Little Harry Frye, who was three years old when the book came out, grew up with strange people coming in and out of his home. It didn't seem to bother him, all this endless talk about a book.

James was in his mid-teens and Anne recalled, "James totally enjoyed it, because he was never a teenager. He was a boy and suddenly grew to a man. He was always a great reader and student of history, and he and his dad were great friends, read the same books and talked about the same things. James always loved to be on hand when these people came. He would listen and take part."

During the busy year of 1964, Anne washed dishes and did countless other things, hosting the hordes that came to see the land where *Night* had come. A writer is compelled to write, and despite all the other demands, Harry managed to write a few pages each week, and Anne wrote correspondence to those requesting meetings, visits, and interviews, and she wrote personal letters to friends and family.

After a year of the extraordinary and intense activity and a busy holiday season, on January 5, 1965, Anne wrote a letter to her dear friend and former college roommate, Lib Williams. The letter captured Anne's personal thoughts, feelings, political views, and life as it was during that hectic, yet stimulating and rewarding time of her life:

This year I just simply could not get all my Christmas letters written. We had an even more hectic time than usual for some weeks just before Christmas, and cards and letters just simply didn't get done. Christmas preparations, though we had a lovely holiday, were the very least of my involvements. I am sending you a clipping from a recent issue of the *Courier-Journal*—the Sunday before New Year's which will show you a little of why I am so busy.

And, Lib, what I want is an opportunity to sit and talk to you all day and all night, as we used to do so long ago. I feel most unsatisfied with just a quick note to say hello, hence no notes at all. I was much interested in your comments about the Birchers of Southern California. Even here, in Letcher County, which went 75 percent for Johnson and in Kentucky, which went 90 percent or more for him, we had the cold sweats until the returns came in. Never in my adult life had I been so really frightened. Never before, of course, had such issues become a really vital part of a national election. The thing that frightened me so was the people I know and associate with almost daily, who have sat around my fire many a time, and who have always been staunch Democrats, who suddenly were Goldwater people, suspicious and antagonistic to all liberal views. I could see the very kind of suspicion and distrust growing between friends and acquaintances that produced Nazi Germany.

On December 15, Harry and I went to Washington to present a gift to President Johnson from the people of Eastern Kentucky, accompanied by the maker of the gift. It was a perfectly beautiful replica of a Kentucky long rifle, powder horn, bullet pouch, and coonskin cap, presented as a thank you for LBJ's efforts to do something about Eastern Kentucky. You asked what this effort will amount to. Time will tell. We had conferences with Shriver and several of his top aides, and were much impressed with their ability and recognition of the depth and complexity of the problems. But whether enough money will be eventually put into the War on Poverty, and whether Washington can figure out a way to keep the new money and new programs from simply augmenting tired old efforts and being used to further reinforce the political machines which feed upon the ignorance and helplessness of our people—that remains to be seen.

If we did not have hope that there are forces at work,

which will eventually rehabilitate and redevelop the area, we would, I think, have left long ago. However, at times it becomes bitterly discouraging. I think you might like to read Harry's article, "The Permanent Poor" in *Atlantic Monthly*, June 1964.

America cannot afford the waste of its people and the terrible destruction of its resources, which proceeds so rapaciously here. The nation needs this green and beautiful area, and it must be saved for future generations. As Johnson said in his State of the Union message, this generation will not see the end of poverty, but at least we have admitted that all is not affluence, and that there are problems here at home in urgent need of attention. We have made a start.

We have been besieged with TV crews, journalists and economists, historians, students, and representatives of big business, who surprisingly seem to be developing the rudiments of conscience. We have been delighted to assist TV crews from England (who have been here three times for extended filming), Japan, Italy, and journalists from Germany and Denmark, Scotland, with another crew coming next month from BBC, London. This has not been very popular with the State Department, but we have recalled that not until Wales became an international scandal did the British Government do something about it. There have been many American TV shows on the area, all of which is adding up to a real national recognition of the problems of an area as large as Great Britain. Next week our friend Charles Kuralt of CBS is coming for an extended trip to do stories on how the War on Poverty is, or is not, being fought. His tremendous show *Christmas in Appalachia* filmed here brought an absolute avalanche of toys, food, and old clothes to Whitesburg over Christmas. The Salvation Army was called in to assist with distribution.

As you can guess, all this has been unpopular with the entrenched power structure and "the other Appalachia"— the merchants and professional people in the county seats, the bankers, and the coal operators who have made a great deal of money. However, I find that even their blinkered eyes are being opened, and television has shown them their own littered backyard.

We have made some talk about a trip to California again this summer. We haven't had a real trip in several years due to the advent of Harry Frye, a book with resultant incredible involvements, and Harry's illness that put him in the hospital for a month last summer. All is OK now, though he must be carefully moderate in all things.

James Kenneth is a great 6' 1", my right arm and mainstay, a very real student, a budding socialist, and his father's constant companion. At Christmas he entertained with an all-night (nearly) chess tournament for friends of assorted ages and sexes. The same evening Diana, who wears all my clothes except skirts and dresses because she is shorter, entertained with a slumber party. Really, chess players are to be preferred to teenage sillies in the form of girls—in so far as entertaining goes. This kind of thing goes on to a smaller extent all the time at our house. This last summer we built on an addition for our own peace of mind. Harry and I have a big library-bedroom-office combination furnished with a huge, handsome, walnut early Victorian bed and dresser. The room is lined with walnut bookshelves and big windows, which look out upon a mountain view you would love, and made comfortable with lounge chairs, a spacious dressing room and bath, and a wonderful big walk-in closet with windows and shelves for my filing cabinet and the collection of "things" which must be preserved.

Little Boy has been a pleasure, as well as a trial to us all. His brother and sister have been blessed and vexed with an absolute dynamo—a Dennis the Menace in the flesh—as affectionate and loving a little imp as ever drew breath. At the time when James goes to college with two more years of high school after this one, Harry Frye will start to the first grade. How's that for avoiding lonesomeness?

Mother is very feeble and is almost unable to walk. She has suffered from Parkinson's disease for many years, and just before Christmas had a bad fall so that she was in the hospital and unable to come here for the Christmas my family has always shared at my house. So on Christmas Day, after the children's parties and my usual Christmas evening dinner and carol sing for friends and neighbors, we drove to Cynthiana to enjoy another Christmas which my dear Aunt had prepared, tree, dinner and all, for Mother's enjoyment.

If we do get to California, I will surely see you.

As always,

"Frye"

Kentucky politics is the "damndest" as James Mulligan's poem says, and the book provided a political feast for politicians, especially Kentucky ones. *Night* is the story and account of the social, economic, and political conditions of this large and neglected part of the state. Politicians go where the action is, and Kentucky politicians began taking considerable interest in the plight of the state's people in Appalachia. In addition to an abundance of coal, the area has voters.

Harry had close associations with most Kentucky politicians. He worked with the state's leaders during his six years in the legislature, and had contacts with many others. Kentucky politicians understood the western, northern, and central parts of Kentucky, which were the crucial political areas. Their philosophy seemed to be, "Don't tax the corporate coal companies in Eastern Kentucky, and you don't have to waste time there." When the book put the Cumberlands back on the map, politicians scampered to the area, shook hands, and asked, "What can I do for you?"

Most of the politicians and government officials who went to the Cumberlands were sincere in assessing the conditions and seeking solutions to the complex problems. The root cause of the problems was political; was politics the answer?

Harvey Sloane was a dynamic young doctor who served on a team of doctors who were conducting a study on children's health in the area. Sloane, who would later become mayor of Louisville, visited the Caudills several times and, on one visit, asked if it would be possible to tour the inside of a coal mine. John Breckinridge, who was running for the US Senate and was a guest of the Caudills at the time, asked to be included. Harry arranged the special tour and Anne recalled:

We all donned coveralls, steel-toed boots, hard hats, and went in on mine cars, flat on our backs, whizzing along with the mine roof just over our heads. I was riding alongside Harvey Sloan, and somehow we got the giggles. Leaving the cars, we entered the workplace and stooping under the low roof, went up to the face to watch the miners continuously cutting away the coal. When our guide indicated it was time to leave, we went single file all stooped over under the low roof. John Breckinridge was just in front of me, then Harry came last. As John turned to go, he shook a miner's hand and said, "I'm John Breckinridge and I'm running for Congress, and hope you will vote for me." As Harry and I passed, we heard the miner, all stooped over, say to his buddy, "Some people will go anywhere to get a vote."

One day inside a coal mine, and the next, Anne was out and into the bright and shiny world that is Washington. She said, "We went back and forth to Washington to talk to people, and try to get support for the idea of developing a major effort to bring the central Appalachians into the mainstream of American life, and not simply as a resource area that was to be continually robbed."

Senator John Sherman Cooper, an elder statesman, former ambassador to India, and a longtime Republican senator from Somerset, Kentucky, served his state and country well. He was highly respected by both political parties and in a position to influence government agencies that could assist the mountain people.

Gordon Ebersole met Anne and Harry at the Washington airport again. Anne, coughing and sneezing, had caught a terrible cold. Tending to their every need, Gordon stopped by a drugstore and purchased a powerful new drug for Anne. She took one that night, slept fairly well, and took another early the next morning in preparation for the visit with Senator Cooper.

"The antihistamine just flattened me like a zombie," Anne said. "By the time we arrived at his office, I could hardly sit up. A funny thing, the senator had a problem, too—a circulation condition in one of his legs. As Harry talked, I was propping my eyes open, and the senator was rubbing his leg up and down and stomping his foot on the floor. It was an absurd scene."

Senator Cooper was very helpful and supportive throughout the years. He was instrumental in establishing the Appalachian Regional Commission, and often conferred and corresponded with Harry. When running for reelection, Cooper made a campaign stop in Whitesburg. After his speech, the senator was whisked off by local Republican leaders for a conference. Anne noticed his wife, Lorraine, standing on the street off to the side and thought it a bit odd that the Republican women were ignoring her. Anne went over, introduced herself, and invited Mrs. Cooper to lunch. When they entered the restaurant, the Republican women were seated and eating. Republicans and Democrats do have good friends in the opposite parties, but in the heat of political battle in the mountains, those friendships are seldom displayed in public. Anne introduced the wife of their chief candidate to the Republican women, and they responded with cool politeness and did not invite the two women to join them.

"I haven't figured that one out to this day," Anne said.

Lorraine Cooper later served with Anne on the board of trustees of the Appalachian Regional Hospital, and Anne was impressed with her gracious willingness to serve and her contributions to the cause.

During the same trip, Anne and Harry met with Sargent Shriver, brother-in-law of President Kennedy and founder of the Peace Corp, Head Start, VISTA, and other organizations in President Johnson's War on Poverty. Following a "most interesting meeting with Shriver," a large contingent of VISTA (Volunteers in Service to America) came to central Appalachia. After the book made its impact, volunteers from several religious groups and other agencies and organizations unselfishly went to the Cumberlands to fight the war on poverty.

In addition to acting as the Caudills' designated Washington chauffeur, Gordon Ebersole's primary responsibility was creating and developing ideas and projects for Appalachia. One idea he proposed was Mine Mouth Power, a project where power plants are constructed near the mouths of mines in lieu of shipping coal long distances. These plants were very successful in the west. The public would own the plants and profits would remain in the local area.

Alex Raiden was the president of the American Public Power Association at the time, and Anne and Harry began conferring and working with him in Washington. On one occasion, Raiden invited the Caudills and some other guests to his home for dinner and discussion. One guest mentioned that President Kennedy had gone to Dallas to speak.

"He should not have gone to Texas," Harry said. "He's going to get himself killed."

The next morning, Anne and Harry went to the Senate Office Building to meet with two senators. When they arrived, they noticed a flurry of activity. Traffic had stopped and people were scurrying around the building. Anne thought perhaps there had been a traffic accident. When they entered the elevator, the operator said, "The president has just been shot."

The room where they were to meet was vacant. A radio blared down the hall. That room was packed until the announcement that the president had died. Anne and Harry returned to their hotel room and prepared to leave for home.

Alex Raiden called and asked, "Harry, how did you know the president would be shot?"

"I didn't know; I was just so fearful."

On this trip, they had decided to drive to Abington, Virginia, and take a train to Washington. The train ride back to Abington was a long, depressing one. When they arrived, they were so disconsolate and drained that they could not continue on to Whitesburg. After a night in a hotel, they drove home the next day.

The sudden, tragic loss affected everyone. President Kennedy had made a commitment to return to Appalachia. He had appointed President Franklin Roosevelt's son, James, to head up the initial plans for Appalachian development. What if the president had lived and followed through with his commitment? After weeks of disbelief and mourning, the nation bounced back. Fortunately, President Johnson took up Kennedy's cause, and the War on Poverty took off, full speed ahead.

In September 1968, Senator Robert Kennedy spent three days in the Cumberlands and held hearings for the Senate Sub-committee on Employment, Manpower, and Poverty. His visit was during a crucial time, as the nation was in intense discussion about race, privilege, civil rights, national identity, distribution of resources, and war. Harry testified at the hearings and escorted the senator around the area. Thus another Kennedy again brought attention, concern, and hope to the area. Within four weeks, Robert Kennedy announced his candidacy for the presidency. He was assassinated four months later in California, eight weeks after Martin Luther King's assassination in Memphis. Those eight history-changing, traumatic weeks stunned the nation, impaired the War on Poverty, and took a toll on the nation's spirit and conscience.

During this low point, the Caudills continued working and accommodating the continuous flow of visitors, with an every-little-bit-helps attitude. Phillip Stern was an undersecretary in the State Department. He contacted Harry to arrange a visit and meeting. Anne planned dinner for him and his photographer, George Vincent.

It had been a very dry summer. At mid-afternoon, when Anne looked out her window, a brush fire was roaring down the hill toward their property. A tall pine tree stood near their home with branches dangling near the ground. If the fire spread to the pine tree, it would go up like a torch. She rushed to call the firefighters at the lookout across the valley on top of Pine Mountain. They informed her they could see the fire and were on the way. Anne called Harry, but he was in court and unavailable. What could she do but fight the fire? She took a bucket of water and an old gunnysack, went out, and began beating the flames and fighting the fire. When the firefighters arrived, they fought the fire until late afternoon, saving the Caudills' home, the pasture, and pine tree. Anne wore shorts during the exhausting and heated battle. When Phillip Stern and George Vincent arrived, Anne's legs looked like she had been tangled in a briar patch, but that was not her primary concern. She had offered them dinner. With nothing prepared, she made tuna fish sandwiches and heated some canned soup.

Several months later, the Caudills were back in Washington at a formal reception hosted by Phillip Stern; the men wore tuxedos and the women were in gowns and long white gloves. The dignitaries were there with Stern in the reception line. Anne said, "Well, Phil, the last time I saw you, we were dressed much differently, and the food is much better here." He laughed and their correspondence continued. His book, *Poverty in America*, and Vincent's photographs of the area significantly helped spread the word.

It was nearing Christmastime and a Manhattan banker had a brilliant idea. Each Christmas, he arranged a spectacular display in the lobby of his bank. One December, the bank president instructed workmen to flood part of the lobby, then freeze it so a Yuletide-clad lady midget could come out and ice-skate to Christmas carols. The banker then went out dressed as Santa Claus to give out presents. Apparently, it was good for the banking business.

Poverty was a popular topic in 1965, so the bank president decided to bring a destitute family from Appalachia to New York, place them in the lobby of the bank for a month, and have them sit there making baskets, quilts, and other interesting mountain crafts. He contacted Harry for a visit.

Anne prepared dessert and coffee for the banker and four of his vice presidents. It was an interesting evening. When the president needed to make an important call to New York, a vice president jumped up, dialed the number, and handed the phone to the president. When the president took out a cigarette, a vice president jumped up to light it.

"Harry, I want you to find me a destitute family for a month," the banker said. All expenses would be paid, and the family would be paid considerably more than what a coal miner made. Harry was dubious, but a quick thinker. He informed the bankers that his good friend, Tom Gish, publisher of the Whitesburg *Mountain Eagle*, could locate a perfect family for the display.

Tom and Pat Gish were UK graduates. Tom grew up in Seco in Letcher County, and Pat in Paris, Kentucky. In 1957, they moved to Whitesburg after buying the *Mountain Eagle*. Tom changed the masthead to "It Screams," and it did. The paper won numerous awards, but was highly controversial for publishing frequent editorials advocating such things as control of strip mining, federal involvement in the local economy, mine safety, and black-lung legislation.

Tom and Harry were of like mind about the exploitation of the eastern coalfields and each gave mutual support in the fight to correct the ills. Tom's controversial editorials brought ostracism, threats, and finally arsonists who burned the paper's office. However, the *Mountain Eagle* continued to scream. In the '60s and '70s, several young enthusiastic journalists were drawn to the ferment in Appalachia and the *Mountain Eagle*. Their work brought to light many important and interesting stories, helping to make the paper a very influential one.

The Caudill and the Gish families were fast friends drawn closer with frequent dinners in their homes and the inevitable amusement and laughter.

However, Tom was hesitant, too, to put a showcase "poverty family" together, but he did, and they went off to New York City with its bright lights, glamour, and city cuisine.

Soon after the Christmas at the New York bank, Harry met

the poverty father out on the street. "Tell me about your trip to New York. Were they good to you?"

"Oh yes, they were good to us and we were well paid, but I'll tell you one thing," he said, "they can't cook worth a damn. I didn't have a piece of corn bread the whole time I was there."

There were other interesting people in the neighborhood. Aunt Ada Combs lived down the road from the Caudills. She was 84, spry, agile, and quite the personality. Aunt Ada was an old-time singer and knew many of the ancient ballads sung in the old-time way. Nothing delighted her more than singing and picking at her guitar.

Alan Lomax was the director of the National Art and History Project. He contacted Harry about visiting Letcher County to record native musicians performing folk songs. Harry arranged for several local musicians to meet with Alan and record their songs. A time was set for Aunt Ada to go to the Caudill home for her recording. Anne sent James to pick her up, but she wasn't there. James asked a neighbor if she knew where Aunt Ada was. "Oh, yes, she's squirrel hunting," said the neighbor.

Another time was arranged and Aunt Ada, dressed in bright red jeans, dangling earrings, with a bandana tied around her long black hair, arrived with her guitar and recorded several old ballads unique to the mountain folk, an informative and most delightful presentation.

John Jacob Niles was Kentucky's preeminent folksinger. In his later years, the Kentucky Arts Council invited him to present an evening of his music. Anne requested "The Death of Queen Jane," an ancient English ballad about the death of the wife of King Henry VIII. Niles, whom Anne recalled was "an elfin character, diminutive, spry with a high-pitched voice," invited the Caudills to his home, but died before the visit could be arranged.

Anne, the letter writer, had many more to write when people came to the Cumberlands, and after she and Harry started traveling to Washington. She had always corresponded with family and friends, and wrote most of Harry's legal correspondence. After the book came out, letters and requests for information increased tremendously. There were letters requesting visits, meetings, and interviews, and many other requests for information. Anne described it as a deluge.

Mrs. Henri Sokolove accompanied Eloise Cohen and six other women of the Washington Democratic Women's Club on a tour of Appalachia and a visit with Anne. A June 16, 1965, letter to Mrs. Sokolove, serves as an example of Anne's style, warmth, and grace:

When we returned a few days ago from a brief vacation, I found your lovely gift awaiting us. Almost immediately, it was put to use for crackers and chips for dip. I don't know when I have ever received anything I thought was more handsome or more useful. I appreciate your thinking of me and shall always treasure the tray as a memento of your too-short visit with us.

Harry and I both have wished that we could have had more time with you. The whole group we enjoyed, but we felt especially that you appreciated the problems of our people, especially the educational needs. I shall always remember your immediate understanding and happy visit with the little girl at Mrs. Ott Hobson's. Oh, would that all our children could have teachers with such ability to understand and care about each child, and with so much to offer in the way of training and experience!

We were in Washington for three very rushed days while Harry took part in the White House Conference on Natural Beauty. Eloise Cohen spent a great deal of her very busy time with me and took me to a number of places that gave me a real lift—places that I would not have visited otherwise. She took me to the school for physically handicapped children, which Mrs. Elizabeth Goodman has developed, to Dumbarton Oaks, and to visit her friend Madam Woytinsky. I would not have missed one of these experiences. Each gave me a lift of a different kind.

In the past week or ten days we have been much involved in advising and meeting with a group of beset people in Knott and Perry Counties who have tried to stand against the strip miners who are destroying their lands and homes. Last week a group of 40 women went out and stood off the bulldozers, in defiance of the law and court orders, etc. The law in Kentucky, as Harry probably explained, is on the side of the mineral holding companies. The only hope our people have to save Eastern Kentucky from complete ravage is to develop enough public pressure to get the law changed. As you know, our people are unorganized, ignorant of their rights, and frequently timid. The third of three public meetings held last night drew a crowd of about 175 people who plan to go in a cavalcade to the office of the governor next Tuesday to discuss the very serious problem with him. Whether enough public pressure can be organized to cause the legislature to stop this horror remains to be seen. The Coal Operators Association, of course, has many millions of profits at stake and is using every method of intimidation, outright contempt for the homes, gardens, wells, graveyards, roads, and watercourses of the people, plus a full-scale propaganda campaign. In attendance with the bulldozers are armed company guards, armed state police, armed deputy county sheriffs to protect the right of the bulldozers to rip up the lands of the people. Of course, when 40 women appear, it is easier to take the bulldozers away to some other area where the resistance is not organized and wait until a later time to return.

One day the Caudills were in Washington, and the next, they were back in the mountains fighting for the cause in Letcher County. Then Borg Visby visited from Denmark. He was a young journalist who decided to work his way around the world, stopping at especially interesting places. When he arrived in Kentucky, the *Lexington Herald* hired him and sent him to write a story about the "storm" in Appalachia. The Caudills invited Visby for dinner and the night. He had dinner and spent the night, and the next night and the next, because a snowstorm dumped two feet of snow over the Cumberlands.

She said, "We had a marvelous time. He learned a great deal about us, and we about him. It was a great experience. Harry picked his brain about the way things were handled in other places, particularly in Denmark and all the many other places he had been."

Dr. T. S. Ko, a director of a province in Taiwan, traveled to the state department in Washington and asked to see some poverty. The state department sent him and Chan, an interpreter, to the Caudills in Whitesburg. Anne described Ko as "a gentleman of middle years, portly, jolly, lots of laughter, and we greatly enjoyed his visit." During the discussions, Anne asked about the form of government in Taiwan and if he was elected. Through Chan, Ko replied, "Yes, very democratic." Were his cabinet and associates elected? "No, I appoint them."

Dr. Ko then began a long oration on something about controlling population.

"What's he saying, Chan?"

"I have no idea what he's talking about."

A reporter from the Tokyo *Asahi* (Sun) arrived in town. Harry was in a circuit court session, so Anne conducted the grand tour. During that time, few counties had established trash collection services, and much of it was dumped in the creeks.

"The creeks and roadsides were terribly, terribly littered," Anne said. "During high water, the garbage attached to the low-hanging trees, diapers and everything. Harry crusaded against that for 40 years, and it's still a problem, but much better now."

That evening, Harry said to the Japanese reporter, "Well, tell me what you think of all those things you saw today."

"I think you have very much garbage."

The guests kept coming, as did the stories. Ben Franklin of the *New York Times* visited the Caudills several times. Anne said, "I cannot tell you what an interesting time it was around my dinner table. These people had much to talk about. They were knowledgeable about what was going on around the country and the world. They had been to many places, seen so many things, and were non-judgmental, except they tended to be rather liberal minded. We were the same way and it made for such wonderful conversation."

Gene Foley of the Environmental Protection Agency had a

story to tell during dinner after the day Harry and Judge George Wooten, who was county judge of Leslie County, took him on the grand tour. They toured strip mines in Leslie County, where all the roads were gravel, including the main street in Hyden, the county seat.

When the group drove to a high point, they got out of the car to look at a devastated strip-mined area. Suddenly, Judge Wooten pulled out a pistol from his coat pocket and shot a squirrel out of a tall tree.

"My goodness, Judge, do you always carry a pistol?" asked Foley.

"Let me tell you, the worst thing that can happen to a man is to need a gun and not have one," replied Wooten.

The people who went to the Cumberlands heard many stories to take back to New York, Tokyo, London, and the US capital. One story Anne told involved Dirty Beard Couch, who lived over in Leslie County. Several years before, Couch was persuaded one Saturday night to go see one of the new moving-picture shows. He went in and took a seat at the back in case this newfangled thing was not to his liking. The show was about a cowboy, who was trying to protect his enormous herd of long-horned cattle from a bunch of dirty rustlers.

When the rustlers drove the herd toward a corral with an open gate near a cliff where they would plunge to their doom, the cowboy hurried to the gate, jumped off his horse, and closed it. When he jumped back on his horse, the gate swung open again. Kicking up dust, the rustlers were bearing in, but the gate wouldn't stay closed.

Dirty Beard jumped out of his seat, ran down the aisle, pointed to the cowboy on the screen, and hollered, "You herd the cattle, and I'll shut the damn gate."

Above, Anne Robertson Frye at age five, 1929. At right, Anne, at age 14, in her Grandmother Frye's second-day dress, 1938.

Cro Carr Caudill, Letcher County Court Clerk, and son Harry Monroe Caudill, 1929.

Anne and her brother Bob, members of the Cynthiana High School Concert Band, 1940.

Anne in her freshman year at the University of Kentucky, 1942.

The cannon at the University of Kentucky, where Harry proposed to Anne in 1945.

Anne Frye and Harry Caudill
engaged to be married,
1946.

Anne, home demonstration agent in Montgomery County,
Kentucky, at a Farm Bureau picnic in 1948.

The Caudill home on the hill at Mayking, where
the family lived from 1948 to 1991.

Strip mine damage near the Caudill home.

Bea Baltimore and Caliph, two members of the Caudill family.

Anne, a confirmed tree hugger, in 1960.

Judge Arthur Dixon and Harry Caudill presenting a replica of a Daniel Boone rifle made by Judge Dixon to President Lyndon Johnson, 1964.

Harry Caudill, Robert F. Kennedy, and Peter Edelman
tour Eastern Kentucky coalfields in 1968.

The Caudills and others prepare to tour a coal mine
with Congressman John Breckinridge (left).

James, Anne, Harry, Diana, and Harry Frye Caudill
spent many happy times in the woods.

Wendell Berry, Anne Caudill, and Governor Wallace
Wilkinson at the presentation of the Governor's Award
in the Arts to Harry Caudill posthumously, 1991.

Anne Caudill's family at Thanksgiving 2012 in New Albany, Indiana.

"I never remember a day when Harry didn't
kiss me and tell me he loved me."

CHAPTER 11

Would It Ever Settle Down?

The guests kept coming and many of them returned for more than one visit. Some of the media returned to do additional stories or films. Politicians and government officials were in and out of the mountains when it was to their advantage, and several authors and writers made visits on one or more occasions, as did professors, students, and representatives from universities. Shortly after the rediscovery (or discovery) of Appalachia, volunteer agencies and individuals began moving in. This "new" frontier captured the interest and imagination of those who came and particularly, those who returned.

When Anne reviewed her guest books, in which she began recording names 50 years ago, she recalled guests who came several times. Sometimes she remembered what she prepared for dinner. One may wonder to what extent Anne's cooking was a contributing factor to the guests' return visits.

Meals at the Caudills were a family affair. They worked in the garden to raise the food, prepare and cook the meals, and wash the dishes afterward. Anne's helper, Bea Baltimore, was invaluable and considered a family member. The chain grocery store provided the staples, sugar, salt, pepper, baking powder, coffee, tea, flour, cornmeal, fruit, seafood, and cheese. Chickens were produced locally, Harry's father raised pigs for the pork, and the Caudills raised a beef. In summer, fruits and vegetables came straight from the garden; in winter, they came from canning jars and the freezer.

Various dips, cheese, crackers, and drinks were served before meals. Although Harry did not drink and Anne only had a sip of wine on occasion, alcoholic beverages were available for their guests.

If a visit was during the early summer, Anne might serve fried chicken with gravy and biscuits, new peas or fresh asparagus, new little potatoes buttered with parsley, carrot casserole, fresh garden lettuce with green onions, wilted with a dab of hot bacon grease, spoon corn bread, and strawberry angel food cake.

Later in the summer, dinner might be breaded veal cutlets preceded by cold zucchini soup, scalloped potatoes with cheese, old-fashioned half-runner green beans cooked with bacon, corn on the cob, coleslaw, sliced tomatoes and cucumbers, and corn sticks or muffins. Peach or another fruit pie with vanilla ice cream topped off the meal.

In the fall, a dinner menu might persuade a visitor to schedule another visit. The menu might include baked ham covered with grape juice-raisin sauce, sweet potato casserole or baked squash, broccoli with lemon curry butter sauce, corn pudding, tossed salad with homemade Roquefort dressing, and yeast squash rolls. The meal would be topped off with apple crisp and vanilla ice cream.

A typical winter meal included roast beef with carrots, parsnips, and onions roasted along the side, mashed potatoes, home-canned green beans, stewed tomatoes with okra, and fruit or cream pie with meringue.

Every meal included dishes of relishes, fruit jams or jellies with biscuits or rolls, followed by hours of lively conversation and delightful stories.

One year after the book, the word was out about the nights in the Cumberlands at Anne's dinner table. The *Courier-Journal* did a story about the wife of the man who had created such a stir.

"Everybody called on us for the grand poverty tour," Anne said in the article. "I used to cook all day when we had guests coming, and now I come in at five, not knowing who the people are, coming for dinner at six." Without Bea's able assistance ahead of time, dinner would have been served much later.

People came in droves, and letters packed the mailbox with requests to meet with Harry. One reporter asked Anne to predict her future. With daily correspondence, legal transactions, articles, and nine more books to type, Anne responded, "All I see in my future is a big blue typewriter." Her future also included untold hours at the kitchen stove and sink.

Eight years later, Lillian Marshall, the food editor of the *Courier-Journal,* interviewed Anne again. When asked about women's liberation, a hot topic at the time, Anne replied, "I'm absolutely for it, but people go off on tangents. I'm a great believer in men and women working together. Something has been lost in this country." During the same interview, Anne described her home as a maelstrom and "a crossroads, where the traffic flows." The journalist added, "The visitors see only the practiced ease with which Anne Caudill entertains them."

"I really like to cook and have people here to eat," Anne said. She attributed her early training in cooking to the summers at her grandmother's farm. At daybreak, the men and boys milked the cows, fed the livestock, and harnessed the horses. Women and girls fried up skillets of cured country ham, sausage, or bacon, and a platter of eggs, accompanied by grits or fried potatoes, and a heaping platter of hot biscuits set beside a bowl of hot gravy. The women knew just when to put the biscuits in the oven and the coffee pot on the stove. A hungry man could smell the breakfast, particularly the cured country ham, when he was still halfway between the barn and the house. Noon meals were served in the dining room during the summer on a table that seated up to 12. To get a good day's work from a farmhand, he had to be well fed. The men finished breakfast with a few biscuits coated with fresh churned butter and topped with sorghum, honey, jams, or jellies. Such a breakfast would hold a man for about five hours, until the big dinner bell, mounted on a high post in the yard, rang around noon. Lighter suppers were served in the cool of the screened-in back porch.

After breakfast, the men headed for the fields, and the women and girls to the chicken yard and garden. A heaping platter of fried chicken with gravy, biscuits, fresh corn on the cob, green beans, new potatoes, tomatoes, and baskets of other fresh foods from the garden, and fresh fruit or berry cobblers topped with freshly whipped cream from the dairy herd, kept a man going until sundown.

One of Anne's first jobs was making tea. Before electricity and refrigerators, hunks of ice were chipped from the block of ice stored in the icebox and placed in large glasses. She remembers when the work hands came in from the blazing hot fields and each drank at least a quart of her iced, sweet tea. Women took great pride in setting a loaded table and feeding tired hungry men. The dishes may not have matched, but the steaming bowls and platters of a Bluegrass farmer's bounty always hit the spot.

From her early experience, Anne learned the vast difference

between heating up a can or package of corn, and picking a dozen ears from the garden, then boiling and serving them with dripping butter. At her house, there was probably more than one New Yorker who nibbled away at ears of corn with butter dripping down their chin. Anne's early training, her study of home economics at UK, and the instruction to her homemaker clubs in Montgomery County were adequate preparation for her life in the rural Eastern Kentucky mountains.

Corn is a staple in the mountains. Almost all mountaineers grew patches of corn on narrow little creek bottoms or up steep slopes. Corn kept their chickens, pigs, milk cow, and horse or mule alive. Corn kept the mountain people alive during the bad times. Many a mountain family made it through long winters living on corn bread, soup beans, and milk. Corn "likker," distilled during the shine of the moon, kept a few other mountaineers alive. Corn bread was the bread of life. Hard rolls cannot compare to corn bread soaked in buttermilk or dripping with butter and sorghum molasses. Corn bread soaked in sweet milk relieves the pain of hunger.

Miners left their homes for work before daybreak six days each week, carrying their carbide lights and dinner buckets. During the good times, baloney and cheese sandwiches provided energy for the afternoon, although baloney was expensive at the company store. During dire times, a miner's dinner bucket likely included a jar of soup beans, an onion, a hunk of corn bread, and a piece of fried salt pork in a biscuit.

Anne cooked corn several ways. She served fresh corn on the cob in season, frozen corn in the winter, corn pudding, fried corn, skillet corn pone, spoon corn bread, corn muffins, corn sticks, and grits made from corn. She also made corn-batter cakes for breakfast, gritted corn bread and corn mush sliced, fried, and served with butter and molasses. Had she smoked, plenty of cobs were available to make corncob pipes.

Until improved roads brought fresh produce to grocery stores, mountain people lived long winter months without fresh fruits, vegetables, and greens. In early spring when plants and trees begin to bud, leaves of various plants were gathered and cooked with boiled eggs and bacon for the first mess of greens in months. In early spring, nutritious poke greens from pokeberry plants satisfy a craving like no other.[15]

Fresh fruit was seldom available in the winter in the mountains except for oranges and bananas at Christmas. When Anne moved to the mountains in 1948, the A&P grocery did sell a limited supply of fresh fruits and vegetables. The people grew apples to make apple butter, and also sliced and dried them for winter use.

Dried apples were used to make stack cakes, which are also called mountain fruitcake, Kentucky stack cake, or molasses stack cake. People often baked these stack cakes at Christmas, and Harry's mother always fixed one.

Anne Caudill's Molasses Stack Cake

    1½ teaspoons baking soda
    1 cup Kentucky sorghum molasses
    ½ teaspoon salt
    1 cup firmly packed brown sugar

---

15. These greens are so popular that Harlan County celebrates a Poke Sallet Festival each year.

2 eggs

1 cup buttermilk

⅔ cup shortening

1 teaspoon cinnamon

1 teaspoon ginger

½ teaspoon nutmeg

½ teaspoon allspice or cloves

3 ½ cups flour (or more as needed)

Grease and flour three or six 9-inch pans. Stir soda into sorghum; add salt. Add all other ingredients except flour. Mix well. Add just enough sifted flour to make the dough stiff enough to roll. Knead as little as possible. Divide dough into six parts. Roll each to ¼-inch thickness to fit into 9-inch pans. Bake in well-greased and floured pans at 350 degrees for 20 minutes. (If you have only three pans, refrigerate the second three portions until ready to roll out and bake.) Cool the layers, then stack them, using dried apple filling between the layers.

Dried Apple Filling

1 pound tart dried apples

1 cup brown sugar

½ cup white sugar

2 teaspoons cinnamon

½ teaspoon cloves

½ teaspoon allspice

Soak the dried apples in water for several hours until soft; drain. Stew and mash the apples; add sugars and spices, stirring well. Cool. Divide filling evenly and spread between cake layers. Wrap the cake and allow it to stand for several hours or overnight before cutting. Refrigerate or keep in a cool place. Serve with whipped cream or vanilla ice cream. Homemade apple butter can be used instead of filling between the layers or on top, a half cup between each layer.

"It was divine," Anne said.

*　*　*

The third week of July 1969 was an exciting one. In preparation, the Caudills bought their first television to watch Neil Armstrong take a giant step for mankind. For the historic event, CBS planned to film the reaction of various people at different sites in the United States. They called and asked Harry to suggest a scene to film during this historic event. Harry suggested they go into a mine where miners were digging coal from a seam where man had never set foot before.

During that week, other guests visited the Caudills, including Wendell and Tonya Berry and David McCullough, who was working on an article about Harry for the *American Heritage* magazine. David was enchanted with Anne's big rocking chair that sat in their library. It was sturdy and exceptionally well made with a ladder-back design nearly five feet tall. Anne suggested that he visit Chester Cornett, who eked out a living making rocking chairs.

The next day, Anne's son James took McCullough to visit

Chester, who lived near Hazard in Perry County. Chester had his own way of making rocking chairs and living his life. He kept track of his orders by writing only the name of the person placing the order in the next blank month on his calendar, because it took a month to make one chair. His blueprint was in his head, so no two rocking chairs ever came out the same, but each was a masterpiece. He knew how to use the best walnut and hickory, how to season it, carve it, and put it together with pegs that would never come loose.

When James and McCullough arrived at Chester's ramshackle work shack, the craftsman was all flustered about the moon landing, and told them he thought it would come to no good. He predicted that it could be the end of time or at the very least, electricity would stop working, guns wouldn't fire, and not much of anything would work. Chester wanted to be prepared, so he had made a huge crossbow. When McCullough asked if it would shoot, he cranked it up—using a small, homemade cranking device—and fired. The arrow cleanly split an oak fence post into two pieces.[16]

Bernie Birnbaum, the CBS producer, and his wife and crew arrived in Whitesburg a couple of days before the moon landing. The crew filmed the episode in the mine a few hours before the landing. During the morning of the historic event, Bernie and his wife drove around the area, and bought two apple stack cakes at a bake sale. The party was set for man's first step on the moon, which occurred at 2:46 a.m. local time on July 20, 1969. The crew assembled in the Caudill living room.

---

16. On another occasion when Anne visited Chester's workshop, he proudly showed her a magnificent figure of Jesus Christ he had carved. Chester had his own unusual way of doing things and had made Jesus's beard with steel wool.

When Armstrong placed his foot on the moon, the camera focused on Harry for his reaction. Anne said, "It was the only time I ever saw Harry Caudill speechless."

*   *   *

For many years after Harry was wounded in 1944, he suffered problems with his leg and knee, and other physical problems stemming from the wound. He had been in and out of hospitals numerous times. The damaged nerves in his leg prevented feeling in his foot, which added to the complications. After his first surgery, a cast was placed on his leg and foot for a lengthy period. This caused a fungus that developed into perpetual peeling of the skin, irritation, and discomfort that plagued him the remainder of his life.

After one operation at the VA hospital, the pain became more intense. Harry decided to seek private assistance and contacted a well-known orthopedic surgeon in Louisville. Upon examination, the surgeon angrily exclaimed, "Those doctors will burn in hell." The surgeon removed a ball of sutures enclosed in Harry's ankle. This enabled him to walk again without a cane. Harry disputed the bill, because it was a mere $90. The surgeon refused to take more, stating, "I'm not accustomed to patients questioning my bills."

In 1957, Harry's father died. He was Harry's best friend, companion, and confidant. His death was devastating to Harry, and he went through a period of deep depression. In addition, he developed a roaring in his ears, fatigue, and loss of appetite and weight. A friend recommended an ear specialist in Pikeville, who asked to see Harry's feet during the examination. The doctor told him that he had also been in the army and had had the same experience. The fungus on his foot had gotten into his bloodstream. The doctor concocted a medicine that included iodine and it relieved the pain. Harry took the medicine for years.

A year later, Harry entered the veteran's hospital in Johnson City, Tennessee, for more surgery. While there, he developed severe chills, fever, and night sweats. Anne thought he might not recover. Although the chills and fever subsided, there was no diagnosis. When he returned home, the chills and fever started again. Harry went to his family doctor, Doc Wright. Doc looked at him and said, "You have malaria." Harry may have contacted it in Africa during the war. Doc gave him some quinine tablets, and he started to feel better on the way home.

Working in the law office or reading and writing placed little stress on Harry's legs. After the book was published, the guided tours, standing for speeches, getting in and out of cars, and moving about added stress and strain to both legs. Consequently, the pain in Harry's good right leg became as intense as that in his damaged one. He put so much weight on his right leg for over 20 years that it became nearly too painful to use. The VA provided an assortment of specially made shoes, but they were of little help. Someone suggested that Harry contact a skilled shoemaker in Vincennes, Indiana; the shoemaker made a special shoe that provided considerable relief for Harry. Frequent standing, walking, and continuous use over the years, however, took its toll. Sprawling on a lounge chair or lying down was his only relief.

Another doctor advised Harry to swim for exercise. Where does one swim in Letcher County—the polluted creeks? Much to the delight of their children, the Caudills built a swimming pool. Anne described the healing waters as a "godsend" that revitalized Harry's physical condition and mental outlook.

"Of course, it was always painful," she said. "He favored his left leg all those years and put more of his weight on his right leg, which wore out the knee joint, because he was walking in a kind of twist. In his later years, the right knee gave him more pain than the left, but both were absolute misery to him, particularly as he got older."

Despite living with pain for nearly 45 years, Harry's spirit, work, and contributions to his people throughout Appalachia and all of Kentucky grew and flourished.

* * *

For several years after the publication of the book in 1963, the Caudill schedule and demands on their time did not ease. Guests kept coming and returning, requests for interviews and speaking engagements continued at a steady pace, and the law office had an increasing number of clients to serve. Two of the children were in their mid-teens, and their activities required time and attention. Anne tended the children and the home fires, including the garden, the stove, and the guests for dinner. She also went to church on Sundays, the law office during the week, and remained involved in local organizations.

During these busy and eventful years, other individuals and groups of people descended on the Cumberlands. Volunteer agencies, including private, public, government, and religious organizations, came in droves, offering their services to the people in Appalachia—and adding significantly to the turmoil.

Harry continued to write and Anne took dictation and typed.

During the flood of visitors and despite the many other demands on his time, Harry squeezed in some time to write nearly every day. He wrote numerous articles and, in 1969, published his second book, *Dark Hills to Westward: The Saga of Jenny Wiley*. Anne wrote the epilogue to the book when it was republished in 1994:

> During the more than four decades that I lived near the headwaters of the Kentucky River, Harry and I traveled, by foot and by car, through and over the maze of mountains that make up the central Appalachians. I came to have a soul-felt respect and awe of those magnificent forested slopes, and their lovely cool hollows and bubbling clear streams. With Harry as guide and teacher, I came to understand something of their history. And I grieved with him at their destruction.
>
> When he wrote the story of Jenny Wiley, it came from his love of that forest vastness and his identification with those early ones, both aboriginal and European, who had inhabited it. *Dark Hills to Westward* expresses his need to share and explain that heritage.
>
> It was not until some years later, during our pursuit of family histories and the reading of early frontier accounts, that I discovered a far off grandmother, Theodosia Vause. With her two daughters, she was carried away by the Indians at the bloody massacre at Fort Vause, at present Shawesville, Virginia. A generation later, another of my ancestors, Jacob Spahr, was killed by Indians in an attack on Strodes Fort near Winchester, Kentucky.
>
> On one of the trips we made to Frederick County, Virginia, delving into our frontier origins, we identified

the Old Zane's forge neighborhood, the site of an early Indian attack. A John Day testified that in his boyhood his mother's brother was there killed and she was abducted along with his two sisters. He was with the party who pursued the Indians. They found his mother dead, scalped, and naked in the woods, but went on to rescue his two sisters. We thought it probable that this was Harry's John Day ancestor though there is confusion in the records as there was more than one "Indian fighting John Day" on the frontier. Another family tradition relates that Harry's great-great-grandfather Branson was scalped as an infant and left for dead, the only survivor of an Indian attack on his family's frontier home.

Thus the story of Jenny Wiley is but one tale in the long and bloody struggle in which our ancestors pushed the American frontier through the mountains of Appalachia, leaving an indelible stamp on our heritage.

* * *

Each day was a new experience and an adventure with new people to meet and new places to travel. Underlying it all, however, was the Caudills' cause—the responsibility, commitment, and effort to help their people and save their land. Interviews, appearances, and serving as hosts for the many visitors were ways to spread the word.

Harry appeared on NBC's *The Today Show* and several other radio and TV programs. On one occasion, Anne and Harry were in New York for interviews, and were invited to attend a party and screening of a film about Appalachia. The director sent a taxi to the hotel for the Caudills and another guest. When Anne and Harry entered the taxi, the other invitee introduced himself. "Hello, I'm Roman Polanski."[17]

David Nevin of *Life* magazine visited the Caudills for interviews on two occasions and brought a prize-winning photographer to photograph scenes for Nevin's article in a 1967 issue of *Life*. Michael McManus of *Time* magazine and his wife and daughter visited the Caudills. They had recently returned from an extended assignment in Greece. McManus's wife explained she was very happy to get back home, because the colors and climate in Greece were so intense and the people highly emotional.

Visitors came to learn about Appalachia; the Caudills learned about the world outside the mountains from the writers, journalists, and producers who, according to Anne, had been "everywhere and done everything." The Caudill home became a haven for lessons in diverse cultures and geography, and endless intriguing and amusing stories. An excellent home-cooked dinner accompanied by lively conversation and laughter made for a perfect evening.

Renowned columnist James Reston made a visit and advised his son, writer James Reston Jr., that a visit would be instructive. Reston Jr. visited during Thanksgiving week, and became so interested in what he had discovered that when Anne asked him to stay for Thanksgiving Day, he accepted.

Anne and Harry met Jack Weller, a minister from West Virginia, at a large church convocation in Kingsport, Tennessee, where Harry spoke. After his presentation, a TV crew asked for an interview, and they went to another room. Anne remained in

---

17. Polanski was a noted movie director who eventually had to leave the United States because of a sex charge involving a minor. His wife was actress Sharon Tate, who was murdered by Charles Manson's "family."

the auditorium listening to the next speaker. She said that Jack Weller gave a "spellbinding account of the people who lived in the hills and hollows and coal camps of West Virginia, which all sounded very familiar because it's not that much different from Eastern Kentucky."

At a reception after the convocation, Weller went over to meet Harry and Anne. Anne told Harry that he had missed a great speech and an account of many experiences that he needed to know about. Weller looked at Harry, handed him a large manila envelope, and said, "Mr. Caudill, I have something for you. I have written about my people, and you owe it to me to read this because your book inspired me to write it." He also added that he had not found a publisher for his book.

It was late when Anne and Harry departed Kingsport. Harry drove and Anne read aloud Weller's book, *Yesterday's People*. Anne said, "Both of us were just fascinated with it." When it became too dark to read, she used a flashlight.

Harry found a publisher for Weller's book and used it in his classes at UK when he began teaching there after retiring from his law practice.

John Fetterman, a writer for the Louisville *Courier-Journal*, visited the Caudills to gather material for a story. He roamed around the area and spent considerable time at Stinking Creek in neighboring Knox County. A year or so later, Anne and Harry met Fetterman again at a Congress for Appalachian Development meeting in Abingdon, Virginia. He handed a manila envelope to Harry and said, "You are the one who caused me to write this, and you owe it to me to read it." Anne felt that *Stinking Creek* was a very fine book about the mountain people and a firsthand look at how they live.

When Harry became a noted Kentucky author, he joined the list of the acclaimed ones. He developed associations and lasting friendships with most of them, including Wendell Berry, Jesse Stuart, Gurney Norman, James Still, Tom Clark, and the publishers, editors, and writers of Kentucky's major newspapers.

Jesse Stuart was a legendary and beloved Kentucky author. He was born in a one-room cabin in W-Hollow near the Ohio River running north of the Appalachian Mountains. He and Harry wrote about similar topics, and were considered authorities and spokespersons for Eastern Kentucky. Like Harry, Stuart had to write. He carried a pencil and scraps of paper with him at all times. While plowing a cornfield on the side of a hill, he would stop to give his mule a rest, and write a poem under a shade tree. He published 64 books. *The Thread That Runs So True* and *Man with a Bull-Tongue Plow*, a book of sonnets, are two of his highly acclaimed works.

Harry and Jesse met and talked a few times, and on one occasion, both spoke at a symposium at Berea College. Anne recalled:

Harry was a firm Democrat. He was a Roosevelt Democrat, and he believed that government had a responsibility to look after the people and to ride herd on the greed of the great corporations and find ways to improve the life of the people. He firmly believed that much of the plight of the people of Eastern Kentucky came about, at least part of it, from the unrestrained exploitation of the resources by the absentee owners who owned the minerals, and that government should find redress for that and put some kind of constraints on the exploitation. Jesse, like

Harry, came from a poor family. Most all the families in Eastern Kentucky were poor, some just poorer than others. Jesse had come from a poor family, and, by his own wits, determination, and perseverance, had become a famous writer, a successful teacher and school administrator, and a very well known leader. But he was of the opinion that if he had pulled himself up by his bootstraps, so could everybody else. Everybody else needed to do that for themselves and government had no part, no responsibility.

Well, at Berea, after each gave a speech, Harry and Jesse got into an interesting debate. After the symposium, some of the people in the audience suggested that Harry and Jesse meet again for a debate and that it be filmed. Here were two people who looked at things in two diametrically opposed ways . . . they both agreed to discuss the issue again.

Jesse agreed to go to Whitesburg and the debate took place later in Harry's office. The moderator began by asking Harry to describe the situation at that time in Eastern Kentucky. Harry explained that it was a depressing time with coal prices way down and the situation was bleak.

When Harry paused, Jesse spoke up. He said, "Now listen here, Harry, if you think things are bad here, you should see what they are like in Egypt." Jesse had recently returned from teaching at the American University in Cairo. Things were terrible in Egypt, but that was not the point. However, Jesse continued on explaining the conditions in Egypt. He went on and on and they couldn't stop him. Finally, he stopped and the moderator asked Harry a question. He is never one to give a short answer.

He'll lead up to it with the facts and an illustrative story, either funny or tragic, but always leading to the point. So he's going along setting the story and all of a sudden, Jesse interrupts. "Well now Harry, if you think things are bad here, you should see what's it's like in Greece."

When this most interesting and divergent discussion ended, the hosts thanked Jesse and Harry for participating, but the program was never broadcast.

The Caudills and the Stuarts had a great deal of respect for each other. However, Harry and Jesse never became close friends, probably because they had such opposing points of view. Anne remembered Jesse as a hardy bear of a man with a big voice, very expressive, a great writer, and fine man. No one who met Jesse Stuart would ever forget him. He was a very forceful person with very definite ideas and, as Anne admitted, "Who knows, his ideas may have been right—at least partly."

Tom Clark is considered the preeminent historian of Kentucky and authored the definitive work of its history in the 1930s. He was a native Mississippian, but lived most of his life in Kentucky and served as head of the history department at UK for many years. He was a highly respected and beloved figure, and worked until he died at age 102. At his 100th birthday celebration, Clark was asked to make a comment about his future. He replied, "At this point in my life, I don't even buy green bananas." Anne recalled, however, that he remained "sharp as a tack until his last breath."

Anne first met Dr. Clark when she attended UK in the 1940s. She did not have classes with him, but one day the dean called to ask if she would babysit the children of a professor. She had never babysat before, but agreed and was directed to the home of Dr. Clark at the designated time and place. Thirty years after that introduction, Anne entertained Clark in her home on several occasions. During one of his visits, he told Anne the story about an incident at UK when he had Harry in class.

Harry was one of the few veterans and one of the few men attending UK during the war years. Harry had a keen interest in history, and enrolled in Dr. Clark's class. An older woman, who had been recently divorced from a member of the faculty and discharged from a mental hospital, was also in the class. She quickly developed a terrible crush on Harry; she would turn around in her seat, and stare and gawk at him. When Harry had had enough, he stormed up to Dr. Clark and said, "If something is not done about that woman, I'm going to kill her."

"Well," Dr. Clark told Anne, "I didn't know this young mountaineer very well, but I did know he had just come out of the army, and I thought there was a possibility he just might do it." The problem was resolved when the woman dropped out of the class.

Years later, Tom Clark visited the Caudills again. It was winter and Anne had removed the screens from the windows. During the night, Anne heard her black cat scratching, a signal that it wanted to go out. It was a somewhat warm night, and Tom decided to get some fresh mountain air and opened the window. Moments later, he was awakened by a black cat nestled in his bed. The history professor opened his bedroom door, put the cat out, closed the door, and dropped back into deep sleep.

All was quiet until Anne's other black cat decided he wanted to roam, so Anne put her other cat out. When the professor came to breakfast the next morning, Anne said, "Good morning, Tom. How did you sleep?"

"Oh, fine, but I was just wondering, how many black cats do you have?"

As the years went by, Anne, Harry, and Tom always had a grand time telling stories and sharing many good laughs. Kentucky was Tom Clark's land, too. He knew its history and understood the importance of preserving its heritage and its beautiful forests and land.

When David McCullough first visited the Caudills, he and Harry hit it off from the start. Each time they met, their conversations would continue long into the night.

"They were just two minds with almost identical thinking, and both were great storytellers and enjoyed each other enormously," Anne said.

After his first visit, McCullough wrote a 27-page article about Harry called "The Lonely War of a Good Angry Man," for *American Heritage* magazine. The article was republished later in a hardback book, *Brave Companions: Portraits in History.* The book is a collection of pieces McCullough had written over the years about people he considered to have particular courage and an influence on history.

Through the years, the Caudills kept in contact with McCullough, and when James made the major move from Whitesburg High School to Harvard, David invited the Caudills to come early and spend a week in his family's 200-year-old home at Martha's Vineyard, which they did.

During another visit with McCullough and his wife in Lexington when he was working on his book about Harry Truman, Anne asked if he knew where Truman's grandparents were buried. He didn't, so she told him they were buried in Shelby County, Kentucky, where Abraham Lincoln's grandfather is also buried. Anne gave the directions and McCullough made the trip.

In 1965, Harry was invited to speak at the Knott County Courthouse in Hindman, Kentucky, where a large number of people had gathered in defense of Old Dan Gibson. Dan's stepson owned some land in the county, but couldn't look after it at the time, because he was off fighting in the Vietnam War. In 1971, Harry published his third book, *My Land is Dying*. The foreword sets the tone of the book and refers to Dan Gibson's plight:

One day in the spring of 1965, I climbed a hill with Dan Gibson, a wrinkled, weather-beaten man of 80. He had lived all his days in Knott County, Kentucky, near the geographic heart of the Appalachian range. He had seen, as the mountain people put it, "many times of trouble," and his eyes were deeply troubled now. Near the top, we came to a halt, and Dan leaned on a heavy stick. For a long time we looked in silence at the valley and across it to the ridges whose crests merged with the horizon. Above those timbered crests, John James Audubon had once recorded how he saw the sky darkened by vast crowds of passenger pigeons in flight. The hardwood forests that clothed the Appalachians in Audubon's day were the largest of their kind and among the oldest and grandest in the world. Dan Gibson had witnessed himself the cutting of their gigantic walnut, oak, and tulip poplar trees to make way for cornfields and pastureland, and later he had watched the prop-cutters sawing down the new growth to be used in the mines. Once again, after the onslaught of the coal industry, he had seen the gashed land struggle to heal itself with new growth, but the stillness that lay over it now seemed to portend, this time, a different fate.

On other hills in that part of Kentucky, nodding in deep coves and over rocky ridges, wild flowers were in bloom, snakes sunned themselves, and squirrels darted overhead. Though diminished from its former magnificence, the forest still pulsed with growth and activity, the marvelous fabric of interdependent life still intact. Here, the scene was altogether different: jumbled mounds of loose earth, slabs of bluish slate, half-buried trunks of dead trees, pools of stagnant, acid-yellowed water, and raw cliffs of sandstone newly scoured; a litter of mechanical relics, already rusting, from the bulldozers, trucks, and power shovels whose work, completed, had left this desolation behind.

Dan Gibson was a coffin maker by trade. Years ago, an accident had severed three of his fingers from his right hand. Death and injury were no strangers to him. But they had not inured him to sorrow. "The strip miners are killing these old hills," he said at last. "When they finish, there won't be anything left. My ancestors lived here, and I've got a stepson in Vietnam who wants to come back here and live out his days, too." He paused. "Yes, sir, this is my land"—the maimed hand gestured toward the landscape— "and my land is dying."

As we walked back to Dan Gibson's house, and I reflected on the millions of acres in America that have likewise been maimed by industry, his words rang in my ears like those of a latter-day Jeremiah.

Anne told the story from there. When a coal company moved in to strip mine the land, Old Dan made up his mind that they weren't going to destroy his stepson's land. Dan took his gun, went to the site, sat down with a cliff behind his back, and waited for the machinery to move in. When the first bulldozer approached, Dan raised his gun and said, "If you move another foot on this land, I'll shoot you." The operator believed him, climbed down from the bulldozer, and walked off the mountain.

It wasn't long until the sheriff and his posse arrived. They said, "Now, Dan, put your gun down, we don't want no shooting here. The law says they have a right to mine this land." The law— the broad-form deed law—generally granted coal companies the right to extract all minerals and lumber from the land with no date of expiration. A landowner might have signed the deed for $50, $75 or $100, a small fortune at the time, and 40 or 50 years later, have his land ravaged and practically destroyed.

Dan Gibson was carted to jail, and the people in the surrounding area became furious. Harry spoke to the volatile gathering at the packed courthouse in Knott County.

"He told them what was happening to them and what could happen might be worse unless they demanded some kind of strong reclamation of their ravaged land," Anne said. "I thought, I'm listening to Patrick Henry. I'd heard him speak many times before, but that was the most impassioned speech I ever heard him give."

Anne was sitting in the back of the crowded courtroom and noticed writer Gurney Norman, a journalist at the Hazard *Herald*, whom she knew. Norman was standing against the back wall alongside a striking figure, who Anne referred to as a "big, long tall drink of water." Norman became an excellent writer, and published several books about Kentucky, particularly about Appalachia. *Divine Rights Trip* is one of his better-known works. He also taught English at UK.

After the impassioned speeches, Gurney introduced his friend, a man by the name of Wendell Berry, to the Caudills, and thus a lifelong friendship began.

Wendell grew up in Henry County, Kentucky, attended UK and did graduate work in writing at Stanford University, as did contemporary Kentucky authors Gurney Norman, Ed McClanahan, and James Baker Hall. He then went to New York to write, but came back to Kentucky. Anne remembers Wendell standing in her kitchen doorway one early morning as she prepared breakfast during his visit. "I can see him now, standing there almost as tall as the doorway, talking with me about having come back to find his place, to completely know his place on earth."

Wendell, his wife, Tonya, and their family found their place near Port Royal beside the Kentucky River, which borders the fertile land of Henry County in Central Kentucky.[18] The Caudill family found their place in the Eastern Kentucky mountains. Geographically, they were different places. However, they were the same, a home to love and cherish, a treasured land to protect and nourish, and a kind of hallowed place where nature's strength connects with the inner spirit—never to depart.

Soon after becoming friends with the Berrys, Anne sent a letter to Haines and Kay Turner in Bloomington, Indiana. Dr. Turner taught in the Department of Economics at Indiana

---

18. Wendell still farms and plows the fields with his team of horses. He has written 25 books of poetry, 16 volumes of essays, and 11 novels and short story collections. One of his early books describes *A Place on Earth*.

University and had visited the Caudills earlier. An excerpt from Anne's letter of March 7, 1968, reads:

> I have delayed writing to you until I had time to make the enclosed copy for you of some thoughts of Wendell Berry. He recently sent us the copy, and I find I go back to it repeatedly. Wendell Berry, poet, novelist, farmer, teacher, and leader of the anti-war movement at UK and a humorous, easy-laughing husband and father is, in the estimation of my son, a mystic. I believe what he has written will have meaning for you, and I felt strongly moved to share it with you. It is good to know that people like you are concerned with saving America's land, as well as its soul. Perhaps the two are one.

Forty-three years later, Wendell Berry had written about 40 more books, most with the underlying theme that America's land and soul are one. His friend, Anne, remained as passionate as ever about preserving the land, an integral part of America's soul.

CHAPTER 12

Why Don't You Stay with Us?

Although the number of guests and visitors decreased somewhat, requests for meetings and interviews with Harry never ceased.

The guest books include more than 4,000 names of those who visited the Caudill home, including those from the local area. Not all visitors are included, because Anne didn't begin using guest books until a short time after the onslaught began. Not every guest signed the book. Harry met a considerable number of visitors at his office, and southern, mountain hospitality required an invitation to one's home for lunch, dinner, or refreshments. Anne was prepared and welcomed these surprise guests on nearly any day or at any hour.

Anne's guest books serve as her storybooks. In gathering the material and information for *The Caudills of the Cumberlands*, her guest books were invaluable. Very few people precisely remember the characteristics and personalities of each visitor to their home 40 or 45 years previously. In reviewing the list of names, she would often say, "Oh, this reminds me of another story." Anne's recall of names, places and events that occurred over four decades ago was amazing.

For the Caudills, business and pleasure were inseparable. The many after-dinner conversations were not only interesting, enriching, and amusing, but also sustaining and energizing. An invitation to the Caudill home for refreshments, lunch, or dinner often resulted in an invitation to stay the night.

Fourteen years after the publication of Harry's first book, a couple of people arranged a visit. It turned out to be unlike any other the Caudills experienced. Anne recalled:

We enjoyed all of our guests, save only one visit during the heat of the intense Cold War. On a most unusually hot summer day, we were visited by a couple of guests who had called a few hours earlier. They said they were on their way back to New York from a visit to the Grand Ole Opry in Nashville, and wanted to stop by for a brief visit. The caller said he was connected with the Soviet Union Embassy. We gave them directions to our home and rather than driving up the lane to our house, the man and woman parked down near the highway by a small service station and walked up to our house.

To put them at ease, as they were rather reticent, I inquired whether they had enjoyed their trip to Nashville and which singers they had heard there. It was immediately obvious they knew nothing about the country music scene and had not been there. I sensed they must have thought this was a way to approach these "hillbillies." Harry glanced at me with a look that said, he, too, thought they were lying. I tried making conversation with the woman. Her responses, although in competent English, were very hesitant and came only after frightened glances to her companion. The man was more collected, and engaged Harry with questions about his writing and the exploita- tion of the people of Appalachia by the coal companies.

The entire visit was tense. She was very frightened and they left soon.

When they departed, Harry and I were both relieved, and I advised him to call the FBI. He called and learned they were aware of the visit, and had followed the couple from New York and had our house under surveillance. They also requested that if the Russian called again to invite him back and let them know as they hoped to enlist him as a double agent.

The next day we learned from a worker at the service station that he had observed this strange car parking nearby with the people getting out and walking up the hill. Soon after, another strange car drove in and two men got out, raised the hood as if they had a problem and then moved the car to a spot where they could observe our home.

The couple called again a few days later, but nothing ever came of it. Harry thought that perhaps they were trying to recruit him to write articles favorable to the Soviet Union, and reveal the exploitation of the masses in our country. No more from that quarter, thank goodness.

From 1964 through the early '70s, the pace of visitors remained steady. Dinner at the Caudills was the highlight of most visits, and there might be up to ten or more in attendance. On one occasion, Anne served dinner to six staff members from the British Broadcasting Corporation, and another time to five members of the Manhattan Savings Bank. Bob Rubin of CBS, Desmond Smith of ABC, and Richard Rogin of Time-Life were guests. Ben Franklin of the *New York Times* made five visits and three other *Time* journalists visited. Anne served dinner to Gene

Foley and nine of his staff members from the Environmental Protection Agency.

Christmas Eve, Christmas Day, and the day after were special and reserved for the Caudill family gathering. However, if friends were passing through unexpectedly during a holiday, they wouldn't be refused an invitation. Anne and Harry had stayed with Dr. and Mrs. David French—a "delightful" visit—when Harry spoke at Brandeis University in Massachusetts. Dr. French was chair of the sociology department and sometime later brought a group of foreign students to do fieldwork in Appalachia during the Christmas break. French called Harry from Alice Lloyd College in Pippa Passes and asked if he could stop by with 12 of his international students. Anne entertained those young sociology students the day after Christmas with turkey salad, Christmas goodies, and spiced tea.

Many major newspapers and many smaller ones sent reporters, photographers, and editors to cover the scene. In addition to the three major US TV networks, five foreign ones, National Educational Television, National Public Radio, and United Nations Television produced programs. Reporters and government officials from several other countries were guests. Calvin Trillin of the *New Yorker* magazine made two visits. The list filled four guest books.

When *Night* came out, James was 14, Diana 11, and Harry Frye two. As the guests came and went, James received a kind of home schooling at a level, particularly in history, culture, and politics, which quite possibly surpassed any educational endeavor money could buy. He also read numerous books on his own and at Whitesburg High before he enrolled at Harvard. Listening intently for years to the discussions and conversations of David McCullough, Wendell Berry, and the numerous other scholars, officials, and authors was perhaps commensurate to, or surpassing, his instruction at Harvard. Diana learned a great deal, too, other than the fastest way to wash dishes. Little Harry Frye was content with his toys in an isolated quiet corner, if there was one, and probably assumed most families ran a bed and breakfast on the side.

The guests discovered that not only were Anne and Harry gracious, personable, and unusually interesting people, their children were, too. James and Diana began receiving invitations from guests to visit their homes and families. Charles Kuralt invited James to his home in New York for a week, but the schedule never worked out.

When Diana was 15, Jack McCrae, president of the E. F. Dutton Publishing Company, visited Harry to inquire about publishing another book. Dutton had previously published *My Land is Dying*. While waiting for Harry to arrive from the office, Anne and McCrae talked. It was late spring and Anne mentioned she was concerned that her daughter was not scheduled for any worthwhile summer activities. During the two previous summers, Diana had participated in Girl Scout activities and had taken two long canoe trips. On one trip, the scouts canoed down the northern part of the Kentucky River. The river's headwaters begin near and run through Whitesburg, meander north past Lexington through Frankfort, and empty into the Ohio.

The scout troop paddled for a day, camped for the night, and then paddled again the next day to reach the destination. In one particular isolated area, the troop had difficulty finding a suitable place to camp. The riverbanks were overgrown and steep with few level spots. Finally, they found a spot, and designated

Diana to search for the owner of the land and ask permission to camp there. When Diana struggled up the steep banks and through the brush, she saw a farmer in his old work clothes walking down the hill.

"Well, Wendell Berry, what are you doing here?"

"I live here, Diana. What are you doing here?"

The lost scout troop had landed near Port Royal, Kentucky, on Wendell Berry's farm.

During McCrae's weekend visit, he also met and talked with Diana. After he returned home, Mrs. McCrae called Anne to inquire if Diana would be interested in going to their home in New York and helping with the McCrae children during their month-long vacation on Block Island off the coast of Rhode Island.

Diana jumped at the chance and Anne put her on a plane for New York. McCrae planned to meet her at the airport, but was unexpectedly called away on business. Mrs. McCrae called to tell Anne she would meet Diana and not to worry. When Anne returned from the airport in Lexington, she turned on the news. Due to problems in the east, planes landing at JFK were backed up and circling the area, and some planes were diverted to other cities.

Anne had several worried hours before Mrs. McCrae called to say all was well.

Anne sent Diana to New York with a set of C. S. Lewis's Narnia books to read to the children. There's no escaping books and reading in the Caudill household. Diana had a grand time and ran into an old acquaintance during her stay. Before going to Block Island, Diana helped the family prepare for their vacation at their home in the Palisades. One day, she was out in the backyard with the children when a man walked through the hedge dividing the two properties.

"Well, Mr. Calvin Trillin, what are you doing here?"

"I live next door, Diana. What are you doing here?"

The '60s were a turbulent time, but they were also years of goodwill and good works accomplished—to a large extent—by volunteer groups from across the nation. Shortly after publication of *Night* and its widespread publicity, and the attention from president and Robert Kennedy and President Johnson's War on Poverty, volunteer groups flocked to the Cumberlands. The federal government sponsored several projects, as did religious and civic groups and universities. Programs such as the Peace Corp and VISTA caught on with the nation's conscience. Kennedy appealed to the young, and service in the New Frontier provided a means to re-establish America's true spirit. Young people were particularly energetic and adventurous during that time. They wanted to volunteer during summer break, see the world, and have fun doing it. Eager students and others discovered that volunteer service not only included foreign countries, but there was a place in America that also had great need. It was a land apart, and it was an exciting and wild place.

Anne and Harry advised and helped direct the volunteers. People who had an interest in or questions about the conditions in the Cumberlands, talked to Harry first. Consequently, most inquirers and leaders of the volunteer organizations arranged appointments with him.

Some of the volunteer endeavors soon became controversial. It was not that the people didn't want or need help and assistance; the controversy arose when the authority of the local political establishment appeared to be threatened. The last thing the powers at the courthouse would tolerate was a bunch of longhaired hippies interfering in their business and putting crazy ideas in the people's heads. During a mass meeting of those in opposition to the volunteers, one ardent speaker said the young intruders "stunk and were communists." The vast cultural, intellectual, and social differences between the locals and the young college students were undoubtedly a barrier from the beginning. It was not the responsibility of a coal miner or an old farmer to relate to those from the halls of ivy, and it took a while to size up the outsiders. Volunteers guilty of mockery, ridicule, or amusement—"they talk and act funny"—had to pack their bags.

Anne and Harry met with Sargent Shriver in preparation for organizing and distributing more than 150 VISTA volunteers who went to Appalachia. Sargent Shriver, married to Eunice Kennedy, the president's sister, was the driving force behind the Peace Corp and founded the Job Corp, Upward Bound, Head Start, and VISTA. Under President Johnson, Shriver was the architect of the War on Poverty and the director of the Office of Economic Opportunity. He was a dynamic leader and worked diligently to improve the lives of millions of impoverished Americans.

The success and results of the work of the VISTA volunteers is perhaps debatable. Anne believed the VISTA volunteers performed valuable services all over the country, but questioned the training, organization, and purpose of those who came. It appeared that the volunteers didn't really understand what they were to do. Some repaired schools and homes of the elderly and taught remedial studies. These efforts were visible and appreciated. They were all enthusiastic young people, who saw problems and were inspired to work and make a difference.

However, there was no definitive plan or preparation to bring about needed change. The '60s were a time when bright, young students began questioning the establishment. Organized protests, sit-ins, and taking over university administration buildings made the daily news. "Make love, not war" was the mantra. The problem in Appalachia was that the political establishment was not ready to change government to a loving one, and it was certainly not going to allow a bunch of hippies to come in and stir up another war.

"The VISTA volunteers who were living in the coal camps on the little farms here, there and yonder, worked to get the people to meet, organize, and talk about what their problems were," Anne said. "As a result, those community organizations began to question whether the political structure was responding to their needs or just using them. It finally got so disruptive that the local power structure began to put pressure on Washington to get these people out of here. The powers accused the volunteers of being nothing more than outside agitators. The place needed agitating!"

Harry said that it was the only time he ever knew when the government recruited people to go into an area, and agitate against the government. Anne termed it a "curious situation, and eventually those young people were withdrawn, but not before the seeds of rebellion had been planted."

Overall, the VISTA volunteers performed many good deeds for the people. A few of the volunteers remained in the mountains, married, raised families, and became community leaders.

*   *   *

When Anne married Harry and moved to Whitesburg in 1948, medical services were on a par with educational services, concern for miners' welfare, and preservation of the land. All were lacking and healthcare services were so inadequate that when Anne's first two children were born, Harry transported her to Cynthiana two weeks before the expected birth dates to ensure she gave birth in a certified hospital with expert care. However, Harry Frye was born in the new Whitesburg Miners Memorial Hospital, which was a tremendous improvement over the three- or four-room so-called hospitals often located in places such as the second floor of an office building.

Until the mid-20th century in remote, rural areas, most babies were delivered by midwives, by nurses of the Frontier Nursing Service, and in accessible places, by country doctors. Country doctors rode a horse or mule to remote places to deliver babies, treat wounds, set broken bones, extract bullets, and treat snakebite. The country doctors took along their "magic" black bag containing the latest in medical equipment and medicine. A pill from a doctor worked wonders. Dentists were scarce. Before teeth rotted down to the gum line, a strong-armed dad or neighbor, using a couple of large shots of potent moonshine as a substitute for Novocain, yanked the tooth stub out with a pair of pliers.

Fortunately, the smaller towns had a few excellent doctors, such as Whitesburg's legendary characters, Doc Collier and Doc Wright, who practiced at nearby Seco. Doc Collier was the man who had given Harry a ride to Whitesburg after basic training. Doc was always in a hurry. On one occasion, bouncing over the rocky roads to "catch a baby," he ran over a turkey. When he was delivering the baby, the phone rang. "Doc, I saw you kill that turkey, but it's plucked and cooked up fine for you, so stop and pick it up on your way back to town."

Another time, Doc hurried way up a hollow to catch another baby. He examined the expectant mother lying in her bed. Doc had so much experience, he knew the hour when he would spank the baby's butt.

"Ma'am, it's going to be a few hours," he said, "so if you'll just scoot over, I'll take a little nap."

Another doctor story goes back to when the public health office began distributing contraceptives to the people. Dr. Francis Hutchins, president of Berea College, and his wife, Dr. Louise Hutchins, who worked in maternal healthcare in the area, were friends of the Caudills. Dr. Louise told Anne that she was guilty of bootlegging contraceptives for her patients when the state prohibited distribution and even counsel about the use of contraceptives.

When Harry was in the legislature, he helped pass legislation making it legal for health departments to distribute contraceptives. Shortly after the law was enacted, Harry saw Doc Collins, the longtime public health doctor, another character with a booming voice and rather brash demeanor. When Harry informed him that the state now permitted distribution of contraceptives, Doc said, "That's good. I'll order some."

A few days later, when Harry was parking his car next to the public health office, a country woman walked out. The office door flew open, and Doc Collins shouted for all on the street to hear, "Honey, come back. I've got some pills for you so you won't get pregnant again."

His patient replied, "I'll be glad to get them, 'cause I've been pregnant for 13 years."

* * *

When Harry Frye was born on May 28, 1961, at the new Miners Memorial Hospital in Whitesburg, his older brother was 12 and his sister nine. During that summer, Anne was in the midst of typing a book Harry was putting together. She spent a major part of the summer at her Royal typewriter out on the big screened-in porch with little Harry in a basket beside her.

If James was the serious and studious one and Diana a perfect little girl, Harry Frye was into everything, when he wasn't literally clinging to his mother's apron strings.

His father nicknamed him "Harrymanzo." Anne said of her youngest, "He investigated everything, climbed everything, leaving a trail of spilled drawers, books, and papers pulled from the shelves and toys strewn everywhere. Never cross or demanding, he was simply on the move."

As Harry Frye grew older, he explored the neighborhood and the surrounding mountains and learned which neighbors would give him cookies. He loved his pony, Judy. One day, a stallion had intimate relations with her while some of the neighbor children watched. Later that day, Harry Frye, about eight, told his mother, "It won't be long until Judy is pregnant," and then the inevitable question, "What is pregnant?"

In school, Harry Frye's studies suffered somewhat in the subjects in which he had little interest. His parents later decided to enroll him in a prep school in Ashville, North Carolina, where he did very well and upon graduation returned to live with his parents when Harry was teaching at UK.

* * *

In *Slender is the Thread: Tales from a County Law Office,* Harry wrote a healthcare story about his fellow lawyer and friend, Steve Combs, who eventually became county judge. It was late on a Saturday night, and Whitesburg businesses and offices were closing. Dr. P. Y. Pursiful ran the town's first hospital, which comprised a waiting room, a few chairs, three or four patient rooms, and an operating room with a skylight and ropes hanging down to hold the lanterns. A small table nearby held an assortment of knives, instruments, and bottles of various liquids.

One day a man doubled up in agony was carried in. Doc Pursiful looked at the man and decided he had appendicitis. He had to operate immediately, but his nurse was gone for the day. He thought of Steve Combs nearby and asked him to come quick. When Combs entered the operating room, Doc informed him he had to administer ether to the man. Combs, hesitant and leery, reminded Doc that he was a lawyer and knew nothing about medicine. Doc explained it didn't matter, because if young Combs didn't assist him and the man died, it would be the lawyer's fault.

The doctor thoroughly scrubbed his hands, and Combs thought he had better do the same.

"Now pour this ether on this rag and hold it up to the patient's nose until he passes out. If he starts coming to while I'm operating, give him another shot."

Reluctantly, Combs followed the directions, the man passed out, and Doc slit open his patient's abdomen. The problem was that the appendix wasn't where it was supposed to be. Doc made another slit and began laying the patient's intestines out on his stomach, legs, and private parts. Combs watched closely with the ether rag in his hand, but the blood, entrails, and everything made his knees buckle and his head swim.

Finally, Doc said, "There it is." Doc snipped the appendix off and threw it in a slop bucket located in a corner of the operating room. The man lived and Steve Combs did, too.

Medical services improved in Appalachia from those early days, but it was a continuing struggle. Anne and Harry worked relentlessly for change and improvement in the healthcare of their people. The work was tedious and frustrating and progress slow, but the Caudills were warriors, and Anne was relentless in her devotion and efforts to make a difference.

The coal companies established the early hospitals. A mangled or unhealthy coal miner can't mine coal. The South East Coal Company located at the appropriately named coal town, Seco, hired the Caudill family doctor, Dr. B. F. Wright, to operate their hospital.

When young James got a splinter in his foot that caused an infection, Anne took him to Seco to see Dr. Wright. Doc took James's foot in his hands, turned away so James could not witness the procedure, and lanced the foot. Blood and pus squirted everywhere. Doc then turned to his attending nurse and said, "What do you mean by hurting that child? Don't ever do that again." The skilled doctor and flamboyant politician also understood child psychology regarding children's fear of men in white coats. The nurse caused the pain, not the doctor.

"I have other memories of the rather primitive and offhand procedures there, but it was a far cry above no hospital service at all," Anne said. "Many a man badly injured in the mines, and their families as well, owed their lives to Doc Wright's skill."

The coal business either boomed or suffered periods of extreme economic depression, greatly affecting the lives of the people. When times were good, healthcare and other services improved. When times were depressed, healthcare was one of the first services to decline.

Bethlehem Mines, a subsidiary of Bethlehem Steel, built the town of Jenkins, which is the largest town in Letcher County. The company also built a well-equipped and modern hospital there, but when the coal economy tanked, company-owned hospitals diminished services or closed.

During boom times, and after the United Mine Workers were organized, UMW built a chain of ten hospitals known as the Miners Memorial Hospitals, Inc. around the area. They imported nurses, technicians, and doctors, and the hospitals boomed until a recession caused much less demand for coal. When mechanized strip mining and mountaintop removal became the prime means of mining coal at considerably higher profits, there was much less need for miners to extract it underground the traditional way. With considerable loss of membership and financial support, the UMW announced they would close the hospitals unless the communities devised a means of supporting them. Anne remembers "Blue Monday" as a time when the future of the hospitals looked bleak, if not hopeless.

The Presbyterian Church (U.S.A.) learned of the dire need and began to explore ways to keep the hospitals open. They pressured the governor for financial help. He called the legislature into a special session, and sufficient funds were appropriated to keep the doors open. Initially, the Presbyterians requested two local people serve on its board from each county in the region. Harry was their first choice in Letcher County, but he was "too controversial," so they appointed the less controversial Anne. "God works in wondrous ways," she said.

On July 19, 1963, Anne received a telegram from New York:

"We take great pleasure in informing you of your election to the board of trustees of the Appalachian Regional Hospitals, Inc. Letter will follow public announcement tonight."

R. C. Day, the local postmaster, served as the other board member.

Anne went to work organizing a local hospital advisory committee, and worked diligently and tirelessly, serving on the board for several years. Staffing and finance were continuing problems. Doctors, many from other countries, and nurses were recruited, and many served a year or two, and then moved on to greener pastures.

Where there is a will, there is a way, and Anne possessed both with a passion and work ethic fortified with boundless energy and determination. She believed that when a lack of finances was critical, it was best to seek help where the money was. She wrote letters to people in positions to assist with the area's healthcare needs. Byron Jay, president of the Great Atlantic and Pacific Tea Company in New York, received the following letter from Anne.

Harry and I recall your visit with us in Whitesburg. We have many times remarked upon the concrete expression of your concern for Appalachia and its people which we see each time we pass the fine A&P store in Neon, Kentucky. We are encouraged to find such a sense of responsibility to a blighted area of America on the part of our great business concerns.

I am a member of the Board of Trustees of the Appalachian Regional Hospitals, a chain of ten hospitals originally built by the United Mine Workers and later bought for the communities with federal funds. These hospitals are absolutely vital to the area, but the problems of their continued operation are many.

I have mentioned your interest in our area to the Board of Trustees and I am taking this opportunity to tell you that Mr. Robert Harris and Dr. Kenneth Neigh of the Presbyterian Board of Missions, and Mr. Robert Reiser representing the board of ARHI, would like to call upon you and discuss the hospitals and their problems. Your willingness to talk with these gentlemen will be genuinely appreciated.

A few days after the letter to Jay, Anne wrote to Dr. Karl Klicka, head of the Appalachia Regional Hospitals in Lexington.

I enclose a copy of my letter to Mr. Barrie calling the attention of Mr. Reiser and those in New York, who are working on fund raising. I have previously mentioned Mr. Barrie and Mr. Byron Jay, president of A&P, and Mr. Phillip Stern, author of *The Great Treasury Raid: Tax Loopholes Open to the Very Rich*. Mr. Stern is a former undersecretary of the state and administrative assistant for more than one senator and has a hand in the administration of the Stern family foundation. In my letter today, I mentioned Mr. Stanley Foster Reed.

Each of these men have made special trips into Appalachia and expressed their concern and interest to us. Each is a possibility in the matter of fund raising.

In a letter to Helen Brown of the Frontier Nursing Service in Wendover, Kentucky, Anne wrote, "The afternoon Mrs.

Westover and I spent with you will always be remembered as a very special occasion on a very perfect day. I have thought a good deal more about your hope of building a new hospital and undertaking the training of rural visiting nurses, and I am more and more convinced that this is the most important basic for health services in our mountain counties."

During the struggle to maintain the hospitals, the Mennonites came to the rescue. They are a group of Christian Anabaptists named after Frisian Menno Simons, who in the 16th century formalized the teaching of earlier Swiss founders. The Amish broke away from the original Mennonites and are considered an "old-order" group, but the two religious organizations have similar beliefs and practices. They believe and practice in both the ministry and mission of Jesus Christ.

The Mennonites ministered in many parts of the world, but had recently concentrated their efforts in South America. They were looking for places to serve in the United States. Shortly after the publication of *Night*, the Mennonite Central Committee in Akron, Ohio, contacted Harry, and later met Anne and Harry at his office. After reading about the dismal state of education in the area, the representatives were particularly interested in helping in that area and suggested sending teachers. Harry explained that good teachers were desperately needed, but teaching positions were political plums for the families that were helpful to those in power. A teaching position could be worth two dozen votes or more, which was certainly deemed more important than qualifications and a degree.

Anne said, "We need hospital administrators, doctors, and nurses."

By way of twists, turns, and dogged persistence, Anne and

the Whitesburg Hospital secured an administrator and staff when the Mennonites agreed to volunteer their services.

During the usual two-year work in the field, the Mennonites were paid a subsistent wage by the central committee. They lived frugally, dressed modestly, and shared housing and transportation. They were educated for both a profession and a skill. A trained doctor might know how to build homes; a teacher might be skilled in auto mechanics.

"They did not proselytize, they were not there as missionaries. They were there to do their work, and all were educated, trained people who had something to offer," Anne said.

As a result of the first meeting with Anne and Harry, the Mennonites served the people of Letcher and other counties for more than 20 years. In addition to their invaluable work in hospitals, they also refurbished homes for the elderly, taught illiterates and prisoners in jails, worked with 4-H clubs and agricultural extension offices, and did many other "wonderful, wonderful" things. Eventually, some were employed as teachers and sent to what Anne called "Siberia." These were the one-room schools up remote hollows in no-man's land, where no one else would go. Many who came served as doctors, nurses, and in health-related fields. They came from many places, including Canada. Those who served spent up to two years in the field before returning to their home base and professions. A few remained in Appalachia and served for several more years.

An old decrepit house stood adjacent to the Caudill property. Anne and Harry decided to purchase it because the property was becoming a junkyard. They repaired the house and rented it at a nominal fee to the Mennonite Central Committee. Up to five occupants and often entire families lived there during those 20 years. The Mennonites became some of the Caudills' dearest friends and neighbors. "We had the greatest respect for them," Anne said.

Guyla Burhans, a widow who had raised five children, came from California to visit her daughter who was serving as a Mennonite volunteer. During her visit, Guyla saw the needs and decided she could help. Although she was a devoted Methodist, the Mennonites accepted others in their program. She was an experienced and innovative teacher, and took a position in one of the "Siberian" schools, but later moved to a larger one. Guyla lived just across the pasture from the Caudills. After years teaching in schools and working with GED students in Letcher and Perry Counties, she decided, at age 80, to go back to California to be with her family.

Anne said of her dear friend Guyla, "I've heard many people claim to be Christian, but of all the people I've ever known, she came as close as anyone I know who practiced true Christianity."

Healthcare services in the region gradually improved and are currently on a par with most other smaller communities across the nation. With the high rate of poverty in Appalachia, Medicare and Medicaid were a godsend (or government send), insuring that a sizeable segment of the population received adequate healthcare.

Along with the Presbyterians and Mennonites, other groups and individuals came to offer their services. A group of architectural students from Yale University went to the Cumberlands to explore the possibilities of producing low-cost housing for the people. There was little flat land available except along the creek banks, and it was used for gardens and crops. The shoddy homes were built on slopes and sides of hills or wherever a small space could be found. Homes built along the creek banks were frequently flooded.

Bill Richardson and his group of fellow architectural students designed and built a unique low-cost home using primarily telephone and electrical poles. The home was built on the side of a hill. It served as an example of providing an efficient and sturdy low-cost home that helped serve the housing needs for many of the area's poor.

Richardson was so intrigued by his brief stay in Whitesburg that he returned after finishing his degree. Due to the depressed conditions in the area at the time, construction of new buildings was limited and architects had little to do, but Richardson stayed on. He had some other ideas and had experience in photography, filmmaking, and documentation. There were vast differences between the Appalachian culture and that of Yale and most other parts of the United States, and he saw the need to preserve that distinct and unique culture.

Richardson initially went into the high schools and recruited students to go out in the community and record and film stories of the people, particularly the older folks. From that beginning, Appalshop evolved.

Founded in 1969 as a project for the War on Poverty, Appalshop has grown into an internationally known cultural center. It was established as the primary hub of filmmaking in and about Appalachia. Appalshop has produced more than 100 films covering such subjects as coal mining, the environment, traditional culture, and the economy. The organization also produces theatrical productions, music, spoken-word recordings, photography, multimedia, and books, and operates WMMT-FM (Mountain Community Radio), which serves much of Appalachia.[19]

When Richardson returned to Whitesburg permanently, his wife started a craft shop selling locally produced arts and crafts. He continued his work as one of the few architects in the entire area, and he designed and built many excellent buildings.

Richardson wasn't the only volunteer who went to the Cumberlands, stayed, and made lasting contributions. Some of the volunteers came as individuals. Jean Martin, a graduate from Indiana University, became an Appalachian volunteer. When these volunteers came to assist, places to live were limited. Jean Martin called on Anne and asked about a place to stay. Anne replied, "Why don't you just come and stay with us?"

The Caudill home was hers, too, for several months. It was a home, not a house, and a place to stay, one night or much longer. It was a warm and inviting place, a brief, but unforgettable home for many guests, including notables and people the Caudills had never seen before.

"Why don't you just come and visit us, and stay a while," Anne would say. "I'll throw some food together, and we'll tell stories and have a wonderful time."

---

19. When Anne moved from Whitesburg in 1991, she donated her collection of films and documentaries about Appalachia to Appalshop.

CHAPTER 13

Where Did the Time Go?

Anne recalled that fourteen years after publication of the book, "It was the same hectic life of visitors, phone calls from everywhere, writing, entertaining, plus a busy law practice and family, gardening and preservation of the garden produce by canning and freezing and filling a 22-cubic-foot freezer each summer. More calls for Harry to lecture in several states, Washington, and the far west coalfields."

Add her ever-increasing correspondence, and the busy days and nights blended into years with little time to stop and catch a breath. Anne's letters addressed everything from lost books and water conservation to the distribution of Christmas presents to the area's poor children. After the book came out, people from various places wrote to Anne wanting to contribute to a needy family or families. She selected the families and identified the particular needs.

Anne wrote to a woman in Maplewood, New Jersey:

I am answering you concerning Isaiah Turner and his family. The checks for each of the doctors were immediately relayed to them, and I appreciate your generosity just as much as Isaiah and his family do . . . then we had to make arrangements to have his eyes examined and get the prescription. I enclose a chart of clothing sizes . . . you might send children's books, paper, pencils, crayons, vitamin tablets, dishes, and cooking equipment . . . I doubt that adult books would find readers in this family. I might also suggest toys like a ball, a doll, and simple jigsaw puzzles.

In a letter to another woman in Dedham, Massachusetts, she wrote:

> Your letter has gone long unanswered, but I have not had the opportunity to visit the Lawrence Hall family until just yesterday. Martha and all are much pleased with the kitchenware, basketball, toys, and coffee pot, etc. which you sent.
>
> Cookie had the cast removed from her arm. Though I did not say it to them, it looks to me as though it has been set crooked. However, she is beginning to use and exercise it, and perhaps it will be all right.
>
> Martha is keeping the money carefully aside that you sent for the wallboard and will use if for that purpose when the time for using coal fires has ended and the smoke involved will no longer soil her newly done walls. This will be a real experience for them. Those walls have never been covered with anything other than old newspapers.

In a letter to Billie Davis, a photographer at the Louisville *Courier-Journal*, Anne requested some photographs:

> This spring I will be talking to various groups, including garden clubs, and for the purpose, I need some

color slides of Eastern Kentucky strip-mined areas. I recall your collection of horrifying shots from which *The Ravaged Land* pictures were selected, and want to borrow or obtain copies of a few.

I want to show pictures of the beauties and possibilities for recreational use of the eastern mountains, and to try to arouse these women to an active interest in what is happening to their state. If you can spare a few shots, I will greatly appreciate your assistance.

Also, if you might have a shot or two of rhododendron, dogwood or redbud, and spring flowers in the mountains, these would be helpful.

As if Anne didn't have enough to do, she received numerous requests to do more. She received another book to read— Tocqueville's *Democracy in America*, but the friend who sent it suggested that she "read Tocqueville's *In America* first as it gives much of the background for the later work." She received a letter asking that she track down two copies of *Night Comes to the Cumberlands* that were lost in the mail. She received a request from the Kentucky League of Women Voters to speak in Chicago on clean water in America.

Anne wrote to Mayor Carl Stokes of Cleveland, Ohio, and received this response: "I wish to convey to you my most humble and grateful appreciation for your kind words of support and encouragement during these troubled times. I cannot adequately express to you how letters like yours have helped buoy our spirits and renew our energies on these long, difficult days as we strive to bring reason and direction to Cleveland's move toward becoming a model city."

Anne wrote thousands of letters—hundreds of her personal letters and ten full boxes of her correspondence are now in the archives at UK.

*   *   *

In June 1968, tragedy struck the community. A film company from Canada, directed by award-winning Hugh O'Connor, wanted to do a story and contacted Harry about his ideas and places to film. The crew made two visits to the area, and, as usual, Anne served dinner to the crew of five when they arrived. After the second visit and several days of filming, they completed their work and were headed back to Lexington, on the way to their homes in New York, Los Angeles, and Toronto. Not far from Whitesburg, they passed by an ideal photo scene at Jeremiah near Blackey and stopped for one last photo shoot.

A row of dilapidated houses owned by Hobart Ison lined the road. A coal miner, covered with black dust, was sitting on the front porch of one of the houses, resting with his little girl in his lap. The miner granted the crew permission to film them and signed a release. When the filming began, a neighbor woman jumped in her car and tore down the road. She found Ison and alerted him to what was going on. He hurried to the houses he owned, arriving just as the crew was loading the gear. Ison pulled out his pistol, fired some shots into the air, and then shot and killed Hugh O'Connor as he stood in the middle of the road.

To say that feelings ran high in the surrounding areas would be a gross understatement. A segment of the people felt that four years of intruders, hippies, and "communists" were enough. The attitude of many people was, "Who do these young people think they are coming in here telling us how to live?"

"Some thought it cold-blooded murder, others that it was fully justified," Anne said. "There were those who never forgave Harry for prosecuting Ison, especially his relatives and those who lived in his neighborhood. It was one more issue on which Harry's position was controversial. As to repercussions, I'm sure there were those who took their legal counsel elsewhere, but we didn't notice it. There were members of the DAR—which I helped found in Whitesburg—who were ever cool to me, but I ignored it."

Harry was controversial and had both loyal supporters and bitter enemies. He had fought to pass controversial issues in the legislature. He fought for his people in opposition to the mine owners and money interests. He fought to levy a severance tax on coal, pass a tax for libraries and education, and was forever trying to save the land. How could other factions fight against these worthy issues? They did and took measures to attempt to put "radical" Harry Caudill back in his place. He was threatened more than once and told that his phones might be tapped, but nothing ever stopped him from speaking out for what he believed was right. He labored for fairness and justice, understanding that justice is, as his book *Slender is a Thread* claimed, as slender as a thread. He believed in doing what was right, and had the courage to speak out and write about that which he believed was wrong and unjust.

"Controversy didn't affect him one bit. He was a man of enormous courage," Anne said. "Of course, he had the great courage to combat his very serious war wound and poor health, which was an ongoing struggle."

Threats to Harry did affect Anne, but his strength and courage strengthened her. Her undying faith in and support of him sustained his crusade for fairness, justice, and the diligent pursuit of that which was right. Anne said of the threats, "We simply ignored them."

*   *   *

After having difficulty in securing jurors and then having three hung juries, the Ison trial was moved from Letcher to Harlan County. Most members of the film crew returned to testify at the trial. The judge resolved the issue by arranging a plea bargain. Ison pleaded guilty to manslaughter and received a ten-year prison sentence. After serving a little over one year, Ison was paroled and returned to Jeremiah a free man.

After Ison's sentencing, the Letcher County Sheriff's Department gave the pistol used in the shooting to Begie "Moose" Breeding, Jr., one of Ison's relatives. It was kept in a lockbox until Breeding retrieved it during Appalshop's filming of *Stranger with a Camera,* which is an intriguing account of the murder of Hugh O'Connor.

Ironically, that same pistol was later used to kill another man on Ison's property. Kathy Walters-Williams worked as a housekeeper for Breeding. She shot and killed Forest Caudill, a distant relative of Harry's, six years later. Police found the gun hidden under a rock on top of Blair Branch Mountain about five miles from the site of the murder. The 1904 Smith and Wesson pistol had been soaked in motor oil to prevent fingerprint identification.

A few years later, one of the film crewmembers, described by Anne as "a very charming man," returned for a visit. He explained to Anne that the place had always haunted him. His name was Richard Black; he was the son of Shirley Temple Black. Richard

Black and Anne were both interviewed and appear in *Stranger with a Camera.*

There were aspects of *Night* that were controversial. The mining conglomerates were not pleased, to say the least, to be portrayed as motivated by greed. Generally, miners who had jobs supported the owners for keeping them alive, although many other miners realized the extent to which they were exploited for profits by the owners. Most politicians waited to see which way the wind would blow. However, the public woke up and realized the need for change.

One point addressed in Harry's book was the effects of out-migration, particularly during depressed times. Thousands upon thousands moved primarily north seeking not only means of survival, but greater opportunity and a better life. Harry wrote that those who didn't move from Appalachia were increasingly ill, less energetic, less ambitious, or responsible for older family members. Time after time, the ambitious and energetic young left because of limited jobs and few opportunities.

He also wrote that perhaps the long isolation and close intermarriage over several generations had produced undesirable weaknesses in some of the population. He was concerned that those who remained might become more compliant and less ambitious. His theory drew the ire of many critics, but it attracted the attention of Nobel Prize-winning physicist William Shockley.

Shockley called Harry asking to meet and discuss the effect of out-migration. Shockley and two other scientists had co-invented the transistor that led to the technology explosion at California's Silicon Valley. His later work became extremely controversial as he devoted his attention and efforts to questions of race, intelligence, and eugenics. He argued that the higher rate of reproduction among the less intelligent was having a dysgenic effect, and that a drop in average intelligence would ultimately lead to a decline in civilization. One solution was to develop a sperm bank where the most intelligent could contribute, thus promoting humankind's best genes to preserve and advance a more intelligent population. Shockley was one of the first to contribute to the "smart bank," a kind of approach to creating a super race. He was referred to in some circles as a "Hitlerite."

Anne remembers Shockley and his group of seven and their visit after touring the county that morning. It was on one of the hottest days on record. There was no air conditioning in the house, and the group went out under the shade trees in the yard. It was very hot—the topic and the weather. Anne happened to notice the extreme weather's effect on her garden. "I was horrified that my tomatoes had completely wilted in the heat."

Anne said that the long conversation with Shockley and his group was "frank, open, and very interesting." Although there was some further communication and correspondence, Harry became dubious, and nothing came of it. Finally, the rains came and the tomatoes thrived again.

One can thrive on bountiful and nervous energy and adrenaline for an indefinite time, but eventually the energy supply runs low, and the body and mind wind down to a crawl. In the summer of 1968, Anne suffered a gallbladder attack. The attack was not severe, but tests revealed she had also suffered a mild heart attack and had some minor damage. She went home to recuperate and spent a couple of months lying on the couch. She had no energy or ambition, and the recovery was slow.

Twenty-three years earlier, Anne and Harry had paused by

a cannon at UK, and Anne heard a boom when Harry promised to take her abroad if she would marry him. She had agreed. It took 23 years for Harry to keep his promise, but she thought that getting away might help speed up recuperation. They decided to take a trip to Ireland, Scotland, and England with no rushing and plenty of resting. Anne returned home rejuvenated and ready to get on with her life.

Three years later, Anne underwent a hysterectomy. The month-long and painful recovery required extensive rest. Two days after returning home, while Anne was still bedfast, sheriff deputies raided the Caudill home searching for alcoholic beverages, and found some that were kept for guests.

A neighbor, who just happened to be a strip miner, swore out a warrant accusing Harry of providing alcohol to underage boys, including his son and nephew. At the urging of the older boys, Harry Frye, age nine, provided them with a bottle of apricot brandy from the Caudill home. The strip miner notified the Hazard and Lexington newspapers to be on hand for the trial "about the scandal of Harry Caudill." The purpose of the charge was to prove that Harry Caudill provided alcohol to minors, and get him to back off from attacks against strip mining. Harry wasn't against strip mining as such. He fought against the destruction and devastation of the mountains, and the political powers' failure to require the strip mining companies to restore the land. However, the scandalous scheme went nowhere when the judge dismissed the case.

* * *

Due to his thriving law practice and many other demands, Harry decided to hire a law partner to ease the load. In 1974,

Forrest Cook, a bright young native of Letcher County and recent graduate of the UK law school, became Harry's law partner. His young wife, Barbara, assisted in the office and became a close friend of Anne's. When the Cook's second daughter was born, they named her Anne.

During that time, business boomed and the result of having a partner to help carry the load only increased their law practice. Business practically tripled and Harry became busier than ever. With the increased workload and the deteriorating condition of his legs and other health issues, Harry announced suddenly, "I quit." Forest Cook continued the successful law practice.

With the law office on sound footing, Harry retired on December 31, 1976. Anne said that he intended to "go home and stare vacantly out the window." When he wasn't staring, he had more writing to do. In fact, from 1963 when *Night* was published, until he retired at the end of 1976, Harry published five other books, all of which Anne typed while still gardening, cooking, traveling, speaking, corresponding, entertaining, mothering, and volunteering. Taking dictation, as she had for the earlier books, lessened because Harry wrote his later ones in longhand on legal-size tablets.

My Land is Dying, published in 1971, is about how surface mining brought about destruction of the land in Appalachia. The fervor with which Harry wrote about the destruction is described in Robert Cole's introduction to the book:

> Mr. Caudill has persisted; he has again and again reminded this nation how much remains to be done: up there in those hollows are families near penniless, and for that to be the case in the world's richest, mightiest nation is a

scandal. But beyond the tragedies Appalachia's people must live with every day—hunger and malnutrition and high infant mortality rate and widespread joblessness—there is yet another tragedy still being enacted there. Thousands and thousands of acres of land have been, are right now being, or are soon scheduled to be cut into—stripped is the all-too-emphatic and suggestive and appropriate word—so that coal can be obtained and shipped to America's ever needy industrial empire. Never mind that beautiful trees are felled. Never mind that flowers and shrubs and meadows are covered over. Never mind that clear streams and creeks and rivers become slow-moving monsters: acid kills fish; poisonous mud is deposited all over and kills grass, not to mention the wildlife that ordinarily sticks close to water. Never mind that farms are destroyed, and homes, and roads, and indeed entire hills, entire settlements of people. Coal is needed by factories and power companies and the TVA, so coal will be obtained—quickly and efficiently and directly. As for those who worry about land being destroyed, water polluted, wildlife killed—they are willful troublemakers, or cranky social critics, or at best, they are romantics, hopelessly unable to appreciate the contemporary needs of an "advanced" nation like ours.

There can be no doubt that Mr. Caudill is a trouble-maker; he objects to the exploitation of man and his environment by companies that behave as if they are a law unto themselves. Caudill is also a social critic and he is indeed cranky, because he cannot stomach what he sees happening every day: the poor being made yet poorer, the rich getting more and more, all under the protection of federal laws and state laws and, ultimately, the guns that sheriffs and their deputies use in those Appalachian hills. And he is a "romantic," too; yes, if a "romantic" is one who has an old-fashioned sense of justice and fair play, and if he is one who treasures the Declaration of Independence and the Constitution and believes they ought to be honored not with lip service but in deed, then beyond any question Harry Caudill is a "romantic."

In this book, Mr. Caudill expands his already large vision; he concentrates his keen mind on the problem of strip mining as a national issue. He warns us that Appalachia's misery is soon going to be appreciated by the rest of us—not because we will have gone there and tried to experience firsthand what the region's people have to contend with day after day, but rather because in the Southwest and in our central states and along our eastern seaboard there are those who want things like coal or oil, and go take them—regardless of the costs to people and their natural surroundings. Meanwhile the rest of us seem destined to stand by in silent dismay or helpless rage. So it goes we say—and hope for the best and often enough expect the worst.

For Harry Caudill there is an alternative, though. As a writer, he wants to bring an outrageous and continuing crime to the public's attention. But as an experienced lawyer and social activist, he wants us all to do something: bring our energies together, make known our sentiments—in order to counter the maneuvers of all those corporate officials and corporation lawyers and subservient bureaucrats, not to mention the all-too-compliant judges and sheriffs who do what they're told to do, namely the bidding of "the big boys, the rich boys," as one mountaineer I know has a way of putting it. (If only some of our sociologists and political scientists spoke half as bluntly.)

I have no way of knowing whether Harry Caudill's struggle is of any avail; I am sure he himself must live with nightmares, must all the time find himself ready to wake up one morning and find the whole of Appalachia leveled—become a sort of vast wasteland of bubbling acid and sludge and dead trees and the litter of homes abandoned and often enough interred in mud. Nevertheless, he keeps on struggling. He writes, he fights in the courts, he speaks to people, he does all he can and more than most of us. A more enlightened nation would honor him as one of its finest citizens; but then, a more enlightened nation would not be so in need of his kind of extraordinary public service.

One sentence in the book says it all: "We live, in short, in a society where a telephone call from the president of a steel corporation carries more influence with those in office than a petition signed by tens of thousands of ordinary one-vote citizens."

Experience taught Harry that lesson. During LBJ's War on Poverty, the Economic Development Administration under Gene Foley's leadership proposed making one Appalachian county a model for economic development. Letcher County was selected to be the model, since it was located near the center of the poverty-stricken area. Roads, water, sewage, and sanitation systems would be improved or developed. Funds for education and healthcare were included, and industrial sites developed to entice new industries. The proposal included planning for effective land use and a few model homes.

Harry and Foley met with the Letcher County judge, who was receptive. Foley told the judge to think about it, and he and Harry would get back with him. Later, Foley called Harry and said, "I met with the judge, and he's against it now, because Bethlehem Steel is against it."

During that same year, a tornado ripped through Central Kentucky, destroying Anne's second childhood home, the Ammerman farmstead near Cynthiana. In addition, Harry's dearly beloved mother fell and broke her hip, and lived with the Caudills for the next four years until her death in 1976. These misfortunes added to their daily demands. To get away for a day or so from the rigorous work, the constant flow of visitors, and the endless requests, Anne and Harry took to the woods, their favorite means of relaxation. Hiking among the trees, woods, and forests revitalized their spirits and provided therapy for their souls. On Sunday afternoons, a solitary stroll out the back door and up the mountain, or across the valley to Pine Mountain, were brief but revitalizing getaways.

They had other favorite hiking places in the area. Lilley Cornett Woods, a virgin forest, was a favorite place to spend a day. Ray Harm, the renowned American wildlife artist famous for paintings of birds, came for a visit to confer with Harry. He was also very interested in land preservation and ecology. Sometime later, he returned to hike the Lilley Woods with the Caudills.

When she hiked up steep mountain slopes, Anne used a walking staff with a curved hook at one end. She would hook a small sapling to help pull her up. Ray Harm told her to forget the hook, grab his belt in the back, and he would pull her up. It worked very well.

There she and Harry were, in a virgin forest with an artist who knew bird life intimately. When they paused in the quiet, Harm might point and say, "That's a warbler," or name another species of bird.

"Where? I don't hear or see it."

"It is way up in that tallest tree."

Anne said, "It was a wonderful experience being with him."

Perhaps their favorite place to spend a day or weekend was the Red River Gorge in Menifee County, about 100 miles northwest of Whitesburg. One of Kentucky's natural treasures, the gorge is a 25,000-acre preserve with sandstone cliffs, wondrous rock formations, and magnificent wilderness. Anne described the gorge as "a fairyland of marvelous trees, wildflowers and rock bridges formed by erosion of the sandstone, and cliff houses and beautiful clear streams with great rocky boulders—it's just an enchanting place, a magical place."

Magical or not, the Army Corp of Engineers had another idea, realistic and pragmatic. Perhaps considering it a wasteland, they proposed building a dam at the gorge to provide a water source for Lexington. The Caudills and many other people were horrified. Harry wrote articles and letters to editors and invited the Bingham family to the gorge for a day's hike. The *Courier-Journal* immediately came out against the project, as did other newspapers. When Harry attended UK law school, Elvis Stahr was the dean. Stahr went on to become the chancellor of Indiana University and later served as the secretary of the army. He ended his career as the president of the Audubon Society. Harry contacted Stahr about the dire matter. Whatever his influence may have been, the Army Corp of Engineers changed its stand, a decision that allowed the Caudills to meet with friends at the gorge for weekend hikes and therapy at its best.

They met Wendell Berry and his family for a day's hike at the gorge. It was a favorite place of Berry's, too. He wrote an essay about camping in and exploring the gorge. "An Entrance to the Woods" tells about his solitary journey through the gorge, and how wandering in the woods changes one's perspective toward a more hopeful life.

On another occasion, Dr. Harvey Sloane, later the mayor of Louisville, called Anne and asked if she and Harry could go to the Red River Gorge and guide him and his wife, and John Davidson "Jay" Rockefeller and his wife through the scenic site. Jay was the great-grandson of John D. Rockefeller, the oil baron. Earlier, he had volunteered as a VISTA worker in West Virginia, and liked the state and its people so well that he returned and made it his home.[20]

Anne packed a lunch, and she, Harry, and little Harry Frye met them for a day's hike. A vigorous hike brings on an appetite, so she served lunch in a beautiful isolated spot known as Tight Hollow. She had packed peanut butter for young Harry, sandwiches, fruit and a big home-baked banana cake. Anne remembers that Jay's wife shared the jar of peanut butter with their son. After everyone had had a piece of the banana cake, one-half remained. It didn't last too long, though, because soon Jay devoured it all, making it another wonderful day in the woods with friends.

---

20. Rockefeller became interested in preserving the land and eventually served as governor of West Virginia and has been in the US Senate since 1984.

* * *

Christmas was always special at the Caudills. Friends and family gathered every Christmas Eve. After a scrumptious meal, the group formed a circle and sang carols, accompanied by Anne on the piano. On Christmas Day, the family exchanged gifts and enjoyed a bountiful Christmas dinner with turkey and all the trimmings.

Anne distinctly remembers three events associated with Christmas celebrations. On one Christmas morning, James threatened to leave home. When he was about six, Santa brought him a pioneer fort, which required assembling. After painstaking work, the fort was finished. Diana, who was learning to ride her new tricycle, came along and knocked it down. Grandfather Frye, known as Granddaddy Pipe, was in the room. James looked up at his grandfather and announced, "If any more baby girls come to this house, I'm taking two bags of clothes and one bag of food and leaving here."

On two other occasions, dogs became involved in the Christmas celebrations. A day or two before another Christmas, Harry hired handyman Lloyd to repair something at his office. Lloyd was skilled when he was sober, and always had his little dog with him. With the work complete, Lloyd locked the office door for the holidays and drove to the Caudill home for his pay. A couple of days later, Lloyd went to the Caudill home again, and informed Harry that he had lost his dog, and might have left him in the law office. Sure enough, he was there. The little dog had chewed up all the papers on Harry's desk and chewed on the furniture and on the door casing, apparently trying to find a way to escape. It was a sad story, but had a happy ending when the dog was rescued.

Another year, friends and family had gathered around the fire to sing Christmas carols when Anne heard a noise on the front porch. Thinking it was another friend, she opened the door, and a big, beautiful collie dog with snowflakes on his coat walked in. He went around to each guest and melted each heart.

Harry Frye said he had seen the dog in their pasture with their ponies a few days earlier. A couple of days after Christmas, Anne asked the neighbors if they knew who owned the dog, but no one knew. Then she put a notice in the paper. Months later, a man called and said he had seen his dog on their property. By that time, Brownie was an integral part of the Caudill family.

Anne offered to buy the dog, but the owner refused. When the owner came to retrieve the dog, Brownie backed away behind Anne and snarled at his former master. A few days later, Brownie broke loose from his leash again and traveled the two miles back to the Caudill home. Anne again offered to buy the dog, but the owner refused to sell.

For a third time, Anne found Brownie on her front porch. This time, the owner agreed to sell. He charged a high price, but Brownie the wonder dog remained in the Caudill family for many years.

* * *

Harry continued writing amidst all the other demands. In *A Darkness at Dawn*, published in 1976, Harry implored UK to seek ways to involve the university in Appalachian solutions. The university did establish an Appalachian Center, but Harry was apprehensive about future major economic and political reforms. He predicted:

I do not for one moment suppose the grassroots program of reform I am about to suggest, or any other major effort will be undertaken during this century. Perhaps no comparable effort will ever be launched. The forces that support the status quo are formidable indeed, including immense transportation firms, fuel conglomerates, some of the nation's largest and most influential banks, and, of course, the legions of leashed and obedient politicians at all levels of government who do their bidding for pay. At this juncture in our history, the American electorate appears too debased to give rise to great and effective leaders or to sustain and support them, the people corrupt and degrade their leaders in the process of electing them, then the leaders corrupt and debase the people to gain their continuing approval. It is a continuous and ultimately ruinous cycle from which there is no present prospect of escape, and which emphasizes at every turn the petty, the commonplace, and the mundane.

Many people would conclude that the above prophecy, written 35 years ago, was exactly on the mark.

During the same year, 1976, Harry published *Watches of the Night*. It received an award from the American Library Association as one of the notable books of the year. It was a sequel to *Night Comes to the Cumberlands*, bringing that "biography of a depressed area" through the years of the War on Poverty up to date. Some critics considered it as influential and consequential as the earlier book.

Harry was only 53 when he retired from his law practice.

The burden of the growing law practice plus the chaos after *Night*, wore him out. His health issues were a continuing concern. The year before his announced retirement, Anne found Harry at home, doubled up in pain. She drove him 160 miles to a Lexington hospital, and fortunately, they immediately removed his ruptured appendix and recovery was quick.

In the meantime, an influential group of people encouraged Harry to run for the US Senate against Thruston Morton. Anne explained that he had no illusions about the difficulty raising the amount of money required and didn't have the physical energy, or the inclination for such an undertaking.

The house was quiet, except during weekends when their most-welcomed guests came. The children were in school, and Anne was doing her thing at the library and involved in other projects. Harry had quiet time to reflect, gather his thoughts, write, and stare out the window whenever he pleased. However, it was a brief retirement, lasting only six months.

CHAPTER 14

The Return to Where It All Began

After Harry retired from his law practice, life for the Caudills settled down to an extent. The house was quieter and calmer than it had been when the phone rang off the hook. Their children were in school or working. After James received his degree from Harvard and a law degree from UK, he spent a year at New York University and received a post-graduate degree in tax law. Diana earned a degree in social work at UK and was working in that field in Lexington. Harry Frye was attending a prep school in Asheville, North Carolina.

Harry devoted most of his time to reading and writing, as his legs remained a persistent problem. Stretching out on a couch with a book or a writing pad provided about the only relief.

Anne seldom sat still, let alone reclined. She had volunteer work at the library and was involved in other community needs and projects, plus the gardening, cooking, and entertaining, which never ceased. At last, they had some peace, quiet time to relax and work at a more casual pace on reclaiming, preserving, and improving the land and the lives of their people.

That all changed during a weekend in May 1976. Earlier, when Dr. Otis Singletary became president of UK, Harry had invited him for a visit to see the orphaned Eastern Kentucky area. Some months later, Dr. John Stevenson, a professor at UK called, asking if he could bring Dr. Singletary for a visit, which was arranged five months after Harry's retirement. Then Mary Bingham called and asked to visit that same weekend. Her daughter was home from school and wanted to visit Appalshop and see their documentary films. Bedrooms were available since the children would all be gone that weekend.

"Well, you don't say no," said Anne. "You say sure, 'come on.'" The calm, quiet Caudill home was becoming just that, except when it was the Caudill Bed, Breakfast, Tour, Lunch, Dinner, Conversation, Storytelling, and Loads of Laughter Home.

That weekend, their guests took the tour and observed the poverty and the increasing evidence of the devastation from the growing strip mines. Earlier that morning while Anne prepared breakfast, John Stevenson, who later became president of Berea College, walked in and asked, "Do you suppose Harry would be willing to come to UK and teach for a semester on a fellowship?"

"You will have to ask him, but I would love to see him do it. He's a natural-born teacher. But don't you dare tell Harry that we had this conversation. I don't want him to think the idea came from me." He wasn't offered a teaching fellowship, but a full-tenured professorship in the history department at UK.

Harry was quite surprised and reluctant at first, explaining he had no teaching experience. He did not want to leave home and was pleased with the way things were in his life. Anne left the decision to him, but hoped he would accept. Finally, Harry decided to try it for a semester and if he didn't like it, he would return home. As it turned out, he liked it. Except during summers and long holidays, Anne and Harry spent the next eight years on the campus of UK.

The weekend resulted in a short-lived retirement. The connection with UK was a tradition and an interim home for nine of Anne's family members, which began when her father enrolled in UK without graduating from high school.

The cannon in front of the administration building remained intact, where, 32 years earlier, the Caudill odyssey had begun. An odyssey is defined as a long journey marked by many changes of fortune, including an intellectual or spiritual wandering or quest. Their journey was long and arduous, accompanied by significant changes of fortune. The intellectual component of the journey defined their purpose. In a sense, the spiritual aspect was a constant in their lives, a right and just cause—serving their people. Harry's brief retirement became an interlude to a significantly contrasting experience in a completely different, but familiar, setting.

The practicality of the move required looking for a place to live. Fortunately, housing worked out quite well. During their eight years at UK, the Caudills lived in seven different furnished homes. They rented the homes of UK staff members who had taken sabbatical leaves for a year; they lived in one home where the owner was away for two years. Most of the homes were conveniently located near the campus. Each year, it was merely a matter of packing clothing, personal items, books, and moving. They returned to their home in Whitesburg during the summers and holiday breaks.

It was quite a change from the mountains to academia. The Caudills made many new and interesting friends in the academic environment. They became close friends with Dr. Joseph Kuc and his wife, Ruth, whom Anne remembered as "two of the brightest and most wonderful people I've ever known." Joseph Kuc was a Catholic raised in Poland and a renowned plant pathologist. His wife, Ruth, was Jewish. When the TV series on the Holocaust first aired, the Caudills invited the Kucs to watch it with them. During the last episode, Ruth told Anne, "There is something I must tell you. My mother and father barely escaped to England before the Holocaust. All my other relatives perished at Auschwitz." As Anne did with most of her dear friends, she stayed in contact with the Kucs throughout the following years.

*   *   *

Eastern Kentucky had been a forgotten land. In 1976, the year before Harry went to teach at UK, he published *A Darkness at Dawn*. The central theme was a plea for recognition and assistance to that part of the state. What better way to bring recognition than teaching the young? Harry agreed to teach a course in Appalachian studies, and the word began to spread.

The campus was an old familiar place where Harry had walked Anne back to her dorm one romantic evening many years before when the war was winding down. The cliché, what goes around comes around, became a reality for the couple, whose odyssey took them back to another home where tradition, commitment, and a part of their hearts remained.

There was one problem in teaching a course about Appalachia. Although UK offered a course in the sociology of Appalachia, a broader course that included the history and culture of the area had not been offered before. There were no guidelines, syllabus, or textbooks for such a course. Harry had to use his own books, and rely on his familiarity and vast knowledge of the area.

Since libraries were like a second home to Anne, she began researching and accumulating materials at the Margaret I. King Library. It was the library where, years before, Anne got to know Harry.

She spent two or three days each week searching for references and materials about Appalachia and made photocopies for use in the classroom. She made triplicate copies of the most useful information and placed reserved copies on reference for his students. She made so many copies the librarians accused her of owning stock in the copy-machine company. The library obtained other works through inter-library loan. The materials filled a filing cabinet. They were later donated to the university, and copies were sent to Northern Kentucky University and the Southeast branch of UK at Whitesburg.

Harry taught Appalachian studies, which included history, culture, and economics. One year, he also taught the course at Kentucky State University in Frankfort, and later taught a course in Kentucky history. He liked it. His trial semester developed into 15 additional ones. Instead of arguing cases before a judge, he argued the merits of adding Appalachia to the map. His new jury included Kentucky's best young minds and those from other states. His courses were always full and popular, because Harry was an interesting and inspiring teacher. Over the years, numerous former students returned to visit, and told Harry how his influence changed their lives and life's work.

The former home economics student at UK became a student again 32 years later. The university had established Donovan Scholars, whereby senior citizens could take courses tuition free. Anne began her study with a course in early European history, followed by modern European history, early English history, and then modern English history. Although she was already well versed in American history, Anne enrolled in early American history, and then took courses on American social history. Time ran out before taking modern American history, but Anne already knew most of that; she had lived it.

The courses were non-credit, but Anne did the work and took the exams. "I only wanted to learn history, not teach it," she said. History is a series of facts. Anne, the storyteller, knows many of the sidelight and human-interest anecdotes, which enhanced the basic facts. Much of her reading and many of her interests were associated with history, and she had had the advantage of sitting around the dinner table and hearing stories from David McCullough and other scholars and historians.

The move was convenient for two of the Caudill children. Diana lived with her parents in Lexington for two years while doing social work at one of the hospitals. Harry Frye also lived with them for four years when he attended UK, except for one semester when his parents went on sabbatical to the British Isles.

During Anne's eight years at Lexington, when Harry taught at UK from 1980-87, she was active in the University Women's Club, the garden club, and an antiques study group, and volunteered for activities and projects sponsored by those clubs. Throughout her life, Anne gave extraordinary amounts of her time to scouts, schools, hospitals, environmental projects, Appalachian redevelopment, churches, the needy, the literacy cause, and libraries.

In addition to participating in clubs, doing research, and studying for her history classes, Anne handled Harry's never-ending correspondence. In later years, Harry would hand her a letter and ask that she respond. "I knew exactly what he wanted to say, since I had worked so closely with him," she said. "I'd write the letter, type it, and hand it to him. Usually, he would sign it without even reading it." During the years at UK, she also typed Harry's articles, speeches, and the manuscripts of the two books he wrote while teaching there.

Lexington was certainly more easily accessible than Whitesburg. Visitors continued coming to confer with Harry, but it wasn't the same. They missed the grand tour and dinner from the garden. However, summertime provided the opportunity to reopen the Caudill Bed and Breakfast, etc., and entertaining continued at nearly the former pace.

Although considered an expert on Appalachia, Harry was less familiar with that part of the mountains in West Virginia, Virginia, and Pennsylvania. The Caudills traveled to those areas several times to do additional research and found considerable information at the West Virginia University Library.

There had been some criticism about Harry's books, particularly *Night Comes to the Cumberlands,* concerning his lack of formal academic training. After he became a full professor, questions arose again as to his scholarly background.

"He was constantly reading, studying, and researching the region," Anne said. "He traveled extensively over the mountains to see the conditions firsthand. What does it take to qualify as a scholar?"

After the first couple of years doing most of the research for Harry, Anne had more time to become involved in those endeavors she loved. While she continued to be active in the University Women's Club and garden club, it was no surprise that she became active in promoting books and reading. However, this time, she devoted her efforts to distributing books worldwide.

At a meeting of retired home demonstration agents, Harriet Van Meter spoke and explained the purpose and details of her new venture—the International Book Project. When her husband was a member of the UK Board of Trustees, she became interested in helping foreign students, several of whom were from India. She helped them locate homes and adjust to the university. When some of the students returned to India, they invited her to visit. She did and observed the conditions pertaining to education and particularly noted the lack of books and materials for their students. When she returned home, Van Meter wrote a letter to a major Bombay newspaper, which they printed. The letter explained that students could contact her if they needed books in preparation for their academic careers. Within one month, she received 400 requests. The project began in her home, but grew rapidly, and required moving to a vacant warehouse. Not only were books solicited, but also financial contributions were necessary to rent the warehouse and pay for packaging and shipping. During Van Meter's talk, she stressed the need for volunteers.

"That afternoon I volunteered and worked several years with the International Book Project," Anne said.

She handled part of the voluminous correspondence as the project grew. She contacted various clubs across the country to solicit involvement, support, and funding. She sent to organizations and individuals instructions and the names and addresses of people who had requested books. Harriet Van Meter's husband had been a noted surgeon in Lexington, and she had access to editions of medical books in the area, and sent many to medical institutions around the world. When a new medical school was established in the Philippines, the book project helped complete the library, which was named the Harriet Van Meter Library.

The project provided a considerable number of books to Peace Corp volunteers, who had requested them for the people they served. Anne usually sent thank-you letters, but one letter she received had no return address. She opened the envelope and found four $100 bills and a note, "This is for the International Book Project."

Each year, around 100,000 books were distributed, along with hundreds of letters containing information and instructions. One year, Anne sent a letter of recommendation to the Nobel Peace Prize Committee in support of Harriet Van Meter, who was a nominee, but the committee chose Mother Theresa.

Although accumulating materials and information for the course and preparation for the classes required considerable time, Anne said, "Harry had more time after leaving law practice and considered university teaching a life of ease compared to his years practicing law." Although teaching is a demanding profession, the daily pressures are generally not as taxing as the rigors of a thriving law office. Arguing a case, speaking, and lecturing came naturally to Harry. His wealth of stories and accounts of life in Appalachia were not only interesting and entertaining, but also educational and inspiring.

Part of the art of teaching is convincing students to develop a desire for learning. Anne said, "Harry was a natural born teacher." This unique gift undoubtedly contributed to his success, reinforced by a subtle, yet dynamic manner of presentation.

The shift to a "life of ease" provided considerably more time to read, write, and relax. Their summers back home in Whitesburg were particularly relaxing times. Their two homes—one in the academic setting in Lexington during winters and the other in the quiet and peaceful mountains during summers—were the best of both worlds.

Perhaps "relax" is not quite the right word; Harry never stopped writing during his work in the law office or the classroom. Anne continued typing, editing, reading, and conducting research. Perhaps writing, in addition to making a living with a job or a profession, is somewhat obsessive or compulsive. From another perspective, writing or another creative endeavor is a form of relaxation as one shifts from formal responsibilities and becomes lost in that which gives satisfaction and gratification. Realizing the social and political impact Harry's writing had, Anne continued encouraging and supporting his time with pen and paper.

Watches of the Night was published in 1976, the year Harry began teaching at UK. The book was a follow-up to *Night Comes to the Cumberland*. *Watches of the Night* was reissued in 2010, ten years after Harry's death. The new edition included an afterword by James and a segment about the author by Anne.

In the June 2011 edition of *The Progressive* magazine, Wendell Berry published an article titled, "A Man of Courage, Constant to the End." In the article, Berry discussed the contents of *Watches of the Night*, noting that it was not a happy book. During the 13 years after *Night Comes to the Cumberlands* and the worldwide attention it received, conditions in Appalachia had changed little. In some respects, conditions remained the same or regressed. To an extent, the War on Poverty intensified the welfare culture.

Night Come to the Cumberlands directly or indirectly brought about change, resulting in improved healthcare, education, and other aspects of the lives of the people. As Berry noted, conditions became worse in other respects. As the stripping of the sides and tops of mountains increased at a rapid rate, destruction of the land intensified. As heavy equipment replaced picks and shovels, unemployed miners had two choices—move away or exist from the largess of the welfare state.

As the human element wasted away, devastation to the environment compounded accordingly. Harry called strip mining "man's most thorough and total assault upon his planet." He said, "The blasting and bulldozing of grass, timber, topsoil, and rock strata kill or put to flight every living creature, destroy every plant, and expose vast quantities of iron, sulfur, zinc, and other trace minerals to follow spoil-bank silt into the river channels and thence into the nation's drinking water. The ill consequences of such water pollution alone are unforeseeable and possibly irremediable."

In his article, Berry recounted the long abiding friendship of the Berrys and Caudills. He greatly admired Harry's endless storytelling, his Shakespearian delight in human comedy, and his eloquent manner of speech. Berry remembered that sometimes Harry answered the phone with, "To what do I owe the signal honor of this communication?"

During Harry's tenure at UK, he wrote *Theirs Be the Power: The Moguls of Eastern Kentucky*, published in 1983. Harry wanted to publish the book jointly, by Anne and Harry Caudill, but Anne objected; she had a good time helping him. He said, paraphrasing what Lincoln had said about his mother, "All that I am and all that I ever hope to be, I owe to Anne."

In the acknowledgments of *Theirs be the Powers*, Harry wrote, "To my wife, Anne Frye Caudill, I am obligated in a very special way. Her patient research in libraries, her endless hours at copying machines, and her toil at her typewriter entitle her to a claim of co-authorship. She rejected that right, but I assert it nonetheless, for her contributions caused the book to emerge from the presses."

Anne never claimed or took credit for co-authorship of any of Harry's works. She said that his writing originated from his own ideas: "He wrote and I just helped him." She helped him accumulate the 205 documented references in the bibliography of *Theirs Be the Power,* typed and retyped the manuscript, edited the book, and encouraged, guided, and insisted that they see it through.

For many years, Harry had been interested in how the so-called moguls, people of money and power, rose to invade a land with such devastating effects. The *Washington Post* said, "A passionate but well-documented chronicle of the rise of King Coal in Eastern Kentucky, *Theirs Be the Power* exhibits how unregulated free enterprise led to the devastation of thousands of human lives."

Dr. Tom Clark wrote, "One of Kentucky's fundamental weaknesses as an organized and political society has been its squeamishness about facing the cold facts of its condition—the state has sweetly looked away while being raped."

Harry, a man of courage, constant to the end, never looked the other way. His writing pulled no punches, told it like it was, and named the names of those responsible Kentuckians—governors, politicians, and the corporate and local power brokers—who became wealthier using King Coal to scourge their land.

The administrators at UK had to play their political cards very carefully. Local coal owners and operators took pride in and supported their university, particularly the Wildcat basketball team. One powerful and wealthy Kentucky businessman and coal entrepreneur served for years as chairman of the UK board of trustees. When Harry, then a UK professor, sought publication of *Theirs Be the Power*, the University of Kentucky Press declined to publish it, which was not surprising to Harry and Anne. The University of Illinois Press published it. When Eastern Kentucky University proposed bestowing Harry with an honorary degree, a wealthy coal baron and EKU trustee blocked it because the proposed honoree was "too controversial." Harry said, "No big deal; there must be several hundred thousand others who won't receive an honorary degree."

Harry's account of the moguls' rise to power in Eastern Kentucky is an intriguing one. Shortly after the Civil War, America's industrial movement began booming. Coal became a very important resource in powering the increasing numbers of steam engines on the vastly expanding railroads across the country. Coal was needed to produce steel for engines and railcars, and it was used for manufacturing the newfangled automobiles and other heavy machinery. Coal generated the electrical flow through power lines that rapidly spread across the land, and coal heated the homes where light shone from the ceilings at the mere pull of a string.

The word spread: Appalachia is a black gold mine. *Theirs Be the Power* described how the coal barons, large corporations, and capitalists industrialized Appalachia, and transformed its immense mineral wealth into enormous personal fortunes. Familiar names—Rockefeller, Morgan, Forbes, Mayo, Mellon, Camden, Delano, Roosevelt, and others—financed the coal, steel, oil, utility, and railroad companies that carved out enormous private profits, leaving behind an oppressive public poverty. Franklin Delano Roosevelt, the former four-term president, made several trips with his uncle, Warren Delano Jr., to Appalachia to check on their financial interests in the coal mining ventures.[21]

Thousands of acres of land were purchased and the rights to mine all minerals and cut all timber were secured for a few cents per acre, under the broad-form deed. The moguls then began building towns—Jenkins, Wayland, Wheelwright, Van Lear, McRoberts, Hellier, Hardburly, Viper, Lynch, Vicco, Seco, and others—all named for capitalists, bankers, and managers involved in the coal business. Hardburly, Vicco, and Seco were exceptions: Hardburley was named after the Hardy Burlington Mining Company; Vicco was an acronym for the Virginia Coal and Coke Company; and Seco for South East Coal Company. Viper was a nearby coal town, apparently named for local wildlife.

An old coal miner told Harry what life was like during the heyday of the coal operations:

Back then, the operators had a ball. They built coal camps all over the place and took money in hand over fist. The biggest show in these mountains was their big special trains. They drove around in White Steamers that would make a Cadillac look tacky. They had the prettiest women in the country and, oh brother, how they did dress! If they wanted anything done, they just called up the judge or governor or whoever had the power, and he got busy and took care of it for them. If they didn't like a body, they told

---

21. During one visit in 1908, Franklin wrote to his young wife, Eleanor, three letters, which are included in Harry's book.

him to get out of the county, and he got out. They told everybody how to vote, and if they didn't like a candidate, he didn't have a chance. They sort of lived like a bunch of kings.

Lynch, named for Thomas Lynch, a high-ranking manager for US Steel, was built on Looney Creek near Big Black Mountain, in an isolated area in Harlan County. Workers, including immigrants from Italy, Croatia, Serbia, Russia, Syria, Sweden, Switzerland, and Albania, flooded Lynch and other new towns. Blacks moved from the South when jobs became available in the mines, and the men living in the countless surrounding hollows put down their plows and took up picks and shovels. It wasn't long until the profits began flowing back to New York, Philadelphia, and other large banking centers far removed from thriving coal towns.

Conceived by Morgan-Rockefeller architects, Lynch was built by the US Coal and Coke Company, a division of US Steel. By 1940, Lynch had grown to a town of over 10,000. Initially, one thousand five-room dwellings lined the narrow creek flats, along with company stores, schools, churches, and a 133-room hotel. Harry described the town as one where there "would be no democracy." Company police enforced the law. The company ran the schools and cared for the sick, and the company undertaker buried the dead. The company-approved preachers proclaimed the Word of God as conceived and approved by the company. The men needed only to work and the women to keep their company-owned houses clean.

Lynch was a thriving, robust, and highly productive town. For years, the Lynch High School football team was a state powerhouse. On one record day at Lynch, workers loaded 10,293 tons of coal on 230 railroad cars—a train 1.65 miles long.

However, in time, the forces that drove economics changed. Oil replaced coal to power engines. Strip mining and mountaintop removal required men to sit behind a steering wheel and load coal, one ton per scoop. Miners discarded their picks and shovels, and sought relief. Moguls moved on to other lucrative enterprises. Today, Lynch is a sleepy little town with a population of about 800, sustained, in part, by welfare. Other once thriving coal towns are now practically ghost towns.

*   *   *

Anne and Harry liked to travel and see other cultures and countries. As a child, Anne remembered living in Asheville and New Orleans where her father worked in the 1920s. Anne also went to Chicago and New Jersey to work during the war. In 1946, it was back to New Orleans for the honeymoon. After their children were old enough, the Caudill family managed to get away for several summer trips to the beaches in South Carolina. Although it took a few years, Harry did take Anne to France as promised.

After *Night* came out, travel was limited to speaking engagements and meetings, which continued for several years. They were on the road with one driving, and one reading a book to the other. When they had to fly, it was a two-hour jaunt to an airport. Anne lost track of the number of times they went to Washington for meetings.

Getting away for speaking engagements and meetings was not a leisurely vacation. When things settled down a bit, Anne and Harry managed to get away in the late 1960s and early '70s.

During four trips, they visited England, Ireland, Scotland, Italy, Switzerland, Portugal, and Spain. The trips were not altogether leisurely and relaxing, but certainly revitalizing and renewing. Not only were the trips opportunities to see other parts of the world, they were ventures to study history, culture, and ancestry.

Recalling their visit to Spain reminded Anne of a story. When Harry was fighting on the Italian front, a large troop of Germans surrendered, and Harry was on the detail to escort them back from the front line. A German officer said something to Harry. Then Harry asked the officer, who spoke perfect English, why the Germans fought for Adolph Hitler and his idea of supremacy. The officer retorted, "Don't you read your own literature?" When Harry asked what he meant, the officer named a particular book, *The Passing of the Great Race*. About 35 years after the encounter, Anne and Harry were touring the king's palace in Spain when Harry saw the book on a shelf.

After they arrived home from their trip, Harry read the book, which was a diatribe about the purity of the Aryan race. After he gave the book to Anne, she began reading it and said, "The farther I got into it, the madder I got, and I got so mad, I couldn't finishing reading it."

* * *

In 1984, during the second semester of Harry's sixth year teaching at UK, Anne and Harry took a sabbatical leave and went to Ireland, England, Scotland, and Wales to study and research the origins of Eastern Kentucky family names. He and Anne spent two months in libraries, museums, and record offices tracing the ancestry of those families who eventually settled in Appalachia.

The next summer, Anne, Harry, and James began a trip by car to the West Coast, but turned back upon reaching Kansas. With his deteriorating physical condition, Harry could not tolerate the cramped conditions in a car for hours at a time.

In 1986, at the end of the second semester at UK, Harry resigned. Anne said:

> In the last years, he was in constant pain from his injured left leg and the even worse misery of his right knee, which had worn out from carrying the extra burden of his walking in a twist caused by his severe limp in his left leg. This last year at UK was a torture and he spent every available minute stretched out on a sofa or bed. In addition, he suffered from the acute miseries of the urinary system so common in older men. Then the tremors and difficulties with speech began and he realized he could not continue teaching.

Anne and Harry returned to their home in Whitesburg. Harry's much-needed rest revitalized him. Without the pressures of teaching, he was more relaxed and his physical condition stabilized somewhat. After resting his legs during the winter of 1986–87, Harry and Anne decided to accompany James on a five-week trip to France and England. After a few days of moving about and seeing the sights in France, Harry's pain became unbearable and the Caudills returned to Whitesburg.

It was back home again and rest this time, but there was work to do. Harry undertook a monumental task—writing a new history of Kentucky. It didn't take Anne long to become active in her community again. There were ongoing civic projects and the library always needed help. The Caudills took occasional trips around the state to attend meetings and give speeches. They continued to host guests in their home, but not the hordes of earlier days.

Anne took care of their home, and above all else, Harry's needs. When she went out, she made sure Harry was comfortable, usually reclining on the couch with his books and writing pad. Writing a history of Kentucky kept him occupied. One day, she came home to discover that he had been writing something else.

Harry had written four chapters of early Kentucky history, which Anne typed. On this particular day after she came home, he handed her a sheaf of papers to type. She recalled, "I typed a paragraph or two, and I thought this is not the history of Kentucky. What is this? This is foolishness. I took it to the front porch where he was writing and asked, 'What got into you to write this?' He looked up at me, and his eyes twinkled and he said, 'The devil got into me.'" *Lester's Progress,* his last book, was well underway.

CHAPTER 15

The Stories Never End

In 1948, when Anne moved to the Cumberland Mountains, she began adjusting to a somewhat different way of life. A Kentuckian is a Kentuckian, and a mountaineer is a Kentuckian, too, but a mountaineer might take some time to get to know. Anne grew up in a rural setting and knew how country people lived. She worked nearly two years with farmwomen in Montgomery County, located in the foothills on the fringe of Appalachia. In the deeper and higher mountains, the native folks, isolated from the so-called mainstream, lived a distinct kind of life in a backwoods and primitive way, and developed a unique culture of their own.

During the early part of the 20th century, when the coal boom began, curious observers began filtering into this previously inaccessible and isolated area. With the arrival of railroads and the conversion of trails into dirt and rocky roads, the area opened to outsiders. Visitors and writers began traveling to and writing about these native mountain people. Observers characterized them as picturesque, quaint, primitive, suspicious, narrow-minded, and ignorant. The mountaineers were also described as brave, chivalrous, noble, generous, and free-spirited. A combination of the two is what Anne discovered when she moved from the lush, rolling Bluegrass to the Cumberland Mountains.

Harry, who grew up in Wat Long Hollow, was a bright young man with an unusual interest in the history of his people and the stories about them, which he heard, remembered, and collected throughout his lifetime. He learned from many of the old-timers who had little else to sustain them other than tradition and the strength handed down from their ancestors. Several of these stories were published in two of his books, *The Mountain, The Miner, and The Lord* in 1980, and *Slender is the Thread* in 1987, the year he left UK.

Anne was a storyteller, too. During her young life, she heard and remembered many stories about her people. Her father told the story about what he called "the most exciting thing that ever happened in Cynthiana" (other than, perhaps, when John Hunt Morgan burned the town).

The Harrison County fairgrounds were located directly across the South Licking River that flowed through Cynthiana. When the circus arrived, the elephant was a big attraction. However, an unwise farmer spit tobacco juice into the elephant's upturned trunk. Enraged, the elephant pursued the farmer as he ran through the covered bridge over the river. Partway through, the elephant was alarmed by the low rafters and refused to go forward or backward. Amidst great excitement, the elephant was finally persuaded to move on through the bridge.

When Anne moved to Whitesburg, she discovered an area rich in history, lore and legends. It became another story land, providing a treasure trove of stories for her. She heard stories about how divided the people were during and after the Civil War. The conflict often developed into feuds, some of which continued for years. One was either a Yankee or a Rebel, a Democrat or a Republican, a miner or a boss, saved or not saved. There was no in-between. Loyalty to the North or the South, to a political party, and to God, was reason enough to fight. During and after the Civil War, roving bands—known as regulators, bushwhackers, guerillas, home guards or partisan rangers—roamed the area, rounding up or killing in cold blood those who had deserted the cause, an unforgiveable sin. A man risked his life fighting the war, and, in some cases, if he refused to join the cause, risked his life for not taking up arms against his own brother, family, and friends.

In 2003, the award-winning book and movie *Cold Mountain* told the story of a desertion during the Civil War. In 2010, Dean and Nina Cornett of Letcher County produced a documentary film, *Guerillas and Bushwhackers: A Different Civil War*, which portrayed atrocities committed by both sides. Some of the historical incidents depicted were taken from Anne and Harry's writings and stories.

Anne learned that James Mulligan was right; politics is the damnedest in Kentucky. She grew up during frequent heated political battles in Central Kentucky. In Eastern Kentucky, political battles, many of which resulted from the equally divided loyalties during the Civil War, occasionally resulted in violence and bloodshed. Armies and militia from both sides passed through the area and committed acts of violence against the hated opposition. The old animosities and antagonisms passed down from generation to generation, and bitter disputes were often settled temporarily by gunfights. After the war, several incidences of feuding continued between families and clans, which resulted in bloody battles. One violent incident in 1914 resulted in four deaths and one person wounded after a school board election at Rockhouse Creek in Letcher County.

For nearly a half century after the Civil War, Eastern Kentucky was known as "the dark and bloody ground." Breathitt County became "Bloody Breathitt," and several other counties had their share of violent feuds. Some of the more noted ones involved these clans and families: Baker-White, French-Eversole, and Turner-Howard. "Devil Anse" Hatfield led the infamous Hatfield-McCoy feud, which claimed 12 lives in ten years. It was the more publicized and notorious one. The Martin-Tolliver feud in Rowan County near the town of Morehead, however, continued for 32 years and claimed 20 lives and 16 others wounded.

Although feelings ran high for years after the Civil War, the cause of some of the feuds was never precisely determined. Legend has it that a dispute over a dog started one of the feuds. Another began over a woman, and, supposedly, the Turner-Howard feud in Harlan County began when a Howard accused a Turner of "speaking badly about Mama." A stolen pig may have started the Hatfield-McCoy feud, but whatever the reasons, it took years for many of the feuds to end. Legend has it that the Hatfields and McCoys laid down their arms when a romance interceded, and a Hatfield married a McCoy. Hollywood even made movies about the feuds.

Anne knew well some of those whose ancestors were involved in the Jones-Wright feud, which began in 1885 and continued for several years.

During the contentious war, armies from both sides passed through the area, and militia groups rode around searching for recruits to fight for their side, or pursued deserters and, in many situations, shot them on the spot. When the longstanding feuds ran their course, battles continued on the political field.

Elections were the event of the year—tense, embittered, and subject to a gunfight or two, often fueled by the readily available, vote-buying moonshine.

Harry fought political battles, as did Anne when she campaigned for him. In 1953, 88 years after the end of the Civil War, Harry, a staunch Democrat running for state representative, went campaigning up on Beef Hide Creek. He told this story in *The Mountain, The Miner, And The Lord*. At a country store, he met a woman, about 75 with a wrinkled, but kind face. Harry asked her to vote for him, and she replied, "I know your opponent and I know a whole lot about you. I think it will be best for the county if you are elected, and I sincerely hope you will win, but I just can't vote for you. My hands are tied and I will have to vote against you."

She explained that her grandfather, Fayette Bentley, worked on his little farm on Beef Hide Creek, and remained neutral and uncommitted during the war. Although slavery was repugnant to him, he did not join the Union army. In 1864, Ephraim Ratliff, a captain and die-hard Rebel returned to the county to prepare for one last stand against the Union. Ratliff and his men began scouring the region for recruits. When they rode up to Bentley's farm, Ratliff summoned him to join with the Rebels. Reluctantly, he joined and marched out with Captain Ratliff and his men. During the night, as the straggling army and new recruits were assembling, Bentley slipped away and headed home. The next day, Ratliff and his men circled Bentley's cabin, called him out, and the Union captain shot him dead.

Fayette Bentley's granddaughter explained that after her grandmother and the Bentley children buried their husband and father, they knelt down and prayed for the longest time that

Ephraim Ratliff would die. Soon after the war ended, a neighbor stopped by to announce that during the previous night, Ratliff woke up, grabbed his chest, and died.

In *the Mountain, the Miner, and the Lord,* Harry wrote:

> The good woman told me, 88 years after the cavalry captain came to the end of his trail, "I am the daughter of Fayette Bentley's oldest daughter, the one who was 13 when he was killed. My grandmother lived 35 years after that, and as a girl growing up, I spent many nights with her. She asked me not to forget the war or the Rebels who caused it. She said they were all Democrats and never to be trusted. She said that someday women would get the right to vote, and when I was 12 years old I promised her I would never—under any circumstances—vote for a Democrat. So now you understand why I can't vote for you, but I will ask God to see you are elected. He answered my grandmother's prayer and I believe he will answer mine, too."

As Harry was leaving the country store, an elderly man stopped him to tell a story. "Another of the loafers—a man of 75 or more, in patched overalls, and with the aroma of moonshine whiskey about him—followed me from the store," Harry wrote. "His name was Wright and he assured me that while the old lady's vote was lost to me, I could certainly count on receiving his own. He asked me to follow him up the road a few hundred yards."

They stopped at the man's old house, which had been his grandfather's cabin. His grandfather fought for the Rebels with Morgan's Raiders and was captured by the Yankees. A few months later, he was paroled; he swore he would never take up arms again against the United States. A few days after returning to his farm and family, Union soldiers rode up looking for members of Ephraim Ratliff's company. Wright's grandfather argued that he fought only for John Hunt Morgan. Nonetheless, they drew their guns and the commanding officer shouted that he had never known a turncoat who obeyed his parole—"once a Rebel, always a Rebel."

Wright's grandfather ran, but a soldier leaned up against a cedar gatepost, took aim, and killed him. Wright showed Harry where the cedar gatepost stood for many years after the Civil War. The old man said, "He stood right where you are now and shot my granddaddy in the back with a Sharp's needle gun. So, don't feel too bad about losin' the old woman's vote. I never go to vote without passin' where the gatepost stood, and I never pass it without thinkin' what happened there. And that is why I have voted for 55 years without ever once markin' a ballot for a Republican."

It all happened on Beef Hide Creek more than eight decades before. The old woman and the old man were living in peace then and loafing at the country store, with many mores tales to tell. The bitter division was not as intense as before, but it was still there many years after the time when neighbor fought against neighbor, family against family, and brother against brother.

The history of coal mining was a series of booms and repressed times marked by struggles, conflicts, and violence. Harry kept a photograph of John L. Lewis on the wall at his law office. John L. Lewis was one of the more important figures in establishing labor unions throughout the United States during the early and mid-1950s. He organized and served as president of the United Mine Workers (UMW) from 1920 to 1960. He was charismatic, controversial, and powerful enough to upset the coal-mining apple cart.

The banks and the steel and mining corporations owned the coal mines along with the camps, houses, schools, stores, churches, and graveyards, and they owned the miners. To an extent, they also owned the souls of at least some of the county, state, and federal elected officials. Consequently, senators, elected officials, and US representatives listened intently to what a coal company had to say. The UMW led by John L. Lewis changed significant parts of that.

Harry grew up during the abhorrent conditions under which the miners worked. After Lewis organized the UMW, miners realized significant improvements in wages, healthcare, safety, and pension programs. For example, in 1924, Lewis negotiated a three-year contract at $7.50 per day, the equivalent of $93 in 2009 dollars. It was not a peaceful transition throughout those years as bitter disputes, strikes, and violence occurred sporadically.

As conditions changed, the UMW became somewhat corrupt, and a faction of the miners felt the union was letting them down by backing out of the promises it had made. These miners brought a class action suit against the UMW. Harry Huge, a lawyer from West Virginia who was representing the miners, asked Harry to assist in the suit.

Anne interviewed the older miners who were losing their pensions and healthcare benefits. A number of older miners explained that in earlier days when the operators learned that certain miners were trying to organize, they would immediately fire them, evict them from their company homes, and move their belongings out on the street. Their names were added to a blacklist, ensuring that no other company would ever hire them. Anne recorded numerous accounts of miners being poorly treated. There was no place to go when the company evicted a miner, his family, and belongings from their home out on the creek bank that ran through a dusty coal camp. Anne said, "It was one of the saddest things I ever did."

*　*　*

Mayking is now a ghost town, but the former coal town had an intriguing history. In the late 1800s and early 1900s, the Ku Klux Klan rode through the area terrorizing the inhabitants and killing a few.[22]

For 43 years, though, Anne's life at Mayking was relatively peaceful. That changed in 1959. Anne, Harry, and their children sat in their home and heard gunfire. Another coal strike was underway.

"There was a coal tipple at Mayking in the big bottom," Anne said. "There was frequent gunfire directed at the site from the wooded ridge just bordering our property to the north, which was within gunshot of the tipple. Often we heard gunfire, but as it was not directed toward us, but away from where we lived, we were not alarmed."

After years of strife, controversy, and dedication to the cause of justice, the Caudills—known for their unfaltering courage— understood the conflict and were concerned, but not unduly alarmed.

---

22. "Bad" Sol Fleming was about as bad as they came. After joining a Klan raid in 1901, he was convicted of killing Jemima Hall and her son. As a result, the Fleming-Mullins feud began and sporadic gunfights continued for almost 25 years.

The most notable uprising between the miners and coal operators began in neighboring "Bloody" Harlan County in 1931 and continued sporadically until 1939. At one point, nearly 4,000 miners marched in protest to the courthouse at Harlan. Gunfire erupted on occasion, spurring the operators to import "peace-keeping" hired guns from northern cities to patrol and keep the miners in line. The miners and their families referred to these men as "thugs." During the worst of the conflict, Governor A. B. Happy Chandler sent over 800 National Guardsmen to quell the hostilities.

When Harry reached the age to drive, he frequently drove his father, who had lost an arm in a mining accident. Harry's aunt Dora Wyatt and her miner husband, Jim, lived at Lynch, a few miles beyond another coal-mining town at Benham. One day, Cro Caudill asked young Harry to drive the family over to Lynch to visit Dora and Jim.

As they were passing through Benham, Harry suddenly whipped the car around and sped out of town. Startled, his father asked, "Harry, what are you doing?"

"We're getting out of here. There's going to be trouble, and we don't need to be in it."

As they had passed through Benham, Harry looked up on the hill near the company school and church, and saw a man sitting behind a machine gun, trained on the company store down by the road. Sure enough, there was a confrontation between the workers and the company.

In *The Mountain, the Miner, and the Lord*, Harry told the story about "Little Thuggie," the son of a miner who took matters into his own hands during the violent dispute between the miners and the coal operators at Lynch in Harlan County.

During the Depression, miners lived on meager wages, barely existing. When John L. Lewis organized the miners, in the '30s, the coal companies fought it with every means at their disposal.

The massive mine at Lynch, owned by the US Coal and Coke Company, a subsidiary of US Steel, imported "industrial policemen" to keep order. The judge of the circuit court, D. C. "Baby" Jones, whose wife was a coal operator's daughter, was determined to keep the UMW from organizing in Harlan County. He directed his county sheriff and deputies, supported by the industrial police, to patrol the area and keep miners from joining a "communist" labor organization. Any miner suspected of being sympathetic to the union or considering joining the UMW would be evicted from his company home and kicked out of the county.

One particular odious thug, fresh from the Alabama coal war, patrolled the area on a motorcycle, equipped with a .45 caliber submachine gun. He kicked children who were in a no-trespassing zone, slapped a women when she sassed him, and pistol-whipped men who wouldn't move on when ordered. The thug bragged about killing five miners in Alabama and said he would probably have to kill ten in Lynch before he left.

Thirty-five years later, Harry assisted in the suit against the UMW when it reneged in paying pensions and benefits to retired miners. On one occasion, Harry conferred with an elderly former miner, his wife, and son, and thought it a bit odd when the wife referred to her grown son as "Little Thuggie." Harry finally asked, "Why do you call him Little Thuggie?"

The husband said, "Go ahead and tell him all about it. Besides, everybody who would have any interest in it is already dead but me, and I ain't got long to go." The wife proceeded to tell the story. It seems she had reached the end of her rope and insisted that her husband take out the thug who persisted in terrorizing the miners and their families. She meant, "I'll never sleep with you again until you do it."

The husband went to the next county to purchase Super X shells for his rifle. One dark night, he borrowed a Model T Ford and drove up on Black Mountain where the thug went each night to watch for any suspicious activity down in Lynch. When the miner had the thug in clear sight and range of his gun, the miner shot him dead, and returned to his wife and family.

Nine months later, a baby was born. The mother said his daddy named him Lewis Delano after his heroes, John L. and Franklin Delano. "His daddy calls him Lewis D, but I nicknamed him 'Little Thuggie.' Most of his friends call him that, but they don't know why."

During his law practice, Harry frequently dealt with moonshiners. They didn't like paying taxes on their product, and the government doesn't like it when they don't. The government employed revenuers to look for smoke from moonshine stills. However, if a moonshiner builds a fire during the night to distill something, he is much more apt to escape the law.

A miner who inhales coal dust for six days needs something to clear his throat, and he needs it fast on a Saturday night. "Ginny barns" were places where a miner could get something to drink to clear his throat and most of his other insides. He could also purchase other items and a woman of questionable repute.

Harry defended some of the unfortunate souls who succumbed to sin on a Saturday night, but became upright after getting out of jail on Monday. There were three brothers in the county who worked out a lucrative business enterprise. One of the brothers was a moonshiner, another was a policeman, and the third was a magistrate.

When a ginny barn got too rowdy, the owner called the law, and the rowdies usually landed in jail. On Monday morning, the magistrate brother fined the miscreants and sent them back to the mines. Harry discovered that the three brothers—the moonshiner, the policeman, and the magistrate—rendered justice in their own unique way by equally splitting the fines.

When he was a young man, Harry knew old Silas (Sy) Cornett, who lived on Line Fork. Sy played the fife in the army during the Civil War. He never married, but had an illegitimate daughter. Harry heard him play the fife a few times after he was furnished with a dram of liquor. Sy collected his army pension in gold coins and stored them in an iron pot. A relative helped him count the coins one time and said the pot was nearly full. When Sy was on his deathbed, his relatives urged him to tell them where he had hidden the pot of gold to leave for his needy daughter. He told them, "You'll never find old Sy's gold." After he died, the family dug up practically his whole farm, but never found it.

Young Harry and his friend, Byrd Hogg, decided they would look. They borrowed an army Geiger counter and went all over Sy's farm. They uncovered nails, horseshoes, and scrap metal, but no pot full of gold.

In *The Mountain, the Miner, and the Lord*, Harry told the story of Bad John Wright, one of the most fascinating stories about legendary characters in Appalachia. Harry did not know him, but he knew several of his descendants, some of whom were his clients. Tilden Wright, John's great-nephew, who died in 1975 at age 92, and other older residents in Letcher County who knew

Bad John told stories about the man, some of which border on the unbelievable.

John was bad when he had to be and good at other times. He served as a soldier, deputy US marshal, deputy sheriff, man hunter, and woman catcher. He had two legal wives, but was believed to have had six to eight common-law wives and 25 to 30 children. Harry heard numerous stories from those who remembered Granpap Wright.

Harry's grandmother told him that his grandfather rode with Bad John and the Confederates at what she called a "right smart little battle" at Gladeville, Virginia. His over-matched platoon holed up in the courthouse when the Union forces surrounded the building. When the Confederates waved a white flag, they were ordered to walk out with their hands up. John, who was 19 and the youngest member of the platoon, pulled out a concealed pistol, shot the Union captain in the face, mounted the captain's horse, and high-tailed it north. Since it wasn't a good idea to ride in northern territory wearing a Rebel uniform, John stopped at a house and stole some civilian clothes.

Although there were frequent desertions during the Civil War, John was probably the only man to desert the Confederate army once and the Union army twice. When he heard that prosperous farmers in Ohio were offering $300 to any man who would take their son's place in the Yankee army, he accepted the deal, joined the troops, put on a blue uniform, and then deserted the next day. Since it was such easy money, John rode to another town, received a federal bonus for enlisting under another name, put on another blue uniform, and deserted the next day.

With several hundred dollars in his pocket, John figured it was time to head back south to his home in Kentucky. He had to lay low, however, since he had deserted his own Rebel army, but while he was passing through the northern part of the state, he learned that the daring General John Hunt Morgan and his raiders were cutting a swath through the area. So John joined up again and fought for the South at the battle of Cynthiana— Anne's hometown. He was wounded during the bloody fight and had to remain there to recuperate. During his recuperation in Harrison County, he met and fell in love with pretty, young Mattie Humphrey. Later, he returned, married her and took her to live at his home in Letcher County.

There are many other stories and legends about Bad John. He was a leader in the noted Jones-Wright feud. His job as deputy marshal required tracking down renegades and bringing them back, dead or alive. Tradition has it that John killed more than 22 men, but he claimed it was more like seven, and "every damn one of 'em deserved it."

When the Ku Klux Klan organized in Letcher County in the late 1890s, the Grand Dragon initiated a campaign against lewdness. During darkest nights, the white-robed Klan rode out to horsewhip and terrify supposedly lewd and ungodly women. John, a noted lady's man, decided to put a stop to it. His plan was delayed when he got word that the Klan was planning to ambush and shoot him. He organized eight of his sympathizers, and they proceeded to bushwhack the 20 or so Klan members during one of their late-night forays. The gun battle claimed the life of the Dragon and three other Klansmen. Several others were shot.

The Klan then set up a way to get John and gave Zack Bentley the honor of shooting him. After careful planning, Bentley hid out near a road, which John usually traveled after leaving a certain pretty young woman's cabin. Zack heard two horses clomping down the road, but neither carried the bad man. Another horse approached and this time it had to be Bad John. Zack was all set until he heard a noise behind him.

"Drop that Winchester and turn over so I can see your face," Bad John said. "So you thought you could outwit the old gray fox. I've killed more trash like you than I can remember."

One good part of Bad John was that he would do most any favor for a Rebel veteran. One old veteran asked if he would help the notorious bank robber, Jesse James, escape from Ohio to Tennessee, and John successfully completed that mission. After the precarious but successful journey through Kentucky, Jesse paid Bad John a goodly sum and threw in one of his pistols in appreciation for a job well done. One of Bad John's granddaughters, who lived near Anne and Harry, told them that Jesse James gave the pistol to her grandfather; no one knows how many men had been killed with it.

There are numerous other stories about Bad John's gunfights, troubles with the law, and various other escapades, but his dealings with a future president of the United States reveals John's good side.

Andrew May, a lawyer from Prestonsburg, was elected to Congress in 1932, and remained in the House of Representatives for 14 years. May later related this story to Harry. During World War II, May served as chairman of the vitally important House Committee on Military Affairs. He was called to the White House on numerous occasions to confer with President Franklin Delano Roosevelt. At the end of one meeting, the president asked May if he had ever heard of Bad John Wright, and May replied that he had been personally acquainted with Wright.

The president told May that he had spent a night in Bad

John's cabin. In the early part of the 20th century, the Delano and Roosevelt families purchased a considerable amount of land in Pike and Harlan Counties in Kentucky. Young Franklin, who was attending Harvard Law School, traveled one summer with his uncle, Wallace Delano, to Eastern Kentucky to abstract land titles for their relatives.

On a rainy night, they were riding horses from Pikeville to Harlan. With no inns in that desolate area, they happened to stop at Bad John's place and asked to be taken in. He agreed, but indicated he only had one extra bed in another room, so Franklin would have to sleep on a pallet near the fireplace while Bad John and his wife slept in their bed across the room. After the lights were blown out, it wasn't long until Wallace Delano began snoring in the other room. Assuming that Franklin was asleep, John began taking liberties with his wife. After about ten minutes or so, all was quiet again and Franklin fell asleep.

Early the next morning, John awakened his guests with a big eye-opening slug of moonshine whiskey followed by Mrs. Wright's heaping breakfast. Before they saddled up, John sold them a quart of his prize moonshine to fortify the rest of their arduous trip through the mountains.

After telling the story to Congressman May, FDR, with his infectious smile and twinkling eyes, said, "I'm probably the only man in the world who ever watched Bad John Wright make love."

During Bad John's later days when most of his adversaries were dead, he heard the voices of the preachers, repented of his sins, was saved, and passed on to eternity on January 31, 1931 at age 88. The old feudist went to his grave without suspecting that his cabin at the head of Elkhorn Creek once sheltered a young man who would become president of the United States. At his funeral, the preacher opened the services by saying, "Now, we don't want any trouble here."

The notorious and the renegades made the news and their legends endure. There were other characters in Letcher and surrounding counties who didn't make big news, but progressed from humble origins and limited opportunities to highly successful careers.

John Elwood Day visited the Caudills. He grew up on Cowan Creek and was determined to finish high school. To travel to Whitesburg High School, he had to walk several miles through the mountains in all kinds of weather, but he never missed a day of school. After graduation, John entered the service during World War II. When it was over, he decided to remain in California and used the GI Bill to go to school. One day, a professor called John aside and explained to him that he had considerable ability and potential, but that he couldn't write or speak well. The professor offered to help, and John began private tutoring sessions from this teacher, who apparently knew talent when he saw it in the raw.

John became a vice president of the Bank of America, and told Anne that he owed his success to the man who devoted his time to teaching him how to communicate. The man was S. I. Hayakawa, who later became a longtime US senator from California.

In 1985, Harry published a 16-page article, "They Climbed the Highest Mountain: The Success Story in the Eastern Kentucky Exodus." After the end of the coal boom during World War II, overexpansion of the industry and competition from cheaper oil and gas caused severe depression and unemployment in the area. Many people were confronted with a choice, getting by on welfare or moving out. About three-quarters of a million people moved out of the Appalachian region between 1940 and 1970.

Anne watched the exodus and observed that many of those who moved away were from families who had little opportunity, but after leaving, they attained success and became teachers, doctors, nurses, lawyers, scientists, and business people. After Anne moved to New Albany, Indiana, she saw many names in the phone book that were common in Appalachia.

"These people came here and educated their children and prospered, which is proof enough that the Appalachian people are not different," she said.

In "They Climbed the Highest Mountain," Harry wrote about the exodus as "a mammoth social transition from remote hollows to urban streets." He noted the "psychological trauma, the heartbreak, and the frequent failure as the baffled and frustrated out-migrants settled down to a relief-subsidized slum existence." He cited case after case of a mountain youngster overcoming tremendous odds to become highly successful despite the social and psychological upheaval. Not every family moved out of the mountains. There were many success stories among those who stayed. Perhaps the basic characteristics of the mountaineers—resiliency, tenacity, independence, and resourcefulness—contributed to achievement and success wherever they lived.

Some of those who climbed the highest mountain were from remote Knox County, which claims three governors, two lieutenant governors, six congressmen, and a Supreme Court justice. Johnson County produced a coal miner's daughter who married at age 13. She left her family and mother (who became a grandmother at age 29), but Loretta Lynn did quite well singing the old mountain ballads. Whitley County produced Edward Faulkner, a noted agriculture scientist and Patricia O'Neal, a Hollywood film star.

Juanita Morris Kreps, who was born in a company hospital at Lynch, grew up in the tiny mining community of Clutts, and became a vice president of Duke University. Orell Collins from Hot Spot in Letcher County became CEO of Nalco Chemical Company and president of the American Hospital Supply Company. Gary Powers from Burdine in Letcher County gained fame when he flew a U2 plane over the Soviet Union. Harrison Garret Jr., born on Long Branch in Letcher County, became chief of the Guidance, Control, and Instrumentation Division at NASA's Space Flight Center.

Kenneth Back of Jeremiah on Rockhouse Creek in Letcher County became director of finance and revenue for the District of Columbia, and Delmar Ison went from Kingdom Come Creek in Letcher County to Washington DC, where he became commissioner of the Washington Metropolitan Transit Authority.

Harry cited many others in his article. Thirteen mountain boys received the Congressional Medal of Honor. Harry himself, a young man from Wat Long Hollow in Letcher County, climbed a steep mountain, too.

CHAPTER 16

A Man of Courage, Constant to the End

On November 29, 1990, Harry Caudill, age 68, took his own life. The family had gathered for their traditional Thanksgiving celebration only a few days before. It was obvious to his children—who lived in other parts of the state—that his condition had worsened. On that day, Harry distributed his gun collection to his two sons and son-in-law. He also told family members to take any of his books they wanted from the shelves in his library. His children realized how much his books meant to him, and were surprised and somewhat puzzled, but they reluctantly took a few.

Harry's decision to take his life was not a shock to Anne. His mother's brother and two of her cousins, after very successful careers, had committed suicide when they became unable to function. He had an older lawyer friend who had committed suicide because he was suffering from Parkinson's disease. In discussions with Anne, Harry had spoken of his admiration for those who chose to end their lives when they became helpless and physically dependent.

"He had suffered too much pain for too many years, and realized that his developing Parkinson's disease and other degenerations of his health were so rapidly progressing that he would soon become helpless," she said.

Anne's mother had suffered from Parkinson's for 15 years. Harry had witnessed her rapid physical decline, culminating in complete paralysis during her last days. Although Anne did not suspect that Harry had Parkinson's disease, she suddenly realized it one day when she and Harry took a car to a garage for repair. She followed him in a second car and noticed he kept swerving to the right and then pulling back. Her mother had done the same thing, and it was then that Anne strongly suspected that Harry had the disease.

After Harry's left leg was wounded, he suffered nearly constant physical pain for the next 46 years. The pain in both legs intensified throughout those years, and the early stages of Parkinson's disease and other complications prompted him to resign from teaching at UK. Harry also suffered from acute urinary problems, and then tremors and difficulties with his speech began. Anne said, "His last years at UK were torture."

After returning to Whitesburg, Harry's condition stabilized somewhat. He continued publishing articles and writing a new history of Kentucky. Sitting and reclining provided some relief, but his condition slowly and steadily regressed. While his faculties declined rather rapidly during the three years before he took his life, he never lost the ability to think.

Harry continued taking trips to specialists at the veteran's hospitals in Johnson City, Tennessee, and Louisville, Kentucky. The amount of time he and Anne spent traveling to and from hospitals was considerable, but he endured this and the subsequent pain until the very end. Anne described his condition during his last years:

His walking became more and more difficult, as the effects of Parkinson's added to the pain in his legs. The prostate difficulties were a constant distress, and his ability to speak began to falter. His mind was clear, but too often he would begin a sentence, then be unable to finish saying what he intended. His depression deepened. Sometimes his arms or legs simply became paralyzed, and he would have a spell of shaking with extreme chills. I would massage and work the limbs back to motion again, bring him hot drinks to help warm him, and cover him with blankets.

In spite of the attention of his doctors, the Parkinson's disease began to advance rapidly. He could no longer write legibly, and I wrote his checks, typed his letters for publication, and signed his name to them. Although he continued to dictate a new history of Kentucky, which he believed needed be undertaken, it was never finished.

Before his handwriting deteriorated, and unbeknownst to Anne, Harry had written *Lester's Progress*. The book is a clever little satire about how the fictitious Lester Warrick learned to profit from the relatively new welfare system that had spread to Appalachia.

Anne and Harry were not opposed to welfare administered efficiently, justly, and where urgently needed. They were opposed to handouts, corruption, and political gain in the name of helping needy people.

One can imagine Harry's delight in concocting that spoof. Ever the storyteller and one who enjoyed the amusing and the absurd, Harry never lost the inclination or capacity to have a good laugh, and perhaps these foolish aspects of life provided a diversion from harsh and insensible reality and allowed him to continue working until the end.

Harry had spent a lifetime addressing the hard issues of his time and place. He had challenged and fought the powerful political forces and the wealthy corporations for decades. Although writing satire is imaginative and amusing, it is often a combination of the comic and tragic. Harry knew the Lester Warricks of his world. He understood that fighting the system was an ongoing battle. Discovering oil on your property or winning the lottery didn't necessarily ensure a happy life.

Harry's life could not be considered tragic in any respect. His love of life was a love for his people, his land, his children—and Anne. Love sustained him, tempered with the pure joy of the foolish and the absurd, and with the recognition of the imperfections of humankind, striving, perhaps feebly, to make the world a bit better place.

When Harry taught at UK, he was asked if he felt frustrated, bitter, or angry at the lack of progress in the causes for which he had fought. In *The Appalachian Interviews*, he said, "I'm philosophical. I've always thought that the world ultimately was something to be chuckled at. As Shakespeare put it, 'All the world's a stage, and all the men and women merely players.' We must never stop regarding the world as—in part—tragedy, but also comedy. When you see people stumbling from one catastrophic situation to another, you can lament it and regret it, but also it has comic undertones, something to laugh at; otherwise you go nuts."

The *Mountain Eagle* published some of Harry's articles about his war experiences, but his first major article, "How an Election was Bought and Sold," was published in *Harper's Magazine* in

1960. Over the next 30 years, Harry published more than 130 articles, fighting worthy fights to the very end. His last article was published in the *Mountain Eagle* two days before his death. In fact, his last two articles were a plea for corporate assistance in financing an adequate public library in Whitesburg. The November 21, 1990, article listed the 62 corporations that owned millions of shares in nine major corporations, and included Bethlehem Steel, Duke Power, and US Steel, among others.

A week later, his last article listed 38 corporations that sell minerals from the 3,814,193 acres they owned in Appalachia. Harry asked, "And what of Armand Hammer, founder and chief official of Occidental Petroleum, whose Island Creek Coal Company has sunk $36,000,000 of Romanian money into a colossal mining network in Buchanan County, Virginia? Should his company be allowed to spread devastation across the Virginia landscape and social chaos among its people in order to provide coal for the Balkans?" He cited other examples of the accumulation of massive wealth in the form of minerals; the mountains had lined the pockets of the great industrial centers and their banks.

He asked, "Do our county officials have the courage to ask those money-making giants to contribute funds to build Letcher County a first-rate public library?"

An editorial in the *Mountain Eagle* accompanied Harry's last article. It pointed out that he addressed the fact that individuals and corporations that owned most of Appalachia's wealth lived in the great northern cities. Libraries and museums in those cities thrived on contributions from the miners who dug and loaded coal after a night's rest in the coal camp house, built and provided by the benevolence of the company with the rent deducted from the miner's wages. A miner would never have the time, or desire to read a book, and many didn't know how, anyway.

With no donations from outside corporations and only one donation—$1,000 from a Kentucky-owned company—the new Harry M. Caudill Library was dedicated four years after his death.

Who was this man of courage? What was his temperament and disposition? His wife of more than four decades said, "For all who knew him intimately, he was ever a major presence in our lives. He was interesting! He was vocal. He was amusing. He was kind and supportive. His interests were always about other people, events, and the natural world. He revealed dismay at the exploitation of the land and his people. His views were expansive, never centered on himself or his problems."

Most families in the mountains possessed little of the world's material wealth. The family was their treasure to honor, support, and protect. Their attitude was, "You got a fight on your hands if you disrespect or harm any of my kin." The young learned early on to honor and obey, and as they grew, the ties with family strengthened. When a youngster left home, or a family was forced to move away in order to survive, there was always the yearning to go back home again. It just didn't feel right living anywhere but in the mountains.

Harry left home, went away to school, and then to the war where he was wounded. Disabled, he returned to UK and met Anne. They married and he took her back to his home, where his mother and father lived. Harry saw or talked to his father every day; Cro made the law office his headquarters. They visited in each other's homes once or twice a week, often staying the night. When Cro Carr Caudill died in 1957, Harry was devastated and became depressed. His close relationship with his father indicated something about his worthy character. He never wavered in his respect and loyalty to his father and best friend.

Anne described Harry as "kind, fair, and friendly," with his clients, colleagues, and friends. However, his adversaries in the courtroom and those he believed were exploiting the land and its people learned that he could be scathing and sarcastic at opportune times, and put an adversary in his proper place.

During his last year or so, Harry's struggle with enduring pain and the deterioration of his speech, maneuverability, and other faculties increased his irritability. Diana remarked that he would get upset with the nightly news. Perhaps it wasn't the preponderance of bad news, but the realization of his limitations to fight back. Fading away as an old soldier was unacceptable to him.

Harry was once asked if there was anything in his life that he would have changed. He replied, "Well, I might have married my wife a little earlier, been a little better to her."

Anne immediately responded, "No you wouldn't have, because I was having a good time. I liked it the way it was."

They had a good time together; the marriage was a true partnership. During a 1981 interview at UK library, Stephen Fisher asked Harry to talk about how he met his wife. "I met her over here at the library and proposed to her."

Fisher asked, "That very same day?"

"Not quite, about ten days after that," Harry said. "She has been indispensable and still is."

Anne and Harry agreed on everything—almost. "Through the years, he constantly expressed his love for me, and was generous as he was able to provide anything I needed or wanted," she said. "He hired whatever help we needed. He was always appreciative of me and never put me down. Occasionally, we disagreed sharply, but he always came to me and we made up. A disagreement never lasted more than an hour or so. We abided by the rule of never going to bed upset."

Perhaps Harry gave the impression of being stoic and reserved. Anne said, "My instantaneous vision of Harry when he comes to mind is his laughter and amused smile." This memory tells the true story, one of deep and abiding love. Through all the trials and tribulations, Anne and Harry shared the lighter side of life, the humorous, and the ridiculous. The dominant memory of Harry's laughter and sense of humor is a healing one, a characteristic that helps lighten any load.

"I never remember a day when Harry didn't kiss me and tell me he loved me," Anne said.

* * *

On November 29, 1990, Anne had an errand to run. She left Harry in his easy chair with his writing tablet. When she returned, she found him in the yard lying on his back. He had shot himself in the temple. He was unconscious, but still alive. She rushed into the house to make the call for help, and noticed a letter Harry had placed conspicuously on a chair for her. "It was a beautiful letter telling of his love and trust for me during our life together."

Anne was all alone with nothing but the letter in her hand. It seemed that she waited for an eternity for the ambulance, and she was not permitted to leave the premises until the sheriff came to process the scene. Word began to spread. The wife of Harry's former law partner heard and immediately went to be with

Anne. When the sheriff finally arrived, she handed him Harry's note. After his brief inspection of the scene, Anne rushed to the hospital.

When she arrived, the emergency room doctor informed her that they had arranged for a helicopter to take Harry to a hospital in Lexington for surgery. Her response was immediate. She understood that life had become unbearable for him. She had the courage to accept and honor Harry's final decision. Like so many times during their long, loving life together, a difficult decision was based upon two courageous minds merging into one.

The emergency room doctor refused to take Harry off life support even though Harry had a living will stating he did not want be kept alive with support. After Anne insisted that he be removed from life support, the doctor withdrew from the case. The hospital administrator brought in another doctor who supported her decision.

Anne's minister, Greg Wingo; the family doctor, Carl Pigman; and other friends hurried to the hospital to be with her. In such emotional and traumatic circumstances, one might have misgivings about deciding life or death for someone else. Her minister said, "Anne, you have the right to make the decision. I think you made the right one." Harry died before Anne's children could reach her, and they, too, supported her decision.

Before all else, Anne cared for their children and for Harry's needs. She understood that Harry needed her help with his health problems, but even more he needed her unyielding support for all the causes to which he devoted his life—fairness, justice, education, and preservation of the land. He had wandered over the mountains, pondering the ills of his people and the land, and struggled to right the wrongs until the end. His wife had the courage to release her husband's soul to lasting peace.

The throngs came to the Cumberlands once again. When Gordon Ebersole heard, he immediately left Washington to be with Anne. The visits from Gordon and her many other friends comforted Anne and meant a great deal to her.

"When Harry was here, I was never lonely. He wouldn't let me be," she said.

*   *   *

The funeral was held on Sunday, December 2 at First Baptist, Whitesburg's largest church. The approximately 350 attendees included family members, friends, and government and university officials from Kentucky, Washington, and elsewhere. Reverend Greg Wingo of the United Methodist Church spoke, and Reverend Tom Stokes of First Baptist offered a prayer.

Harry's son James read one of his father's favorite passages from Shakespeare's *As You Like It:*

> All the world's a stage,
> And all the men and women merely players.
> They have their exits and entrances
> And one man in his time plays many parts . . .

James said that his father, "died with his boots on, such as they were . . . those terrible, ugly shoes that carried him through many good years, and some bad ones, but mostly good, and so he played his part."

Wendell Berry gave the eulogy. He said:

To know Harry only as an advocate would be to know him less by half. One did not have to be around him long to discover that his argument in defense of his region grew out of a deep knowledge of it and love for it, and out of a lifelong fascination with its history and its stories. He was a marvelous storyteller, a master of the subtle art of lawyerly overstatement. Strangers impressed by the gravity of Harry's argument were undoubtedly surprised by his utter glee in the storytelling that relieved the argument, and by the delighted laughter that floated the stories along. There was the story of the man who, to his too-late regret, took his infallible retriever along when he went to dynamite a fishing hole. There was the aphorism—"The law is the only net ever devised to hold the little fish in and let the big fish out"—which Harry made up himself for use in a certain court trial, but which he attributed to Mark Twain, much to the consternation of the presiding judge. When Harry got started, there was nothing to do but listen, and hope he would not stop. And he would oblige by not stopping, until forced to do so by circumstances beyond his control.

Twenty-five years earlier, Wendell Berry had written a poem for Harry, whom he had recently met. Wendell ended the eulogy for Harry with the poem.

The Sycamore for Harry Caudill

In the place that is my place, whose earth
I am shaped in and must bear, there is an old tree growing,

A great sycamore that is a wonderful healer of itself.
Fences have been tied to it, nails driven into it,
Hacks and whittles cut into it, the lightning has burned it.
There is no year it has flourished in,
That has not harmed it. There is a hollow in it
That is its death, though its living brims whitely
At the lip of the darkness and flows outward.
Over all its scars has come the seamless white
Of the bark. It bears the gnarls of its history
Healed over. It has risen to a strange perfection
In the warp and bending of its long growth.
It has gathered all accidents into its purpose.
It has become the intention and radiance of its dark fate.
It is a fact, sublime, mystical, unassailable.
In all the country, there is no other like it.
I recognize in it a principle, an indwelling
The same as itself, and greater than I would be ruled by.
I see that it stands in its place, and feeds upon it,
And is fed upon, and is native, and maker.

Wendell concluded:

Now, in the minds of all of us who loved and admired him, Harry Caudill begins his emergence out of mortal difficulty and suffering into his greatness, and into his absence. His absence is large and demanding; for us, it is a trial. My fellow citizens, if we are suitably to honor this man, it is not enough merely to recognize what a happy gift his life was to us and to this place; it is not enough merely to be grateful. We must complete his work and his hope.

We must redeem our land and with it ourselves. We must become better than we are.

*   *   *

The burial took place two days later in the Battle Grove Cemetery at Cynthiana, Kentucky. Anne and Harry had discussed this matter a number of times.

He didn't want to be buried up there on that lonesome hillside [on Pine Mountain], which had been a community and family burial ground way up above Cowan Creek. All those people were buried up there, beginning with his grandfather, Doc Franklin Blair. We'd been at that graveyard on the mountain many times, and he said that someday it would be overgrown and forgotten. He had talked about being buried in a military cemetery, but decided on Battle Grove Cemetery in Cynthiana. We had already bought lots near where my parents are buried. His grandfather, Henry R. S. Caudill, serving under General John Hunt Morgan, had taken part in the battle of Cynthiana. The hundreds of soldiers killed at the battle were the first to be buried in that cemetery. When we visited my parents, Harry liked to go there, wander around and look at the tombstones of the soldiers who had paid the supreme price. It is a peaceful place now up on that hill with trees all around.

A carving of a mountain and a pine tree are engraved on one side of Harry's tombstone. He rests in peace in the shadow of those two symbols of the land he so loved. At James's suggestion, there is inscribed a slightly modified line from *Macbeth*: "After life's fitful fever, they sleep well." Anne's name is also engraved on the stone, lacking only the final date.

News reports of Harry Caudill's death spread across the land. It made the newspapers throughout the United States. The *Troublesome Creek Times* in Hindman, Kentucky, and the *East Kentucky Sun* in Inez reported his death, as did New York's *Wall Street Journal,* the *New York Times,* the *Washington Post,* and the *Los Angeles Times.* The headline in the metro section of the *Cincinnati Post* read "Author Inspired President" and the subheading was "Caudill instilled hope despite Appalachian despair." Most of the announcements included a photograph and an account of the major aspects of Harry's life, work, and contributions. Several of the articles quoted a passage from *Night Comes to the Cumberlands* that defined his lifelong commitment to correct the wrongs inflicted on his people and the mindless devastation of their land: "Coal always cursed the land in which it lies. When men begin to wrest it from the earth it leaves a legacy of foul streams, hideous slag heaps, and polluted air. It peoples this transformed land with blind and crippled men, and with widows and orphans. It is an extractive industry, which takes all away and restores nothing. It mars but never beautifies. It corrupts but never purifies."

During those dark and dreary December days in the Cumberlands after Harry's death, calls, cards, and letters flooded the Caudill home, and Anne spent weeks responding and thanking her dear friends. Personal notes, letters to editors, essays, and articles remembering and honoring Harry appeared in the media all over the country.

"I guess I never knew anyone who cared more about people than Harry Caudill," wrote Charles Kuralt of CBS News.

John Stephenson, president of Berea College, who convinced Harry to teach at UK, wrote, "A monument has fallen."

Stuart Sprague described Harry as "a giant . . . and if you read *Night* for the fifth, sixth, and seventh time, his writing power is just incredible."

Mary Bingham wrote, "Harry was a wonderful man, passionate, gentle, and full of fervor you seldom see these days."

Stewart Udall, who wrote the foreword to *Night*, said, "Harry reached the whole country."

Harry was remembered by others as "a 20th-century Jeremiah," and as a "David among corporate Goliaths. His weapon was his pen." Another said, "I doubt I'll ever have the privilege of meeting an Old Testament prophet, at least not in this lifetime, but I can tell my grandchildren I met the next-best thing."

Other writers compared *Night* to Stowe's *Uncle Tom's Cabin*, Steinbeck's *The Grapes of Wrath*, Rachel Carson's *Silent Spring*, and Michael Harrington's *The Other America*.

On the Sunday of the funeral, the minister of a church in Huntington, West Virginia, lit a candle to light the way in tribute to and symbolic of Harry lighting the nation's conscience.

William Keesler of the *Courier-Journal* wrote, "Harry Caudill cast a spell on me, and wouldn't let go."

"His work and courage putting his thoughts into print gave me courage to start this newspaper," wrote Ron Daley in the *Troublesome Creek Times* in Hindman.

One admirer claimed, "It is not an exaggeration to say that Harry Caudill's classic book changed my life."

Several former students wrote about the impact Harry had on their lives. One wrote, "I'm not famous and you don't know me from Adam, but I'm a great admirer of your late husband.

As a former student of his, I have such fond memories of being in his Appalachian studies class. Mr. Caudill was magic in his classroom and I hung on his every word and fell for the lore of his land hook, line, and sinker. Mr. Caudill was a kind man and one of the few professors who tried to provide an encouraging classroom atmosphere. I have such respect for your husband, and a tender place in my heart."

A friend from Missouri wrote, "In my mind, I've written you a hundred letters since your terrible tragedy, but can't seem to put it on paper. I can't express to anyone how much I respected Harry as a man, friend, soldier, and warm caring human being. I was in awe of him for all he was able to do in changing some of the miseries of the human condition around him. He was one of those rare individuals who made a difference for the better in this imperfect world."

An acquaintance and former Letcher County native living in Michigan wrote, "You probably don't remember me, but I remember you and Harry. I loved him like a brother. I think he was the greatest man those mountains ever had. I think he would have made a wonderful president for this country. I have read all his books. I spend half my time reading, and I have never read anything to compare to *Night Come to the Cumberlands*. I think it is there for all the ages, unless one of your sons can carry the torch for their dad . . ."

Anne received boxes of letters from people she didn't know or remember, and from people from all over who had met the Caudills when they went to the Cumberlands to take the grand tour, and then spent a night or several nights at the green house on the hill.

On December 7 1990, Ben A. Franklin of the *New York*

Times wrote, "Harry's lasting legacy to journalists is astonishing, and will be, I hope, some comfort to you and the family and him. He was that very combination of a visionary and a cynic, an inspirational persona and, to us inky wretches, an empathetic self-doubter—a heroic failed perfectionist. Reporters loved Harry in a way I recently (and accidentally) found described in E. M. Forster's *A Passage to India.*"

Franklin wrote that Forster believed in an aristocracy—not one of power, rank, and influence—but an aristocracy that was sensitive, considerate, and represented the true human tradition, a victory over cruelty and chaos. He closed his letter by saying, "Harry was—and you are—that aristocrat to the end, and we who were so salubriously influenced by you both salute you."

David McCullough wrote on December 9, 1990:

Harry Caudill was one of the finest men I've ever known. I've traveled a lot of the country, because of my work, and I have spent time with a number of exceptional and accomplished people, but Harry had no match.

If ever there was someone who could influence others, inspire, and encourage in a greathearted way, it was Harry. I know he influenced me to my great benefit—he still does—and I will always be grateful, always proud, he was my friend.

He was not just a good man, but an American of a different kind, who comes along once in a while. Talking with him, I used to get the feeling that I was in direct contact with something very much like Abraham Lincoln or Mark Twain. I would go on about this—we all could— and soon, I suspect, he would be laughing, too.

Some people make you feel better just by being with them. You and Harry both do.

Rosalee and I feel a terrible loss, but we count ourselves blessed that we knew Harry, that our time here on earth and his happened to coincide, that my work and his work made our paths cross, and that our older children had the chance to know him and will remember him.

Legislatures and other governmental agencies passed resolutions honoring Harry Caudill, and on December 7, 1990, the city council in Los Angeles adjourned to pay tribute to him.

Tom Gish and Harry went to school together and both returned to Whitesburg to resume their careers. They were great friends and Gish probably knew Harry better than anyone other than his family. Gish published the *Mountain Eagle,* and *Newsweek* honored him in 1986 as one of the "100 New American Heroes."

Of course, there was speculation about why Harry took his life. Gish explained that some thought he was despondent, because, despite all his efforts, so little progress and change had come to the Cumberlands. In a lengthy tribute to Harry after his death, Gish wrote, "About two months before Harry Caudill died, he suggested that we spend a day or two taking a joint look at some of the well-known creeks and hollows of Eastern Kentucky. Caudill said he had been driving around a lot by himself and was excited by all the changes he saw taking place. There's a new home up just about any hollow, a lot of them brick. Things are a lot neater, too. They're beginning to do something about garbage. You just don't see it along the roadside like you did a few years ago."

Loyal Jones of the Appalachian Center of Berea College remembered Harry's wit, wisdom, and charm:

I remember being in the Office of Economic Development in Washington once when he came in and started to tell about the wondrous passenger pigeons now extinct, that were once so plentiful in Eastern Kentucky. When he got into full cry, his eloquent but mournful voice (as someone called it) could be heard throughout the place, and soon doorways were filled with the heads of secretaries and poverty experts, and they were drawn irresistibly in a tight circle around him. He related several stories to the amazement, puzzlement, and delight of these earnest poverty workers before going off to the White House to present President Johnson with a Kentucky rifle.

In *Kentucky Living,* Al Smith, a noted journalist, paid tribute to Harry and Anne:

His career as a public scold began as a GI law student at the University of Kentucky, when the school planned to name an engineering facility for a Swedish industrialist who had business ties with Nazi Germany. "Harry had a fit," Anne remembers and he greatly provoked the president, who told the papers that Harry was "emotionally unstable."

But it was Anne Frye, from Cynthiana, who had the fit when young Harry Caudill took his bride-to-be on her first trip to Eastern Kentucky. One night she saw a burning gob [a pile of mine refuse] sending gassy flames to redden the skyline, a scene from hell. Her revulsion opened his eyes;

later in marriage they would share perceptions that formed his vision of the whole region in decline—poor schools, sorry roads, hungry children, and jobless miners violently lashing out at those indifferent to their plight. Everywhere you looked, human wreckage was staring you in the face.

* * *

After the funeral, Anne was overwhelmed with the numerous details involved in making the sorrowful and dramatic change to her life. She and Harry had previously decided to sell their home and move closer to their children. Diana lived in New Albany, Indiana, across the river from Louisville, where James lived. Harry Frye lived in Lexington, 75 miles from Louisville. Considering their ages and Harry's condition, continuing care and upkeep of their home and grounds would have become a considerable burden to Anne. Although Harry did not discuss his primary reason for wanting to sell their home, she understood he did not want to leave her living alone in the country with the responsibility of managing the property.

A young couple had made an offer on their property, contingent upon financing. The day before Harry died, the young man called. The green house on the hill had sold, necessitating the enormous task of packing or discarding 44 years of accumulated furniture and accessories, 3,500 books, file drawers full of papers, and Harry's personal belongings.

The family began by cleaning out the closets and deciding what to do with the books on the shelves. Diana started with Harry's closet, intending to save any of his clothes that could be used by others. There were certainly enough men around who could use a good coat. When Diana reached down for Harry's shoes, she had mixed feelings. The family had spent years trying to find shoes to help him walk. The veteran's hospital doctors tried, but with little success. Finally, a shoemaker in Vincennes, Indiana, had used his skill to make a shoe that made walking much better for her dad.

When Diana held the shoes, her reaction was to toss them. She remembered how her dad had cut, scraped, and adjusted them all those years. And then she remembered how they had helped him walk—to his office, his classes, and through the woods. He was happiest amongst the trees, and that's where he loved to be. The woods seemed to free him from his cares and renew his strength. She thought of walking in the woods and his leading the way as she, her brothers, and mother followed. Leaning on his walking stick, he would pause, not in pain, but because he had a story to tell. Those were the best times, but now he was gone. She could hear his voice, forceful and yet gentle and reassuring. She knew he would want her to believe that when night comes, it is followed by a bright new day.

Anne sat at their desk, surrounded by all his books, which lined the walls of their combination library-office-bedroom. It was a rather unusual arrangement. Anne and Harry slept together surrounded by their books, which served as protection and insulation from the elements of ignorance, greed, and injustice.

The Caudills had added this room soon after Harry Frye was born and after *Night* came out. It was a large room, 25 by 30 feet, and built from walnut logs Harry had previously purchased, milled, and stored in his father's barn. The room had a high ceiling, paneled in walnut, with four alternating amber and turquoise stained glass windows. A large bathroom and two large walk-in closets were attached. One closet served as Harry Frye's bedroom when he was very young and was later used as storage for Anne and Harry's files and papers. When the guests who came for dinner filled the dining and living rooms, card tables were set up in this haven-type room. Their furniture included a large walnut Victorian bed, which had belonged to Harry's parents, a matching dresser, a large desk, Harry's favorite lounge chair, and other comfortable chairs and tables. The room was cozy, spacious, and practical, with a magnificent view of Pine Mountain through the sliding picture windows across one whole side. It was a room—a shrine and sanctuary—for rest, conversation, laughter, contemplation, study, and work, and a room to display all the books that lined the walls.

"Parting with Harry's books was the hardest thing I had to do," Anne said. His favorite activities were being home with his family, walking in the woods, and sitting in his study with his books. When a visitor had a question, Harry often selected one of his books, turned to a specific page, read a passage, and then added his own comments and interpretation. He read to his children and he read to Anne in the car, on the porch, and in the kitchen.

"I see him in the kitchen in his rocking chair," Anne said. "I'm preparing dinner and he's reading to me. He read to me because he loved and respected me. I never felt alone when he was with me."

Harry had planned for the days when Anne would be alone. He had decided they should give his books to Northern Kentucky University. UK, Eastern Kentucky University, and Berea College already had collections of books on Appalachia. NKU was a relatively new university, and shortly before Harry died, they honored him. He spent the day talking to classes, and giving radio and TV interviews. That night they had dinner with the president and other officials before the reception and ceremony attended by an audience of 300.

When Harry died, it took Anne months to get her life back in order. There was so much to do. She realized, however, that she had to make a move and, no matter where, carry on Harry's legacy. It took courage to call NKU to come get the books. They sent a large van full of empty boxes and people to pack and load approximately 2,500 books. Anne distributed most of the other 1,000 books to her children and the Letcher County Library.

"When they took his books away, I think it was the loneliest day I ever spent," she said.

*   *   *

After the funeral, her children went back to their homes and work. Her daughter-in-law Rosemary stayed with her and helped for several days. Anne responded to each of the letters she received, and they wrote for days on end. Then her dear friend Hazel Quillen came for about ten nights to help and to keep her company during those long, cold winter nights.

Then Anne was all alone again, in the quiet. She remembered that the crazy green house was never quiet, but the silence now was mystifying, paralyzing. With no one to talk to, her thoughts would not leave Harry. She recalled those days:

> When he was reading or writing, strangely, it was as if he were talking to me, doing it for me. It was as if we thought the same. His work was my work, and mine his. We worked together, and if he were here, he would want to help me. I'd say, 'No, Harry, you write; I want to read it.'

He knew I did, but sometimes, he surprised me with what he wrote or what he thought, but I think he wanted to run it by me, hoping it would please me. He depended on me and had confidence in me, and I always wanted him to be free to do what was so important to him.

Anne remembers thinking:

There's so much to do I can't concentrate, can't think with all these papers and lists on my desk. There are all of his things and my things to sort out. Which do I keep? I can't throw away his walking stick or the old crumpled hat he wore. When I pick something of his up, I just hold it, and don't know what to do. It's so quiet here. He liked listening to music. He never liked the television, considered most of it a waste. I need a sound, a voice, other than the cold wind blowing through the trees. The TV . . . that's David McCullough's voice! He's narrating a series on the Civil War. Harry and I watched it together before. What a clear and commanding voice he has, warm and soothing. Oh, my, I hear David and Harry in the other room. What discussions they had and the joy!

My loss will never be replaced, but I have other treasures stored, the many memories of those grand times. It will take years for me to sort through them all, and not one will I ever throw away. There were those trying times, but Harry never seemed to let them bother him. The disappointments only made him stronger. I learned that from him; I'll do the same as best I can.

The comfort of McCullough's voice prompted Anne to write to him: "Dear David: You'll never know what you did for me. I heard the voice of a friend when I was lonely. You accompanied me as I worked. It was such a help to me."

There was so much to do, but Anne was determined to sort out things, pack up her memories, and take them with her. She asked Diana and James to look for a house for her, "something woodsy."

On May 1, 1991, five months after Harry's death, Anne moved to New Albany, Indiana. It was spring. The azaleas and the pink tulips were in bloom, the birds were singing in the trees, and a clear bright sun shone down on Anne's new home. Her big window in the back looked down into a wooded hillside, much like the beloved hollows back in the mountains of Kentucky.

CHAPTER 17

The Great Joy

How many letters did Anne write in her lifetime? How many trees cover the Appalachians? A major part of the narrative of Anne's life is recorded in her letters, which tell a part of her story. Seldom did a day go by that she did not write at least one letter. Writing letters never ceased. "I still enjoy the process of correspondence with snail mail," Anne said.

In 1945, when Anne moved to New Jersey to work for Standard Oil, she wrote volumes of letters to her family and Harry, her fiancé. A year later when she moved back to Kentucky, she shipped a box of his letters and *The Rubaiyat*, Harry's first gift to her. The box never arrived, a most disappointing loss. She wrote letters associated with her work as home demonstration agent.

Anne was a part-time secretary to Harry for 34 years, and he frequently instructed her to write to this client or that company or to those who inquired about Appalachia. She would write and type the letter, and, in most cases, he would sign it, and in the mail it went. In 1958, with Diana in kindergarten and James in grade school, Anne enrolled in shorthand at the high school. The boss then dictated letters and his other writings to his faithful employee; she was one the few in any office who worked without pay.

She wrote long personal letters to family, friends, and her children (after they left the cozy nest), and to her houseguests from places far and wide. With her extremely busy schedule, particularly after *Night* was published, she found or made the time to correspond with those she loved. The tone of her personal letters expressed her thoughts and feelings authentically from the heart.

When *Night* and Harry's other books came out, the volume of her letters increased many fold. For decades, Anne continued corresponding with several of the numerous guests from the many places who visited the Caudill home. Throughout her life, she received letters and requests from individuals about Harry's books and work.

The Anne and Harry Caudill papers in the archives at UK contain copies of most of their correspondence before 1991, except those dealing with his legal practice.[23] Anne typed these letters on her trusty 1941 Royal typewriter, until modernizing with an IBM Selectric in 1972.

In 2005, writer Rudy Abramson began a biography of Harry. Due to Abramson's untimely death, the biography was not completed. He interviewed Anne extensively and sent many questions for her response. In one letter back to Abramson, Anne (80 at the time) wrote, "I beg your kindness in overlooking my too many typos. My hand grows ever more stiff, painful, and unresponsive. Trying to make all the corrections is just too much trouble. This has been far too long delayed, and I want to get it to you now. Sixty-five years at the typewriter has exacted a

---

23. Most of her letters received and sent since 1991 are filed in the boxes and cabinets in her home.

penalty." In another letter to a friend, Anne apologized for any mistakes caused by "my arthritic hands not functioning very well on my arthritic typewriter."

She tried modernizing again in 2005, but it didn't work out. Her children insisted she throw the ancient typewriter in the garbage and update to modern technology. James placed a sleek, up-to-date personal computer on Anne's desk. She knew precisely how a typewriter performed, but her bright new computer was full of surprises, producing strange results and messages she didn't understand, want, or need:

> I attributed my many errors to my typewriter, but, actually, it was my hands and I thought, well, I need to replace this typewriter and I'll just get a computer. James helped me get one and brought it here, and I worked with that thing for about a year and a half, and found that it absolutely dried up all my creative juices. I was so involved in how it worked that I would get distracted, and finally one day, I got so aggravated, I just pulled the plug out of the wall and I pushed the whole thing to the back of my big desk and I said, "Sit there." And it sat there for some months and then James was here one day, and I said, "Take this thing off my desk and put it in the trunk of the car. I'm taking it to the Salvation Army, printer and all."
>
> And I took it down there and said, "This works fine; I don't want it." I never have gotten another one and people keep saying, "Oh, you're missing so much, so much information." And my reply is, "I've already got more information than I can use and if there's something especially needed, I call one of my children and say look it up."

Anne's personal letters were seldom less than two or more single-spaced pages. She covered pertinent news from home, and often injected amusing and humorous observations. She commented about the books she read, the speeches she heard, and offered views and opinions, political and otherwise. She frequently quoted other writers and slipped in an occasional story to emphasize a point. Underlying the content of almost all her personal letters was the positive philosophical and spiritual dimension of her life. Without fail, she always expressed her appreciation and gratitude for a good life, sustained and enhanced by her cherished friends.

How many friends did Anne have? How many leaves were on the trees outside her window? When their many guests from all parts of the world settled in for a night at the Caudill home, numerous enduring friendships ensued. Anne felt fortunate to have had the distinct opportunity to develop friendships with authors, journalists, government officials, scholars, Appalachian volunteers, and others. She also continued corresponding with some of her friends in the Cumberlands, the "common" folk, who meant so much to her and who revealed the value of living the simple life.

The following are examples extracted from her letters.

Harry went to school in Whitesburg with William Newton Cornett, or "Sir Isaac" as Harry always called him. As did Harry, Sir Isaac fought in Europe during World War II. He was a ball-turret gunner on a B-52, flew 51 missions, and had several narrow escapes. After the war, he and Harry often met, and talked about their experiences.

Sir Isaac had been a friend of Anne's for more than 60 years. They corresponded and he visited Anne once or twice each year. In a letter to Sir Isaac on November 10, 2011, Anne wrote about an article that paid tribute to Harry, as "a modern day Jeremiah," and she sent an article on the Ku Klux Klan activity in Letcher County in days gone by. She closed the letter by writing: "We have had a beautiful autumn. My woodland has been glorious for two weeks ending with the brilliant orange of the two rain trees at my back deck. Alas! Big winds yesterday and today have stripped most of the leaves, but the weather is still bright blue and only slightly chilly. Take care, keep on having a good time, and hurry back here."[24]

Anne wrote to Tanya and Wendell Berry shortly before Harry's death:

> The arrival of your *What are People For* and *Great Possessions* so soon after your departure has served to assuage in great measure my sense of loss and disappointment that your brief visit allowed so little time for real conversation. *Great Possessions* I look forward to savoring presently. So much we need to learn from a study of the ways of the Amish and their understanding.
>
> But your conversations set down and put before me have been joy in the late evenings on the porch amongst the night sounds, or early in the mornings. Like Martha, I become cumbered with much serving. Your essays have afforded the opportunity to be like Mary, who "sat at his feet and hath chosen the good part which shall not be taken away from her." You have communicated, and I have replied, though you may not have heard.

---

24. They will visit again, but maybe not this year. Sir Issac, age 90, is going back to see Germany. It's been more than 65 years since he saw it from the air.

Your picture of Mr. Henry Besuden riding across his pastures in the morning freshness brought to me another picture I cherish in my mind of my mother's father whom I never knew. One time my little Aunt Anne, who left us at 96 still loving the land, told me of how he used to ride over his farm early, and always carried a short-handled hoe on his saddle. Whenever he saw a thistle, he got down and chopped it out, she said. He surely was mindful of the scriptural injunction that the Lord God took man and put him in the Garden of Eden to dress it and to keep it. I know he was mindful because the farm in after years still bore the imprint of his keeping when the family sold it nearly a hundred years after he first began to work it.

Hyde Bailey stands in my mind as an ideal, not only for his great work, but his understanding of the Holiness of the Earth, and his unflagging interest in it. I have always cherished the story that he celebrated his 92nd birthday on the headwaters of the Amazon where he had journeyed to investigate the report of a type of palm tree previously thought to be extinct. Can my own delight in God's good earth survive so long intact?

Your comments on Harry and his work are a beautiful tribute to him and to the idea of a man and his idea of his Place on Earth. I remember vividly the meeting in the Knott County Courthouse, and in seeing you, Wendell, leaning against the wall at the back as we listened enthralled to another Patrick Henry. That all led to a tremendously active and effective life for Harry, but one which has exhausted him, and along with his war wound, left him to suffer much pain and frustration because he cannot continue.

Tanya, did you rescue the peas? My neighbor brought me a great mess yesterday. Our garden did not get turned early enough—rain, rain, and more rain.

Please come here when you can find opportunity to get about. Beyond our trips to the medicine men, we will come to you.

Much love,

"Wife"

Anne signed "Wife" in reference to the article, "What are People For," which Wendell had published in *Harper's*. In the article, he said his wife typed his manuscript and offered advice, whereupon feminists sent letters to the editor. Wendell then explained at length that he and Tonya had a cottage industry and a shared effort. Anne considered her partnership with Harry the same, and in this context, the term "wife" was a badge of honor.

After reading his book, *Lost Mountain*, Anne wrote to Dr. Erik Reece of the UK English Department:

Dear Erik,

It seems I cannot address you as Dr. Reece, for I have hiked every step you told, stopped at every lovely secret place, loved every plant along the little creeks and branches, heard every bird song, all in your company. At least in my mind I have accompanied you, as I accompanied Harry and so many others deep into the mountain forest. All through the years, it was our joy to be constantly in the woods. For we had only to cross our pasture and go up through the trees we'd replanted, then go on up and to the next hollow to be with the great oaks, hemlocks, and all the rest. All this for any day's walk, and Harry spent so much time alone in the woods. But it was also with our children, sometimes with friends and their children, often stopping to sit on a ledge or an old log to listen to Harry tell stories or talk about the forest and its history. We spent many a weekend exploring those magical places.

Merrill Keller, an aeronautical engineer living in Florida was, Anne said, "another of my friends who has blessed my days on earth. He's also something of a Renaissance man, a great reader, writer, poet, and artist. He reveres Leonardo da Vinci and has made a lifelong study of his genius."[25]

Keller had read most of Harry's works and visited the Caudills shortly before Harry died. After that visit, he wrote the following to Anne: "All human beings are one and the same. From the most civilized to the most savage, from saint to dire sinner, we all share a common identity—MANKIND. Each of us are part of the continuity of life from one billion years, survivors of unimaginable challenges, heir to incomprehensible wonders, oblivious to the theme or scope of our destiny. I have great faith, my friends, that we will span the star-strewn reaches of space, litter the universe with our empty shells and find our splendid destiny together—You and I."

Anne continued corresponding with Merrill and they visited a few times. They often exchanged thick packets of poems, articles, quotations, and sketches.

In November 2009, Anne wrote to Merrill, "The words from

---

25. Anne owns a large framed rendition of the head of one of the angels in da Vinci's "Angels of the Rocks," done by Merrill.

your mind and pen always stir my thoughts and imagination. I marvel at your many talents. Poetry is surely not the least of the accomplishments, for you are truly a Renaissance man. And to say that, is to say you have led a rich life. Never since first reading John Keats's 'Adonais,' have I known such tribute to a friend whose soul . . . 'like a star, Beacons from the abode where the Eternal are." Fortunately, Merrill, to share such friendship is an understanding born of the shared knowledge of spiraling through 'that Steely blue.'"

Anne wrote Merrill in February 2010, informing him of her latest effort to restore the land.

Recently, I have given two talks to groups concerned with the dreadful process of mountain top removal of coal. The Kentuckians for the Commonwealth organized a march on Frankfort to urge legislators to vote for the Stream Saver Bill, which would limit the ability of the coal companies to fill the valleys with the spoil they blast from the tops of mountains. I talked to a large group from the Louisville area about the history of the struggle against strip mining. It was Louisville people who put the pressure on their legislators that got the first bill to demand some restoration of strip-mined lands. Harry and I had made countless trips to Louisville to talk to anyone who would invite him. Now the process of mountain top removal is so terribly and totally destructive that whole regions of the mountains will be turned into desert. The nation and the world have come face to face with the consequences of our profligate overconsumption of resources. The future will hold severe adjustments, which we only begin to see.

You and I, Merrill, have lived through a golden age, though it has been rocked by dreadful wars. It has been an age in which we thought we understood where we are, and where we seemed to be going. Now I do not feel that we as a people have that certitude.

Anne's positive outlook was ever a part of her innate character. Two lingering concerns, however, disturbed her: the political scene and the continuing disregard for the land and its limited resources.

Al Smith, a noted journalist and a longtime host of the popular TV program, "Comment on Kentucky," wrote a memoir, *Wordsmith: My Life in Journalism.* On January 6, 2012, Anne wrote:

WORDSMITH you are indeed! If I had accidently run across your memoir, as a non-Kentucky reader, I should have found it a page-turner indeed. But I am a Kentuckian, and almost every page resonates with a memory, or a story I have heard about events before my time.

I never expected to disagree with Tom Clark [a noted Kentucky historian] on any score, but I recall that he told you shortly before he died, "My God, Al, nobody wants to read two books about the same man." I could read twice as much about your life's experiences as you have thus far published.

Though all my family, both sides, were confirmed Democrats, except my mother, a history teacher who disagreed with FDR's monetary policies, none were ever actively involved in party politics. It was after I married Harry, and he finished law school and returned to Letcher

County, that I began to learn about the vagaries of party politics. His father, Cro Caudill, was a longtime county court clerk and sometime chairman of the Democratic Party, and close friend and henchman of Dr. B. F. Wright, political kingpin of the county. On several occasions, Doc Beauchamp [a colorful longtime Kentucky politician] visited overnight with Cro, and I heard many eye-opening stories, plans, and plots. One night I cooked dinner for them and served a chiffon pumpkin pie for dessert. For years after, whenever we encountered Doc in Frankfort or elsewhere, he never failed to announce to all within earshot, "Anne Caudill makes the best pumpkin pies in Kentucky." He was ever the skillful politician like unto Carl Perkins about whom I know a similar story. When Harry commented that Doc had been accused of voting the names on the tombstones of the Logan County cemeteries, he replied, "We didn't do a thing they wouldn't have done for us."

Arthur Hammer owned a textile business in New York and lived on Fifth Avenue. Anne recalled that he was "tall, handsome, vivacious, well-traveled, and with a sympathetic and generous turn of mind, he devoted himself to helping the less fortunate after he retired." One day he picked up *Night Comes to the Cumberlands* in a public library, read it, and then went to Appalachia to offer assistance. He began by providing resources to worthy children who had no means of continuing their education. During his first trip to the mountains, Arthur called the Caudills, asking to stop by. A friendship began that endured until his death.

He visited the Caudills in Whitesburg a couple of times and Anne twice after she moved to New Albany. Their correspondence is voluminous. In excerpts from two of his letters, Arthur wrote, "Thanks for your warm hospitality, and for the exciting discussion. 'Go out into the highways and compel them to come in, that my house may be full.' Luke 14:23. The two of you do fill your house with kindness, friendship, and excitement, and I love visiting you.

He later wrote, "Please excuse the occasional flood of letters. I cannot help it. It's an addiction. Someday I'll throw away my stamps and stationary and go cold turkey."

When Arthur died, Anne wrote to his wife, whom she had never met. The letter perhaps embodies a significant part of who Anne is:

This morning at the Unitarian-Universalist church, which I attend, the service was dedicated to the great traditions of the Hebrew faith. During this time of meditation, our marvelous cellist played the achingly beautiful Kol Nidre, and during that time with closed eyes, I celebrated the life of my friend, Arthur Hammer. The music is both deep and beautiful, sensitive and longing, with elements of the great joy of living. This was my farewell to a beautiful life.

This afternoon, I have been looking over some of the collection of his letters and the copies of things he sent to me and to Harry at an earlier time. Always he lifted our hearts with his enthusiasm for life, and his participation in the lives of others, especially those who needed a helping hand. I have just been looking at snapshots. The last time I saw him was two years ago when he came down to visit his protégés in the Kentucky mountains. He took some pictures of the high school we visited because he had read of the innovative teaching there. It was a memorable day. Arthur was so excited by the school and by the integrated success story he saw there. That day, he provided a $500 prize to be given for the best short story written by a student.

Always in his letters we received from his adventures, the emphasis was on the people he met, who were in need, and those who were rising to demand change. I recall his jubilation when he wrote that Evelena le Brun in South Africa had finally been freed, and that his campaign to get letters written had helped bring about her release.

It's a sorrow that he had to suffer so in the end. I have been grieving for him ever since I first learned of the illness, as I grieved for another dear friend who died this summer, another great spirit, a doctor who devoted his life to service in the Kentucky mountains and in Korea. He was a founder of the Quaker (Friends) Medical service, whose wife I just spent a week with in Concord, Massachusetts. Both men were rare treasures and both suffered the same fate. Would that our race could produce more of their breed. Arthur's spirit is desperately needed to love, to teach, to challenge. There is no way to calculate or measure the effect his life had on all those he taught, all those he encouraged.

I am so glad he had you close by during all these many weeks of illness. I'm sure it made it all more bearable, not being alone. And you will find, I am sure, that as time passes the remembrance of these last weeks will diminish and you will dwell more and more on all the joyous, beautiful wonderful times you had as you adventured together. How fortunate that you could share all those trips with the enthusiasm and interest that you both possessed. A rare privilege indeed.

I seem to recall that Arthur said you have a friend in Louisville. I remember that I was disappointed that you could not come the last time he visited. Please find occasion to come this way and come to see me. I have a room and bath awaiting you and only 15 minutes from Louisville. Driving in Louisville is no problem for me as I have learned to get around the city fairly well. It would be a pleasure to have you here.

I shall never cease to be blessed because I knew Arthur.

On August 11, 2011, as she approached 88 "wonderful" years, Anne wrote a letter to Susan Scott Downs, daughter of her friend, Elmer Downs:

As the song says, "I don't get around much anymore." I find myself much more stable and secure using a walker as my balance is very uncertain. I drive only around the neighborhood, to the grocery, medical appointments nearby, the library and such, in the daytime. I get to go to church when my daughter can take me, as I do not feel safe driving on the interstate. However, I stay busy and occupied at home with many visitors. Currently, I am working with a committee to produce a book about Scribner House for the

2013 bicentennial celebration of the town's founding. And there is no way I can keep up with the books that are given to me, or that I want to read.

In an earlier letter to Reverend Jim Chatham, Anne wrote, "I continue to learn and enjoy. Legs do not insure me a good balance, fingers do not flow over the keys with assurance, and everything is at a slower pace. Thus, there is more time to stay home and enjoy visits from family and friends, and READ. Thanks for your July 4 article, 'A Larger Concept of the Patriotic Call.' I reread it numerous times."

Several years ago, Anne wrote a letter to Virginia Combs, who was a pillar of the Whitesburg community. She taught English at the high school for decades, was a mainstay at the Methodist church, and the wife of Circuit Judge Steve Combs. Anne's letter expressed her thoughts about Virginia's celebration of her 88th birthday. (She lived to be 102.)

We have the invitation to your eighty-eighth birthday. What a wonderful achievement—to be eighty-eight years young!

Nobody grows old living a number of years; people grow old by deserting their ideals. Nor is youth simply a matter of ripe cheeks and supple knees. Youth is a temper of will, a quality of the imagination, a vigor of the emotions and a freshness of the deep springs of life. Years may wrinkle the skin, but to give up enthusiasm wrinkles the soul.

Whether eighteen or eighty-eight, if there is in one's heart the love of wonder, the childlike appetite of what's next, and the courage to play the game as the rules are written, that person is young. We do not quit playing because we grow old; we grow old because we quit playing.

Oliver Wendell Holmes said, "To be eighty-eight years young is sometimes more cheerful and hopeful than to be forty years old."

Shakespeare wrote, "To me, dear friend, thou never canst be old." Virginia, no one I know has more enthusiasm and joy in what is next, more pleasure in friends and society, more love of wonder in what is beautiful. You are an inspiration to us all.

Anne's letter to Virginia Combs perhaps foretold her own philosophy upon reaching her 80s.

CHAPTER 18

The Unsteady Belief
That Life is Good

The months after Harry's death were busy, hectic, and trying. It was five months of running on adrenaline as Anne moved into her new home in what is known as the "knobs" high above New Albany, Indiana, in the Ohio River valley.[26]

Amidst the tedious and seemingly endless task of preparing for the move, Anne had little time to reflect on the events that had dramatically changed everything. Her life had always been filled with bustling activity, but it was suddenly and profoundly different—Harry wasn't there to help and support her. Having nearly more to do than can be done became a means of surviving, which partially alleviated the powerful emotions that accompanied her loss. Anne had a few quieter moments when grief, loneliness, and emptiness took hold, but Harry's strength had given her strength. She never felt total despair or sorry for herself. It was a time of release and a time to accept and embrace what Harry would want for her—a complete and happy life.

Before the move, Anne was consumed with tying up loose ends, closing one home and opening another, and deciding what

---

26. Knobs are rounded, isolated hills.

to keep and what to discard. There was the tendency to take everything, but she understood that all the furnishings and mementos would not fit into a smaller home. She would take the memories of the good times, and leave behind those of their struggles, disappointments, and painful moments.

There were the moments of solitude, a time to reflect on her life with Harry. She remembered the deep, bold voice from the back of Kincaid Hall, and sitting on the steps with him and talking. She remembered him quoting poetry to her, and his promise, "If you'll marry me, I'll take you to France." She recalled going to his home in the mountains and stopping by the little coal town of Vicco. It was so different from her home in Cynthiana. She remembered his Aunt Larce Hogg asking, "Lord, honey, can you cook?"

Anne recalled building their home and making curtains from tobacco canvas, Harry working at the office, and the two of them working in the garden. Soon the children arrived. Anne didn't put an ax under the bed to relieve the pain or rub groundhog grease on her baby's throat, but she learned that if she ever needed anything, her neighbors would give what they had.

When it was quiet, she heard Harry reading to her as she worked. He never stopped thinking, nor did Anne. Harry wouldn't let her.

When he took that walk up the mountain in the spring of 1960, Anne knew something worried him. He released it when they wrote down his thoughts. They didn't think his book would amount to much, and then the phone began to ring. "Come and see for yourself," he said and they did. Anne remembered fixing dinner, and hearing the stories and the laughter. She heard it throughout the rooms and on the porch, under the trees, as soothing as a gentle summer breeze.

Harry took his life looking at Pine Mountain. He loved the mountains, and he loved Anne. He didn't want to be a burden. That's not what love is.

The first several months of Anne's life in her new home were very busy ones, following the pattern of her life. She had to put the house in order and adjust to a new and different community and environment. She wanted to meet new people, make new friends, and become active in community organizations. How better to do this than as a volunteer?

Anne began building her life without Harry, but was ever conscious of his influence and love, which gave her support and confidence. Throughout her years in New Albany, questions and discussions about Harry continued. She corresponded with several of Harry's former friends and with others requesting information about him and his work. The file fills a four-drawer filing cabinet.

Eleven months after Harry's death, Linda Stahl of the Louisville *Courier-Journal* interviewed Anne and Diana to gather information and their thoughts for a feature article titled, "Death Wish." In the article, Stahl wrote about all aspects of suicide, including assisted suicide. She quoted several authorities who dealt with life-and-death issues, particularly among the elderly. She wrote that losing control of one's life and living in a debilitating state is a fear shared by most of the elderly, many of who develop chronic illnesses, feel isolated, and experience depression after the loss of a spouse.

A photograph of Anne and Harry sitting on their front porch

accompanied the article, with a caption by Anne: "After he was gone, I didn't have a feeling of grief. I had a feeling of release for him." In the article, Anne said, "My mother finally died—completely, absolutely, and totally helpless. She could not move, she could not speak above a whisper, but her mind was very clear. Harry loved me dearly. He didn't want that for me and he didn't want that for himself."

Diana, a nurse, expressed her views, which embraced the hospice philosophy of making terminal patients comfortable and pain free, but neither prolonging life nor accelerating death. She said, "I have more liberal views, and I believe there are situations where there might be assisted suicide and you could be with your loved ones and say goodbye." She expressed regret that she could not have somehow said goodbye to her father. The family respected those who maintained control of their lives, and although Harry's death was a great loss, they recognized and honored his courage in maintaining control.

Anne said that she missed him the most "when I'm having a good time, when there are things I want to share with him—trips, friends, and experiences. It just comes to me; I want him back so much."

*   *   *

The final letter Harry left for Anne reminded her of the letters he had sent to her during their brief courtship. Among Harry's early love letters to Anne, she recalled one written when he was finishing law school. He wrote about having dinner with two professors and their discussion of the Civil War. One of the points he made was that it wasn't only the generals and leaders who determined the outcome of wars and major events. It was the unknown and unsung heroes, like the fifer Sy Cornett who made a lasting difference.

Harry's theme in the letter was prophetic, except that he was noticed and remembered. He devoted his life to reconstructing and rebuilding his land and its people with the belief that life is good. With that shared belief, Anne began renewing her life, determined to carry on his legacy and live the good life, as he wanted for her.

* * *

The drive from downtown New Albany the short distance up to the knobs where Anne moved was similar to driving up a winding, narrow road in the Cumberlands. The knobs are on a forest-covered plateau at a maximum elevation of 771 feet. Although Anne couldn't look out her window and see the 3,200-foot Pine Mountain, she could look out the wide windows at the back of her home into a beautiful, dense forest. Anne spent considerable time in the large living-dining room, observing the seasonal color changes in the thick woods and visits from wildlife guests, including blue jays and brilliant red cardinals feeding against the backdrop of the trees.

Her new comfortable, well designed home was conveniently located a short walk from her daughter Diana's home, and a short walk from a spectacular view of the Ohio River Valley and the greater Louisville area. She could drive to downtown New Albany in five minutes and to downtown Louisville in fifteen. It wasn't the same as living in the Cumberlands, but for someone who wanted to move to Indiana and still be near Kentucky and Kentuckians, the knobs in Floyd County were a good choice.

Anne moved some of her prized possessions to her new

home. "The things I cherish most go back to the relics of bygone generations," she said. "Since childhood, I have valued the things my ancestors used in their everyday lives, and enjoyed having them and using them in my everyday life. Some of the things that I grew up with or that came to me after I married and moved far away into Eastern Kentucky, have long since been given to my children. They also value them for the same reasons."

Many pieces of the Caudill furniture had a history and a story. Anne's bedroom furniture from her family dated back to 1875. Her guest bedroom furniture came from Harry's family.

The portrait over Anne's fireplace mantel depicted Harry sitting in a rocker holding a book. His confidence, strength, and infectious smile seemed to invite all who enter to come and listen to a story.

Anne's oak table in her living-dining room sat eight, and was quite a bargain. She bought it for a dollar at an auction in Cynthiana many years ago. She also bought another large oak table later for ten dollars; it sat in her screened-in porch. Miners crippled in the mines had made the chairs that sat beside it.

Dr. Bennett Wall, one of Harry's history professors at UK, gave Anne her walnut corner cupboard.[27] One day Dr. Wall drove up the lane at Mayking pulling a trailer loaded with a gift for the Caudills. It took five men to carry the walnut corner cupboard into the house.

Although several rocking chairs graced the Caudill home through the years, three had special memories. Anne remembered

---

27. A small group of students who were veterans often went to Dr. Wall's apartment in the evenings to discuss Kentucky's history, politics and its future. Ned Breathitt, Harry's fellow student and friend, was a member of this informal group and later became governor of Kentucky.

being rocked as a child in a rocking chair made by the Shaker religious sect at Shakertown, Kentucky, in the 1800s. The chair dates back to her great-grandfather who bought it at an auction for five cents.

Harry often sat in a rocker in the kitchen reading and talking to Anne while she worked. During the Depression, Harry's father, Cro, loaned a man five dollars to pay his taxes. A year or so later, Cro saw the man walking up the hill to his home carrying a rocking chair. The man asked Cro if he would accept the chair as payment for the loan. The chair remained in the Caudill family as a reminder that most people are honest and honorable.

Chester Cornett made his living by making twelve rocking chairs each year, and he made a special one for Anne and Harry, which they revered. Anne gave each of her three children one of these special chairs.

"In my home I have reminders of those generous and welcoming people of other generations," Anne said. "I enjoy using every day some of the dishes that belonged to grandmothers on both sides."

Anne's treasures also included four pieces of sandstone:

On my window ledge by my desk are four little fragments of sandstone carved and pierced by the elements. They were brought to me by Wendell Berry. On his way to visit us back in the 1960s, he spent time hiking in the Red River Gorge, which we had told him about. He said that climbing up over a rocky ledge, the pieces broke off in his hand. Their presence there in my window are a constant reminder of my deep respect and affection for Wendell and Tonya, and my memories of the times we have spent together in the Red River Gorge and elsewhere. The fragile weathered stones are also a reminder of how important to all of us it was to save the gorge from being dammed by the Corp of Engineers as a water source for Lexington. That is one battle we won. I also treasure a whole shelf of Wendell's books sent to me and inscribed with affection.

The woods outside her window were a treasure, and the books neatly stacked on her coffee table and lining the shelves in her study were special ones. She couldn't keep all the books she read, but she kept those written by her friends—Wendell Berry, James Still, David McCullough, Al Cornett, David Dick, Jim Chatham, Al Smith, and others. She often remarked, "I don't when I'm ever going to have the time to read all these books. An author sent me this book today, and I can't wait to read it."

It seems that every few months she delighted in announcing, "Wendell sent me his latest book today."

Anne's new home was full of mementos in honor and in remembrance of those who blazed the trail to make this nation what it is. She continued a keen interest in history and politics, despite the buying and selling of elections, past and present. At times, her faith in government and politics waned. However, she lived through wars, depressions, and the poverty and coal wars in Appalachia. She understood how our nation weathered those troubling times through faith, perseverance, and sacrifice. Her deep sense of pride in the nation's history and heritage was a positive and significant influence on those who knew her and her continuing work.

* * *

When Anne moved to Indiana, she knew only three people in the area other than Diana and her family, and James, who lived across the river in Louisville. She had met Mary Bingham and Beverley Rosenblum when they visited the Caudills in Whitesburg. Mary was the wife of Barry Bingham, owner and publisher of the Louisville *Courier-Journal,* and Beverley was the president of the Louisville League of Women Voters. Anne had also previously met Margo Reynolds, Diana's neighbor. Soon after Anne moved, each of these three friends invited her to meetings of various community organizations and events. She quickly became involved and her friendships grew in leaps and bounds.

Anne's warm, gentle, and friendly nature flowed naturally from a sincere and authentic character. Her delightful sense of wit, intelligence, and natural charm invited people to pursue continuing friendships. The value of a true and lasting friend was immeasurable.

Mary Bingham was one of Anne's true friends, and their friendship grew and prospered for 33 years. It began in 1961, when Mary and State Librarian Margaret Willis visited the Caudills to assist them in establishing library and bookmobile services in Letcher County. The lives of the Caudills would never be the same. Mary and Margaret stayed overnight and it was during this visit that Harry gave Mary a stack of his writing. She took the papers to bed with her and read most of the night. As a result of her visit, *Night Comes to the Cumberlands* was soon published.

Months later, the Binghams visited the Caudills for two days and saw firsthand the problems in the neglected third of the state. Mutual trust and deep respect strengthened the developing relationship and friendship of the Binghams and Caudills. When Harry felt a particular issue needed attention and publicity, he would contact Barry Bingham, whereupon a reporter and usually a photographer would descend on the Caudills posthaste. Anne recalled hosting many of the *Courier-Journal's* acclaimed journalists, including John Ed Pierce, John Fetterman, David Ross Stevens, Fred Luigart, and photographers Billy Davis and Phil Strode.

When the Caudills had business or meetings in Louisville, they occasionally stayed with the Binghams. On one occasion, Harry spoke in Louisville at a conference of the South Eastern Garden Clubs. It was held in a big tent, and when the Caudills arrived, Anne was amused to see a bar set up with Kentucky bourbon and other drinks. Back home in the mountains, alcohol was available in liquor stores in "wet" counties, but was never on the menu at garden club meetings.

Anne and Mary corresponded through the years: Mary in a distinct and elegant longhand and Anne in single-spaced typed letters, often two or three pages long. Anne's file of the Binghams' letters and clippings was a thick one. Although the long distance across the state from Whitesburg to Louisville prevented regular visits, they arranged to meet occasionally and spent wonderful times hiking in the woods. They hiked together at Bad Branch Falls on Pine Mountain, the Lilley Cornett Woods, and the Red River Gorge.

Barry Bingham died in August 1988. Harry died two years later in 1990. When Mary heard the news, she called Anne immediately and reassured her, "It is better this way." Barry had lingered with a brain tumor. Harry suffered enduring pain and rapidly declining health during his last days. Mary flew with Governor Bert Combs to the funeral. Five months later, Anne moved to New Albany, Indiana, a short distance from the Bingham home and her friendship with Mary grew.

Both were lovers of the arts, and the two widows often met for dinner followed by a concert, ballet, opera, play, lecture, or civic meeting. After one concert, Anne wrote Mary the following:

All of yesterday and today, my soul has soared as I remember the concert. Dame Kiri Te Kanawa is a presence I shall long recall. It makes me proud of the human race that such a magnificent combination of beauty, charm, and the superb voice that she has can all coalesce in one personality.

As I listened, lines of poetry kept running through my head, and I could not complete them, nor put them rightly together, though they described what I was hearing. Today, I looked them up and find they come from two separate poets:

O Nightingale! Thou surely art

A creature of a fiery heart

These notes of thine—they pierce and pierce;

Tumultuous harmony and fierce!—William Wordsworth

The song that oft-times hath

Charmed magic casements, opening on the foam

Of perilous seas, in fairy lands forlorn.—John Keats

In a letter to Mary on October 4, 1991, Anne wrote of her dismay at the slovenly manner in which people appeared in public.

Your gift of the tickets to *Romeo and Juliet* brought an event of special beauty and delight to my daughter Diana and me. Every moment was riveting, a feast for the eyes and ears. Ever since, there have been visions dancing in my head, not of sugar plum fairies as in *Nutcracker*, but of dancing girls in flowing apricot chiffon and of Gypsy girls in brilliant and richly colored dresses and ribbons; of gentlemen dressed as gentlemen should be, in brocades and velvets, long fanciful robes or magnificent swooping sleeves, displaying their rapiers and marvelous physiques. Alas! We have degenerated to running shoes and knit jogging wear worn over bulging tummies, to be seen on any and all occasions, apparently.

Mary died four years after Anne moved to the Louisville area. She was giving a major address at a gala Rotary Club Toast in Louisville, when near the end of her speech, she gasped, collapsed, and died later in the evening. Her speech scorched the media for its "self-righteous pomposity" and she blasted the "talk-show rabble-rousers and the primates on the far religious right." Before collapsing, her last public pronouncement was a call for support of the effort to raise $4.4 million for the Louisville Free Public Library.

Shortly after Mary's death, Anne wrote a letter published in the *Courier-Journal*, expressing her own sorrow at the loss, but also enumerating the benevolence of the Binghams, their sincerest interest in the forgotten third of the state, and their charitable work benefitting southern Indiana:

The loss to Kentucky of Mary Bingham's guiding presence leaves a very lonesome space. So much of the vital progress of this last half century has come about through her direct interest and personal support.

The small part of her manifold efforts I know best concerns Eastern Kentucky. Thirty-five years ago, she visited Letcher County at the headwaters of the Kentucky River to contribute personally and financially to upgrading the public library and the establishment of the bookmobile services. There she saw firsthand the devastation of uncontrolled strip mining and came again with her husband Barry to walk over those blasted and stripped hills and valleys. They then launched the *Courier-Journal* on a campaign, which culminated in legislation for control and reclamation. Later they tackled the problems of the Kentucky River pollution control and the long campaign to gain severance taxes on coal for the state.

They found time to hike through Lilley Cornett Woods and they contributed sizeable funds necessary to ensure its preservation in the public domain. They walked also in beautiful Red River Gorge, and then aroused public demand, which prevented its flooding by a dam. Through the years, the concern of Mary and Barry Bingham continued focusing the attention of the *Courier-Journal* on the region. In recent years, under her guidance, funds from the family provided large sums for establishing the Whitesburg Community College and for the purchase of the headwaters of Bad Branch Falls on Pine Mountain for the Nature Conservancy. They also provided the major impetus for the new Harry M. Caudill Public Library in Letcher County. Mary's interest was a vital support to the work of my husband and other mountain writers for three decades. In addition, their children's interest supported Appalshop and other Eastern Kentucky projects.

I mourn the loss of Mary Bingham, for myself, and for Kentucky. A guiding light, bright to the last moment, has been extinguished.

The last time Anne and Mary were together, they had dinner followed by a concert. They talked, and although they did not dwell on the past, they discussed the reality of life as it nears the end. In referring to Barry's long illness, Mary expressed the hope that she would "just be taken."

Before her address at the Rotary Club, the toasters showered her with accolades; her daughter referred to as a "remarkable little giant." Responding to the stirring comments, Mary said, "I couldn't be happier if a big pink cloud came and carried me off to the sky."

Seventeen years later, Anne said, "I thought our friendship came from being perfectly open and honest, sharing so many ideals and having no undercurrents of past history to burden our companionship. I have only good memories other than our shared grief of losing two exceptional men we had loved."

Books and libraries initially brought Mary and Anne together. The *Courier-Journal* published a cartoon the day after Mary's death depicting her standing before St. Peter at the gate. She says to him, "First, I'd like to inspect your library, young man."

Anne would undoubtedly do the same when a big pink cloud came to take her away. In the meantime, she happily continued the work of the man she loved, as her dear friend Mary Bingham continued the Bingham legacy.

"My life in New Albany has been a wonderful chapter in my life," she said. "I've had a perfectly lovely time in this lovely town. Of course, I came here to be near my daughter and her family and my son James. As soon as I got settled in this wonderful little house in the woods, I began to look about for ways to volunteer, because that's always been an enriching part of my life, and I had the time to devote to it."

Soon after settling into her new home, Anne drove down from the knobs to the New Albany-Floyd County Library, where she completed a volunteer form describing special skills she might have. Since she had initiated a history and genealogy program at the Whitesburg Library, they assigned her to the Indiana Room, which contains a historical collection, and she worked off and on for a couple of years indexing the Floyd County 1880 census. She sat in front of a microfilm reader and indexed the names, which was about as tedious as the first job she ever had, binding books. Sitting there indexing names hour after hour made her head swim.

Anne also became a member of the Friends of the Library. People in the community donated used books to the Friends, which then sold the books at public sales twice a year. Paperbacks sold for 50 cents and hardbacks for a dollar. Each sale brought in from $600 to $900. When Anne became a volunteer, she met with the other volunteers once each week to catalogue and box the donated books, many of which were like new. The volunteer friends found that empty beer cases made perfect containers for the books, but were reluctant to be seen entering a liquor store. Anne volunteered. She became friends with a liquor-store owner, and when the library needed more boxes, she drove around to the back of the store and collected an ample supply of empty beer cases out near the garbage pile.

Anne had been associated with the Daughters of the American Revolution since childhood. Her mother became a member in 1922, and her aunts about the same time. Beginning at about age six, she often accompanied her mother to the meetings and helped with their projects. In 1976, Anne helped organize the Pine Mountain DAR chapter in Whitesburg, and later organized a genealogical society as a DAR project. Both organizations grew and thrived.

Soon after moving to New Albany, Anne transferred her DAR membership to the Piankeshaw Chapter, which owned the Scribner House. In 1813, three Scribner brothers—Joel, Nathaniel and Abner—came down the Ohio River, stopped below the Falls of the Ohio, and decided to buy land and build a town. The Scribners bought over 800 acres, surveyed it, and sold lots. They named it New Albany after the capital in their home state of New York. In 1814, Joel built the Scribner house on a sloping bank above the river. It was the first major brick and frame house built in the town. The DAR bought the house from Joel Scribner's granddaughter, Harriet, in 1913. The house is located near the center of New Albany on historic Main Street.

The Scribner house was a delight for Anne. Helping preserve the 200-year-old house gave her something more to do. For 21 years, Anne sewed new curtains, cleaned, dusted, and painted, tediously repaired antique dolls, washed and mended antique quilts, and served as a docent during tours for thousands of schoolchildren and adult groups. The inside of the house took constant care, as did the outside, so Anne helped care for the garden on the grounds surrounding the house.

Anne was featured in two *Courier-Journal* articles about the Scribner House on November 10, 2010, and December 6, 2010.

When asked about the boost in the building's profile, Anne said, "I'd say it's high time." She also helped write and publish a history of the house, *The Scribner House: A Bicentennial Commemoration.*

Soon after she moved, Margo Reynolds invited her to attend the First Unitarian Church located near downtown Louisville, and Anne joined the church. She said, "I had felt for many years that my religious understanding fit better with the Unitarian practice, and, of course, living in the mountains there were no Unitarian churches, and for 40 years I sat in the Methodist church there and enjoyed it enormously." She and Reynolds rode together to the church for 12 years until Margo moved away. Anne decided later to begin attending Thomas Jefferson Unitarian on the outskirts of Louisville where she felt at home in the warm, inviting, and enriching spiritual environment.

Mary Ellen Elsbernd, a librarian at Northern Kentucky University, had conducted a lengthy interview with Anne a few months before Harry's death. In the interview, Elsbernd asked Anne to describe Harry as a husband:

> His first thought is always his family. He is a very loving and very kind husband. He has sacrificed himself in many ways and not done things he would like to do because of concern for his family. He can be sharp tongued at times because he is a perfectionist. He has the feeling that people should always do things and do them right, do them when they are supposed to. He always finds it frustrating and irritating when that doesn't happen. Sometimes that makes people short tempered particularly when they are under the kind of pressures he has been under from an incredible law practice and with all this [*Night* aftermath] on top of it.

There would be times when the phone rings all day at the office, and when we walked in the door at home, it rings throughout the evening.

Anne said that the family finally adopted a hard and fast rule—never answer the phone during mealtime. The rule annoyed some of their dinner guests who frequently heard the phone ringing throughout a meal. One guest asked, "Aren't you going to answer the phone? What if someone died?"

Harry replied, "If they're dead now, they won't be any deader after we're finishing eating."

Anne had tremendous respect for her parents and family, who were "people of ability and strength." She also said that one of her teachers "did more to enrich my life than any other of my many great teachers." At UK, Ann Callahan taught history and art appreciation. "With her boundless enthusiasm, I learned to see in the world around me so much beauty. I learned to appreciate line, form, color, and design in painting, architecture, and nature. Of all I learned at the university, that stayed with me and meant more to me in my personal life than anything else. Now it didn't help me get a job, but it made my life beautiful."

In addition to her many other interests, Anne painted still life and landscapes. Her painting of Bad Branch Falls flowing down Pine Mountain hangs near her dining room table. The painting is a daily reminder of those grand times when the Caudills trudged up the mountain, then paused to rest and listen to a story.

Anne said that Harry had a tremendous influence on her because of his constant interest in history and issues. Harry taught Anne from his favorite rocking chair in their kitchen while she cooked and cleaned. (She did give Harry credit for his fair share of washing dishes.)

"Over the years, he educated me from that rocking chair by reading aloud to me or retelling me something he had read and then commenting on it," Anne said. "I think unconsciously he used that to fix it in his own mind, helping him to remember it."

Elsbernd asked what values Anne hoped to instill in her two grandchildren. She replied, "I think that a sense of responsibility and service to their fellow man, a sense of whatever each person is, is a result of all those who have gone before. None of us is ever anything in ourselves, and we owe so much to those who have gone before. The only way we can repay is to serve those who are here. Whatever society believes is good and beautiful and worthwhile has been built at the sacrifice of time and strength and energy in the lives of others. We owe that back. I believe it with all my soul."

When Elsbernd asked Anne to describe herself, she said, "We like to talk to people of all faiths and find out their thinking. Once a Mormon couple visited us and the woman said something to me that I've always cherished. She said, 'I can tell by your hands that you are a woman who works, and mine are the same.' Harry complains and grumbles at me all the time and says I never stop."

Elsbernd asked, "Why do you do that?"

"Because there are so many things that need to be done!"

Anne Caudill is Fine, Thank You

When Anne moved from the mountains, she was 67, an age when the energy level usually begins to decline, but her vigor and enthusiasm declined only the tiniest bit. She continued doing the things that needed doing, and had more time and opportunity to do some of the things she had always longed to do. With fewer demands and obligations, it was a time to live fully in the present:

> I don't think that much about the future, there's no use worrying about it. I decided a long time ago that the best you can do is to enjoy every day and be useful. If you live in fear of the future or in bitterness over the past, then it erodes your soul. None of us is given that much time on earth, and we should make the most of what we have. I keep saying, "Here I am, a sweet young thing just out of college, and I've got a son more than 60 years old, grandchildren, white hair, and a Medicare card." John Adams lived to be very old and jolly. Someone met him one day and asked, "And how is John Adams?" And he said, "John Adams is very fine; his body is old and tired, but John Adams is fine, thank you."

Adjusting to a new and different environment, Anne began making friends and attending civic meetings, church functions, and arts performances. In spare moments, she read and wrote letters, scads of them.

Five years after arriving in New Albany, she met Elmer Downs at a luncheon with her church friends. She discovered he lived only three blocks from her home. From that introduction, Anne and Elmer formed a companionship that lasted about eight years until his death. Anne remembered him as "ever elegant in dress, manner, and speech. He had a delightful sense of humor and was a lover of poetry and music." As near-constant companions, they attended church, concerts, plays, ballets, and other programs and meetings together.

Anne's children accepted Elmer as an integral part of the family. One Christmas, Diana prepared a lovely gift for him and drew up an ersatz legal document formally adopting him as a grandfather. One evening, he came to join Anne wearing his 1913 New Albany High School cheerleading sweater, still a perfect fit for his slender form. Anne took his picture. When the family celebrated his 90th birthday, the photo was reproduced on his birthday cake. He was delighted. He worked in the food brokerage business until age 90, and retained a spry mind and sense of humor until his death at nearly 95. Elmer Downs filled a void in Anne's life. They had similar interests, dispositions, and wonderful times together.

In New Albany, Anne had considerably fewer family obligations and responsibilities, which permitted time to travel and pursue new interests. Four months after the life-changing events before and after her relocation, Anne accepted an invitation to visit Jane and Huston Westover, her friends from Whitesburg who had moved to Concord, Massachusetts, after their years of working in Appalachia. The getaway proved to be a renewing one. She spent several days with them at an old Victorian hotel at Pemaquid Lighthouse Point on the coast of Maine. Anne "simply relaxed on the sea cliffs, watching the waves roar in, visiting art galleries, eating lobster and reading. I needed that and they knew how to find peace and share it with me."

Once settled in her new home, Anne's interests and activities broadened and grew. She and Harry had traveled considerably. Harry kept his promise to take Anne to France, and then they took seven other trips abroad during the next 18 years. However, Harry's declining health prevented further long trips. After Anne moved to New Albany, friends kept calling asking her to fly with them to faraway exotic places and she did, several times.

In 1992, Anne and Harriet Van Meter, founder of the International Book Project, took a trip to Spain and Portugal. They had a wonderful time. Anne said, "Madeira is as close as what I expected heaven will be as ever I'll see, except Kentucky and Indiana."

The next year, she spent two months with James and his wife, who were living in Wimbleton, England. James traveled back and forth negotiating trade agreements in Central Asia for the British American Tobacco Company. Anne's visit was an excellent opportunity to wander around the museums and galleries in nearby London. The next year, she took a bus tour with a Mennonite friend to East Germany, Poland, the Czech Republic, Hungary, and Austria.

Anne had seen her college roommate, Lib Williams, only twice since their college days. While she was in California visiting James and his wife, he took her to see Lib at Del Mar and they discussed places they had been. Neither had been to Egypt. Anne said, "Let's go," and they went to Egypt and Greece for three weeks. A couple of years later, a friend from Bloomington, Indiana, called to invite Anne to tour northern Spain with a Unitarian church group. Anne remembered it as an exceptional trip. She then accompanied Jane Westover on a tour of England and Wales. A couple of years later, she accompanied her Unitarian friends on a trip to Romania and Transylvania, where they stayed with Unitarian families, and had a "unique and wonderful experience." It was Anne's last trip abroad, but not her last trip.

Throughout those years traveling abroad, she also traveled the United States and Canada to visit friends and attend Elderhostel programs, usually related to art and history. She went with friends to the Shakespeare Festival in Stratford, Canada, and visited James a couple of times when he returned to the states to work in Los Angeles.

Anne's move to Indiana, a 15-minute drive from the Falls of the Ohio, provided a new historical interest in another geographical area. The history of the falls region began 375 million years ago during the Middle Devonian period of the Paleozoic era. The falls contain the largest exposed Devonian fossil bed in the world. For hundreds of years, the Ohio River has been a means of transporting people and goods. The river was a primary route in the expansion of the West in the early 1800s. Along the Ohio River from Pittsburgh to the Mississippi, the falls were the only truly difficult part of the river to navigate, and many early settlers stopped and settled there. Consequently, the towns of Louisville, Kentucky, and Jeffersonville, Clarksville, and New

Albany in Indiana sprung up, grew, and became thriving centers of commerce. In the mid-1800s, dams, locks, and a canal were constructed to open the river from Pittsburgh to the Gulf of Mexico.

Anne began learning about how the early settlers established the area and subsequent historical events. Thomas Jefferson, an early environmentalist, proposed and sent a checkerboard plan with open green spaces for establishing Jeffersonville (which the builders ignored). George Rogers Clark founded and lived in Clarksville, located between Jeffersonville and New Albany. In 1803, Meriwether Lewis first met William Clark at the Falls of the Ohio where they began their three-year western expedition. John James Audubon and a partner ran a store in Louisville, but Audubon spent most of his time painting birds, which were abundant around the falls. When Kentucky outlawed dueling, some famous duelists took their grievances across the river to New Albany. Two of Anne's ancestors were among the very earliest settlers of the falls area.

Much to her delight, Anne, the history buff, began a second historical field day when she moved to the region.

An interpretative center or museum sits beside the falls in Clarksville. For several years, the museum exhibited a likeness of a Welsh explorer, the legendary Prince Madoc. Devil's Backbone is a high bluff a few miles upriver from the falls where an ancient stone fortress and mounds once stood. There is other evidence—light-skinned, blue-eyed tribes and other stone structures and artifacts—throughout the Mississippi and Ohio River Valleys, which point to a pre-Columbian civilization. There is no definitive proof, however, to substantiate that Prince Madoc or any other voyagers settled around the falls or anywhere in America before Columbus, but the Ancient Kentucke Historical Society believes there is considerable evidence.

Anne remembered something her sixth-grade teacher had said that Anne didn't believe. "I recall vividly an incident, a flash of revelation, which came to me. My teacher had been explaining how Columbus discovered America, and she said that no one before knew that America was here. I recall looking out my school's second-story window into a blooming locust tree, and thinking, 'I don't believe that.' I still don't believe it. Since that day, I have been intrigued by indications of earlier peoples who may have come to America before Columbus."

In 1976, her friends the Westovers gave Anne *America B. C.* by Barry Fell, and she was hooked on searching for evidence of earlier peoples who may have here before 1492. Books on the subject are a current part of her library and she subscribes to pre-history magazines. Ancient walls, artifacts, and cave carvings intrigue her. She began attending meetings on the subject, met other interested people, and corresponded with them. She met her longtime friend Virginia Hourigan, who traveled each summer on a motorcycle with camping gear to assist in archeological excavations at various sites. They shared an interest in pre-Columbian history. During her travels, Hourigan stopped by several times for two or three days to visit Anne.

Anne read the literature and attended monthly historical programs of the Ancient Kentucke Historical Association at the Falls of the Ohio Interpretative Center. She also attended Ancient Artifact Preservation Society meetings in Michigan and Ohio, and the Conference on Ancient Voyages to America in Halifax in 2009.

Anne said, "Travel does indeed broaden the mind, but now I am content to stay at home, to read, study, and reflect on all that I have seen and experienced. Variety is the spice of life, and my life has been well-seasoned."

Anne was not content to stay home all the time. There were friends to visit, meetings to attend, and projects to complete. In 2010, she had planned to attend the Epigraphic Society Conference in Ohio, but family came first; one of her two grandsons was getting married that day. She had considerable time to be with her three children and two grandchildren. She was proud of them and felt "blessed" that all were well.

Her son James had an interesting and unique career. He had graduated cum laude with a degree in history from Harvard, received a law degree from UK and a post-graduate degree in tax law from New York University. He remained in New York for two years working for a firm on Wall Street and then took a position in Louisville as a tax lawyer for a firm of which former governor Bert Combs was a partner.

James then accepted a position with British American Tobacco US. He served as their director of corporate finance until moving to London to negotiate contracts in countries of the former Soviet Union. He spent much of his time in Central Asia. When the negotiations were complete, the company sent him to work in Los Angeles as treasurer of their Farmer's Insurance Group, which was negotiating earthquake insurance after the 1994 disaster.

Seven years after Anne moved to New Albany, James retired and returned to Louisville. He takes his mother to artifact society and save-the-mountains meetings and other places.

Diana graduated from Whitesburg High School and later

UK with a degree in social work. She worked with the severely handicapped and then for the North Carolina Social Services for a year. After that, she returned to Lexington and worked as a social services coordinator for disabled people. In the meantime, Diana had met Jack Grace, a graduate of the UK School of Forestry. They married and eventually moved to Morehead, Kentucky, in the foothills of Appalachia, where he worked for the Division of Forestry for seven years.

While Diana worked as a social worker making home visits to remote hollows in the area, she found a serious need for better nutrition and healthcare. During those seven years, Diana gave birth to two sons, and received a degree in nursing from Morehead State University. When Jack took a job in Louisville with a lumber company that exports lumber to Europe, the Grace family moved to New Albany. Diana has worked in nursing and with hospice, and for the past 15 years, she has worked in a psychiatric ward.

Anne's first grandson, who lives close by, presented his grandmother with two precious gifts. Anne's first great-grandson was born on July 11, 2011, and the second on June 19, 2013. These two babies lifted Anne further up into the heavenly clouds.

Anne's second grandson has had a varied and interesting life. He has worked for Americorps, helped repair damage from Katrina, served in two Conservation Corps, and counseled attendees at the Space Camp at Huntsville, Alabama. After receiving his degree from Prescott University, he has worked in sustainable agriculture, organic farming, and green living—a chip off the old block in a way.

A few years after the Grace family moved to New Albany, Anne moved a half mile away. She says, "Diana has been a constant help and companion to me. Scarcely a day has passed that she has not stopped by to bring in my mail, groceries, water plants, or other small chores, or just find time to visit. If her schedule is too busy, she calls to check on me and see if I need anything. She is truly a good, kind, warm, and entertaining woman of wide interests and reading choices, all making for good conservation."

Harry Frye had majored in geology, and worked for a building company during the summers. He liked the work and finished college at the Lexington Technical Institute, an adjunct of UK, to learn other aspects of the construction business. Eventually, Harry Frye formed his own business and built ever larger and more palatial homes. The business grew until the housing bubble burst during the recession that began in 2009, which practically ended new home construction.

Anne is very proud of her children's accomplishments, and says, "Each of my children have different talents and interests. I have been so fortunate that all three live not far away and each is of such pleasure and help to me. Harry Frye's special affectionate contribution is an ever-ready ability to repair things around my home that need to be fixed and he has the skill to do it right. His ongoing concern about the state of the nation and his well-informed views make his visits with me a pleasure."

Years after Harry's death, his writing and work continue to be recognized. The 1993 spring edition of *Appalachian Heritage* published by Berea College was a commemoration of the 30th anniversary of *Night Comes to the Cumberlands*. Tom Clark, Ned Breathitt, Loyal Jones, Kate Black, and nine other writers contributed articles to the publication. Anne wrote a four-page article, "Life with a Polemist." She wrote, "He was disappointed, sometimes discouraged to the point of bitterness, that apathy and ignorance combined to obstruct needed change. Then again, he was hopeful as he saw ignorance dissolving and efforts beginning to bear fruit here and there. His were large visions, practical ideas worth pursuing, worth the doing. I believe deeply that his life made a real difference, and his imprint is visible in the region he loved."

Night Comes to the Cumberlands continues to sell. A new edition was published in 2001, which included an afterword by James K. Caudill. His writing style is similar to that of his father. In the afterword, "The Gray and Cloudy Present," James summarized the intervening 28 years:

The tragedy of central Appalachia is that it is becoming more and more marginalized in American life just when the country needs more than ever what it has to offer. At a time when the bonds of community and family are visibly failing and people feel more alone than ever, and as they are bombarded from all sides with more demands and more data than they can possibly digest, Appalachia offers a model for a less frenetic and more measured way of life. People of Appalachian descent elsewhere in the nation—and they number millions—still feel deep ties to some Appalachian hamlet or hollow as to an ancestral homeland, though they may never have even visited it. As they make their way in the big world of getting and spending, they know that something valuable has been lost for all they may have gained. That less frenetic way of life is deeply embedded in Appalachian culture, which has proved incredibly tough and enduring. Yet Appalachia has now been so thoroughly bypassed and forgotten that it cannot give, because the rest of America will not take what could be its greatest gift.

Watches of the Night, a sequel to *Night Comes to the Cumberlands,* was published in 1976, and a new edition in 2010. James wrote an afterword and Anne added the "About the Author" section. James summarized the conditions of the Cumberlands in 2010:

> The decline in the standard of living foretold by this book [in 1976] is now upon us. It is past time for the American people and among them the people of the Cumberlands, to put aside childish things and to face up to the realities, economic and otherwise, of their situation. It is past time for the telling and understanding of the plain unvarnished truth, the kind Harry Caudill so cherished and tried to tell. I close with a quotation from one of Dad's favorite poems, James Russell Lowell's "The Present Crisis" written in 1844 when another era of upheaval and change was coming into view:

> Once to every man and nation comes the moment to decide
> In the strife of Truth with Falsehood, on the good or evil side;
> Some great cause, God's new Messiah, offering each the bloom or blight,
> Parts the goats upon the left hand and the sheep upon the right.
> And the choice goes by forever, 'twixt that darkness and that light.

James concluded, "So it is. So it has ever been. So it will ever be."

Anne wrote "About the Author" for the second edition, and closed with this statement: "It was a wonderful life we shared for 44 years. I count myself truly blessed to have been a partner in all the undertakings of a unique, complex, and gifted statesman, a man of courage, constant to the end."

* * *

In recognition of her longtime volunteer service, Anne received numerous awards through the years from various organizations. In 1967, UK held a conference and published a book about *Women: Equal but Different*. Anne and nine other Kentucky equal-but-different women were recognized and honored. The moderator introduced Anne, saying, "There are those . . . who not only keep up, but who provide a never-failing support, encouragement, and sharing. Through the mass media, Harry Caudill has come to be one of the best known and most knowledgeable spokesmen on the problems on Appalachia. What happens, Anne Caudill, when you find yourself with speaking dates and *New York Times* reporters, network broadcasters, and congressional committees on your doorstep? You have coped exceedingly well. How does it come about?"

Anne explained to conference attendees why and how she became involved in working for the people in Appalachia. She closed by saying, "Always there appears another issue to be brought to the attention of the state and nation in the fight to bring people abreast of the rest of America, and to ensure the wise use of its resources and the preservation of its incredible wild beauty."

Anne has received several certificates of appreciation, Helping Hand and Woman of the Year awards, and a Gold Leaf Award from various organizations, including the VFW Auxiliary, the Community Foundation of Southern Indiana and others.

In 1991, Anne accepted on Harry's behalf the Governor's Award in the Arts awarded posthumously from Governor Wallace Wilkinson and Wendell Berry. In 1995, Anne presented the Harry Caudill Conservation Award of the Sierra Club to a longtime conservationist, Elizabeth Jones, wife of Governor Brereton Jones. In 1997, she presented the award to Frank Elsen in memory of Mary Bingham.

In 2008, Anne was recognized for her years of service and support of the Harry M. Caudill Memorial Library. A newly redecorated and furnished Anne Caudill Community Room was dedicated in her honor. Three years later, the Whitesburg Heritage Festival committee invited Anne to be the grand marshal in their parade. On September 24, 2011, she led the big parade through the streets of Whitesburg.

* * *

The year after she moved to New Albany, Anne suffered a recurrent heart condition, which required angioplasty. The recovery was quick and her health and energy level improved. Nine years later, she had breast cancer surgery followed by chemo and radiation, which left her fatigued for a year. All went well until she fell and broke three ribs, followed by a painful recovery, and then underwent gallbladder surgery, and had an easy recovery.

During the past few years, Anne's health has been generally good with no major illnesses. However, she is experiencing the general physical problems accompanying aging. When she stands and walks, her balance is unsteady. For several years, she used a cane to help maintain balance, but now she uses a walker to move about. Her eyesight is failing somewhat, and she uses a magnifying apparatus for sewing and reading fine print.

Anne's fingers are not as flexible as they once were. In a letter to one of her friends, she wrote, "I have just this moment made a decision, had a revelation. I have made so many typos in my effort to write this letter that I think I am going to have to forgo my beloved typewriter and go back to longhand. It surely is not from a lack of experience that I make so many errors, as I have been typing in great volumes since about the age of fourteen. No, my fingers have betrayed me and no longer do what I think is going to be automatic. Oh, well. I'm not *complaining*, just *explaining*."

As of the writing of this book, Anne is 89. She is aware of the eminent pink cloud that will eventually come and take her away, but not anytime soon, because there's more work to do. Her spirit is willing and her mind is keen. Her only disappointment is that her former abundance of energy has diminished somewhat.

She does not get around as much anymore, but she does get around. She can't live without family, friends, books, trees, and at least one ongoing project. However, her recent project is complete. She contributed to the writing and publishing of *The Scribner House: A Bicentennial Commemoration*, which came out in 2012. Although Anne does not drive her car anymore—the one with the "I Love Mountains" bumper sticker on the back—she'll continue supporting the efforts of the Kentuckians for the Commonwealth.

Anne's story is found in her stories that reveal her convictions, her love of the land, her compassion for others and her reverence, gratitude, and obligation to those who came before.

She said, "All of my adult life, I have had the feeling I wanted to be of service in some way for the general good. Over the years, I've taken part in many charitable efforts of various kinds. After college, I worked for a while teaching farmwomen in a way that was useful. Then I married and became occupied establishing a home and starting a family, but always in the back of my mind, I had the feeling I wanted to do something that was more important than just the ordinary things."

Assisting one's husband is usually considered an ordinary thing. Anne's part-time job at Harry's law office evolved into more than she had ever anticipated. She recalled:

As it developed over the years, I found my career. It was a very satisfying one for me, and a great joy in my life to be the assistant and the backup for Harry, who was an eloquent and impassioned voice for the Appalachian region, its problems, and its potential. For over 40 years, he was an outspoken advocate for the Appalachian land and its people, and it was my great joy to help him any way I could. I served as secretary, as a research person, and as hostess for the countless people who came to visit. I served as companion on the many trips we took and in many other ways.

The great joy in my life was being able to be of real service to him, and I do not feel that it was—as the feminists would have it—deferring to a male. I was not deferring, I was supporting and assisting a rare and able spirit, and it was a privilege. It's been a rich and wonderful life with never a dull moment.

In 1945, a young man just back from the war met a young woman, who had the most sparkling eyes he had ever seen. Sixty-eight years later, those eyes still shine.

Selected Sources

Abramson, Rudy and Jean Haskell, eds. *Encyclopedia of Appalachia*. Knoxville: University of Tennessee Press, 2006.

Bates, Artie Ann. "I'd Sharpen Your Ax." Special issue, *Appalachian Heritage* 21 (Spring 1993): 26.

Bethell, Thomas N. "A Wise Man and Very Brave." Special issue, *Appalachian Heritage* 21 (Spring 1993): 38.

Black, Kate. "The Anne F. and Harry M. Caudill Collection." Special issue, *Appalachian Heritage* 21 (Spring 1993): 45.

Breathitt, Edward T. "On the Cutting Edge: the Gadfly and the Strong Voice-Raising Hell." Special issue, *Appalachian Heritage* 21 (Spring 1993): 21.

Brosi, George. "Harry M. Caudill: An Annotated Bibliography." Special issue, *Appalachian Heritage* 21 (Spring 1993): 47.

Anne and Harry M. Caudill Collection, 1854–1996, 91M2, Special Collections and Digital Programs, University of Kentucky Libraries, Lexington.

Caudill, Anne. Interviews by Rudy Abramson, December 2001–January 2004

———. Interviews by Terry Cummins, February 2009–March 2010

———. Interviews by Mary Ellen Elsbernd, February and March 1990

———. Personal files and private collections

———. "Life with a Polemist." Special issue, *Appalachian Heritage* 21 (Spring 1993): 9.

Caudill, Harry M. *Dark Hills to Westward: The Saga of Jenny Wiley*. New York: Atlantic Monthly Press/Little Brown, 1969.

———. *A Darkness at Dawn: Appalachian Kentucky and the Future*. Lexington: University Press of Kentucky, 1976.

———. *Lester's Progress*. Berea, KY: Kentucke Imprints, 1986.

———. *The Mountain, the Miner, and the Lord, and Other Tales from a Country Law Office*. Lexington: University Press of Kentucky, 1980.

———. *My Land is Dying*. New York: E. P. Dutton, 1971.

———. *Night Comes to the Cumberlands: A Biography of a Depressed Area*. New York: Atlantic Monthly Press/Little Brown, 1963.

———. *The Senator from Slaughter County*. New York: Atlantic Monthly Press/Little Brown, 1974.

———. *Slender is the Thread: Tales from a Country Law Office*. Lexington: University Press of Kentucky, 1987.

———. *Theirs Be the Power: The Moguls of Eastern Kentucky*. Champaign: University of Illinois Press, 1983.

———. *Watches of the Night*. New York: Atlantic Monthly Press/Little Brown, 1976.

Clark, Thomas D. "Harry Caudill, A Native Son." Special issue, *Appalachian Heritage* 21 (Spring 1993): 14.

Drake, Richard B. *A History of Appalachia*. Lexington: University Press of Kentucky, 2001.

Eller, Ronald D. *Uneven Ground: Appalachia Since 1945*. Lexington: University Press of Kentucky, 2008.

Ellis, Ron, ed. *Of Woods and Waters: A Kentucky Outdoor Reader*. Lexington: University Press of Kentucky, 2005.

Greene, John W. and Rosanel Owen Oswald, eds. *Women: Equal But Different.* Lexington: University of Kentucky Press, 1964.

Jones, Loyal. "Harry Caudill and *Night Comes to the Cumberlands* Revisited." Special issue, *Appalachian Heritage* 21 (Spring 1993): 42.

Kramer, Carl E. *Visionaries, Adventurers, and Builders: Historical Highlights of the Falls of the Ohio.* Jeffersonville, IN: Sunnyside Press, 1999.

Perrin, Alfred H. "Letter to the Editor." Special issue, *Appalachian Heritage* 21 (Spring 1993): 8.

Salatino, Anthony J. *Will Appalachia Finally Overcome Poverty?* Kuttawa, KY: McClanahan Publishing House, 1995.

Schmitt, Edward R. "The Appalachian Thread in the Antipoverty Politics of Robert F. Kennedy." *Register of the Kentucky Historical Society* 107 (Summer 2009): 371.

Smith, Al. "Remembering Harry Caudill." *Kentucky Living* (August 1991): 14–22.

Stephenson, John B. "Harry Caudill: He Was Who He Was." Special issue, *Appalachian Heritage* 21 (Spring 1993): 19.

Whisnant, David E. "Harry Caudill: A Remembrance." Special issue, *Appalachian Heritage* 21 (Spring 1993): 31.

Williamson, J. W. and Edwin T. Arnold, eds. *Interviewing Appalachia: Appalachian Journal Interviews, 1978–1992.* Knoxville: University of Tennessee Press, 1994.

About the Author

Terry Cummins was born in the hills of Pendleton County, Kentucky, in the house his great-grandfather built. He grew up on this family farm, which is about 20 miles from where Anne Frye Caudill grew up; both have similar rural backgrounds.

Cummins has a bachelor of arts degree from Transylvania University and a master of arts from the University of Kentucky. After two years in the US Navy, he started a career in education—two years as an English and physical education teacher—followed by 31 years in administration, primarily as a high school principal in Kentucky and southern Indiana.

After he retired, Cummins began a second life following Helen Keller's creed that "Life is an adventure or nothing." His adventures include running marathons, climbing mountains, trekking through many parts of the world, and his compulsion—writing. He ran his first marathon at age 63, climbed his first mountain on his 64th birthday and reached the summit of a 20,000-foot peak three days later. He published his first of more than 625 articles at age 66, and published his first of five books at age 69.

Cummins traveled through Siberia and trekked above the base camp at both the north and south faces of Mt. Everest. He is the oldest person to reach the advanced base camp at K2, the second tallest mountain in the world. He lived in India for a month, climbed mountains in the Andes in South America, and recently hiked through part of Patagonia.

His previous books include *Feed My Sheep, How Did Back Then Become Right Now, Briny's Gift,* and *Retirement is a Blast Once You Light the Fuse.*

Cummins has been married to his wife, Vera, for nearly 60 years. They have four children, five grandchildren, and two great-grandchildren.